GENESIS AND APOCALYPSE

Books by Thomas J. J. Altizer
also published by The Westminster Press

The Gospel of Christian Atheism

Mircea Eliade and the Dialectic of the Sacred

Oriental Mysticism and Biblical Eschatology

GENESIS AND APOCALYPSE

A Theological Voyage Toward Authentic Christianity

Thomas J. J. Altizer

Westminster/John Knox Press
Louisville, Kentucky

© 1990 Thomas J. J. Altizer

Book design by Gene Harris

First edition

Published by Westminster/John Knox Press
Louisville, Kentucky

PRINTED IN THE UNITED STATES OF AMERICA

9 8 7 6 5 4 3 2 1

Library of Congress Cataloging-in-Publication Data

Altizer, Thomas J. J.
   Genesis and apocalypse : a theological voyage toward authentic Christianity / Thomas J. J. Altizer. — 1st ed.
        p.   cm.
   Includes index.
   ISBN 0-664-21932-2

   1. Theology, Doctrinal.   2. Creation.   3. Eschatology.   I. Title.
BT75.2.A45 1990
230—dc20

90-24059

For

Barbara Walters Altizer

Contents

Preface

Apocalypse is at the very center of an original Christianity, just as it has been a primal ground of a uniquely Western and Christian history and culture, and has even been reborn in our contemporary world. Yet nothing is a deeper theological mystery than apocalypse, as we are the inheritors of a theological tradition or traditions which have banished apocalypse to the periphery of theological thinking, traditions which are fulfilled in that overwhelming body of modern theology which has dissolved the very category and identity of apocalypse. Nevertheless, it was the historical discovery of the original apocalyptic or eschatological ground of the New Testament which has been the most profound challenge to twentieth-century Christian theology, a challenge unmet by all of our major theologians, who thereby foreclosed the possibility of a contemporary Christian theology which is or could be a biblical theology.

Apocalyptic faith or vision is not only the historical origin of Christianity, however; it has been renewed or resurrected in each of the great revolutionary transformations of Christian and Western history, as reflected not only in the epic poetry of Dante and Milton, but also in the prophetic and apocalyptic poetry and vision of Blake, a vision which gave us not only the first imaginative enactment of the death of God, but an apocalyptic death of God which is a resurrection of the apocalyptic Christ. Indeed, the most profound philosophical understanding of the death of God, as realized by Hegel and Nietzsche, occurs by way of a uniquely modern apocalyptic enactment of the death of God, an enactment calling forth a final and apocalyptic age or aeon.

At no point has modern Christian theology been more reactionary than in its refusal of an apocalyptic ground, and just

9

as this refusal occurs in every major modern theologian, that is an occurrence which is a reenactment of our theological traditions, traditions which themselves arose out of the dissolution or reversal of an originally apocalyptic Christianity. This theological dissolution of an apocalyptic ground is now clearly manifest as a dissolution of the deepest ground of the New Testament itself, and if it was only in the world of late modernity that a historical discovery of original Christian apocalypticism occurred, this was also a world that was born with the advent of a uniquely modern apocalyptic vision. That vision occurs most purely in Blake and Nietzsche, and if Blake and Nietzsche are prophetic precursors of our world, they are most fundamentally so in their very apocalyptic vision.

Yet that vision is also and even thereby a resurrection of genesis, a genesis which is a new creation, and an absolutely new creation which is the consequence of an apocalyptic ending of an old world or an old totality. This is that very genesis which is the deepest even if most elusive ground of Hegel's purely dialectical thinking, for it is the ultimate origin of that self-negation which is the center of Hegelian thinking, a self-negation which is the first philosophical realization of a uniquely Christian kenosis or self-emptying. While nothing is so isolated and apart in our given theological thinking than genesis and apocalypse, genesis and apocalypse are essentially and integrally conjoined in the epic visions of Milton, Blake, and Joyce, just as they are in the philosophical thinking of Hegel and Nietzsche, and that very conjunction may yet prove to be a decisive way for a theological recovery of the Bible, and for a rebirth of theology itself.

This book is an attempt to evolve a purely apocalyptic theology by way of a full conjunction and even dialectical identity of genesis and apocalypse. At the very time when Christianity was most profoundly alienated from all modern thinking, most certainly including scientific thinking, Karl Barth unveiled creation as a theological secret, and a secret that is reversed only through a purely Christocentric theology. Here, the ultimate victory of the crucifixion and the resurrection is a repetition of the creation, and a repetition of creation out of nothing. If Barth's theology in its deepest ground is a profound conflict with that Nothing annulled by the creation, it remains most elusive precisely at this point, for the Nothing is finally unspeakable in our given and classical theological languages.

Yet a Nothing or pure Emptiness is at the very center of Buddhist language and meditation, just as a pure and all-comprehensive nothingness has been realized or resurrected in the most powerful imaginative languages and visions of the twentieth century. While there appears to be no way by which to bring these languages and visions together with a biblical and theological language of genesis, that is a decisive sign of the alienation of our theological language from our contemporary world. So likewise is our theological language alienated from a purely mystical vision. If Meister Eckhart inaugurated a uniquely Western mysticism, that is a mysticism revolving about a uniquely Western self-annihilation, a self-annihilation of a creature who is finally a pure nothingness, and is a pure nothingness by being identical with the divine nothingness, a divine nothingness which is nothing less than the Godhead itself.

The opening chapters of this book are a theological meditation upon genesis from the perspective of an apocalyptic faith and a contemporary apocalyptic situation. In large measure they are a continuation of a theological dialogue which I have conducted with Mircea Eliade for almost thirty years, for I continue to be persuaded that Eliade is the purest religious thinker of our century, and that his phenomenological understanding of the primordial myth and ritual of eternal return is a genuine theological understanding of that original Nothing which genesis reversed. Thereby Eliade has given us our only true theological understanding of "paganism," a paganism which is a universal religious phenomenon, and a paganism which is the intrinsic "other" of genesis and apocalypse alike.

These opening chapters are also and equally so a continuation of my theological dialogue with Hegel, for even though Hegel was never able to openly and systematically draw forth the full meaning of the once and for all and irreversible event of genesis (and this eludes him even in the opening sections of the *Science of Logic*), it is genesis that is the origin of that pure negativity which dominates his thinking. For genesis is the origin of an original self-alienation and self-estrangement of Spirit, and thus is the origin of that "labor of the negative" or that self-negation in which absolute Spirit or the Godhead of God actually becomes and realizes itself as its own inherent "other." While these opening chapters are more abstract and less historical than the other chapters, they are essential to a project of realizing a fully apocalyptic theology, and are so if only because *apocalypse can finally have no meaning if it is divorced from genesis.*

Lying at the center of this book is a quest for a theological conception of the eternal act or actualization of God, an actualization which is fully genesis and is fully apocalypse at once, but is so only insofar as it is simultaneously incarnation, crucifixion, and resurrection. That bald and cursory statement has very little meaning, and can only have real meaning as it is theologically enacted, an enactment that here intends to be theological and historical at once. For this book intends to bring together the thinking of my earlier books, *The Self-Embodiment of God* and *History as Apocalypse,* and to do so by attempting a coinherence of abstract or systematic and historical theology. Historical theology itself virtually disappeared after the first world war, and largely did so at the hands of Barth and Tillich, and yet this disappearance was a genuine theological response to the end of Christendom, a response which was first and most profoundly realized by Kierkegaard.

While such thinking made possible the theological preservation of faith in the modern world, it did so only by establishing a purely negative and nondialectical relationship between faith and culture or faith and history, with the consequence that theology has become wholly alienated both from culture and from history. Yet a theological refusal of historical thinking is inevitably for us a theological refusal of the Bible, and nothing more fully reveals the ultimate failure of Barth's *Church Dogmatics* than its alienation from the world of biblical criticism and scholarship, an alienation that is even more manifestly present in all forms of fundamentalism. The Bible is the only scripture in the world which is profoundly and comprehensively historical; nothing more fully makes manifest its uniqueness, and yet theology as such continues to remain estranged from a truly historical ground. Thus we are confronted with a truly new situation in which for the first time theology is alienated from both Bible and culture, from both its own source and its own contemporary world, and so much so that theology itself has seemingly come to an end.

Yet this new situation is integrally related to a universal apocalyptic condition in our world. Once again we are confronted with the end of history upon our real and actual horizons, an ending that was at the center of ancient apocalypticism, that was reborn again and again in Christian and Western history, and that even inaugurated the full birth of the modern world in the new epic vision of Blake and the new philosophical thinking of Hegel and Nietzsche. So likewise a Heidegger and a Derrida can enact the end of philosophy, just as Joyce and Beckett have enacted the end of literature, and contemporary painting and sculpture are seemingly enacting the end of art.

Who can now believe that a truly new imagination or a truly new nonscientific or nontechnological thinking is possible in our world? Or who can now believe that a truly new society or a new humanity is any longer possible? Why then should one think that a new theology is possible? Perhaps because theology was the first discipline or "science" to perish in the modern world, or if not to perish to go deeply underground, and while it has been culturally or publicly invisible in that underworld, perhaps it has been undergoing some kind of regeneration, or, at least, a very modest rebirth. That is the most we can realistically ask of theology today, but perhaps even that is now impossible, and impossible if we are now being engulfed by a new and total silence.

Now any rebirth of theology today can only be a rebirth occurring in our own contemporary world, and that is a world which is a profoundly atheistic if not nihilistic world, a world that has issued from the uniquely modern realization of the death of God. Not the least of that which has perished with that realization is everything we once knew as *authority*, and not only the authority of God, but all sanctioned authority, or every authority presenting itself with an ultimate claim, or even every authority which is in-itself or as-itself authority. All too significantly, what we know as scholarly documentation only arose after this historical realization, and perhaps nothing so clearly gives witness to that vacuum which is a consequence of the death of God than does scholarly documentation, a scholarly citation replacing what was once a scriptural citation, and implicitly claiming that very authority which once was present in scriptural citation. One need not deny that such documentation is also a consequence of a truly new critical and historical consciousness, but that consciousness is itself a consequence of the death of God, as both Hegel and Nietzsche knew so deeply, and therefore a truly critical and historical consciousness is by necessity the embodiment of the dissolution of an ultimate and absolute authority, and hence the dissolution of any authority embodying such a claim.

A decisive loss which has occurred in the world of modern scholarship is that of a text which is solely and only a text; here a text has authority or power only insofar as it is conjoined with texts that lie far beyond it, and then it becomes impossible for the reader to read a text that is wholly meaningful within itself. That impossibility is also the impossibility of the reader's fully exercising his or her own autonomous judgment. It is not insignificant that our poets and philosophers refuse to employ documentation, a documentation that would make their projects impossible, because they are seeking to realize a text that is only a text, or a text whose power and authority lies solely within itself. These are the texts that call for pure reading, a reading that is impossible in scholarly and academic worlds, and impossible just because these are institutional worlds that foreclose the possibility of a truly autonomous or solitary judgment. All too naturally, academic worlds are alien to purely philosophical and theological thinking, or surely so in the contemporary world, but they are also alien to solitary and autonomous judgment. But that is the very form of judgment which is at the center of a purely religious or theological consciousness, a consciousness which is liberated or distant from every center or ground which is not a purely religious or theological ground, and thus a consciousness that can be itself only by way of an absolutely solitary judgment. From this perspective, truly theological writing cannot be scholarly writing, just as truly theological reading cannot be scholarly reading, and this is true not only of theological reading and writing, but of philosophical and poetic reading and writing as well.

Nevertheless, this project does entail a conjunction of historical and theological judgment, and it is certainly true for us that historical judgment is possible only through modern scholarship, just as the historical realm itself can only be fully meaningful to us through such scholarship. But it is to be remembered that our first great historical thinker was Spinoza, whose *Tractatus Theologico-politicus* created a modern historical understanding of the Bible, just as it was Hegel who more fully realized a conjunction of pure thinking and historical thinking than any other thinker, and Nietzsche who embodied a pure historical thinking that created whole new historical horizons. No one could doubt that Hegel was immersed in historical scholarship, as is most fully manifest in his university lectures, which comprehend virtually the whole world of the historical scholarship of his time; and yet Hegel in his published work virtually never engages in scholarly citation, and one sees this absence even more purely in Nietzsche's writing. Now even if a Spinoza, a Hegel, or a Nietzsche would clearly be impossible in our world, ours is a world that is profoundly grounded in their thinking, and not least so in our historical understanding. There is no inherent reason why historical thinking cannot be an abstract or systematic thinking, as witness Spinoza, Hegel, and Nietzsche, to say nothing of our Christian epic poets who have so fully incorporated a revolutionary historical understanding and vision. If it is precisely the presence of a full historical ground that is the clearest sign of a uniquely Christian vision, *Christian theology must finally be either historical or not theology at all.*

This book is foregoing all scholarly citation, and is doing so with the intention of striving for a purely theological thinking. There is no authority whatsoever present in this book which is not at least potentially present in the reader; here judgment can only be a mutual judgment, but a mutually solitary judgment, and if this must occur through the historical and theological perspective of the reader, let the reader make the judgments that this historical and theological voyage entails, and do so on the basis of his or her own historical and theological understanding. While it is true that there are a few texts here which are crucial to this inquiry, these are always specifically cited, but no arcane or esoteric understanding has any relevance to this inquiry. This book is not simply addressed to everyone, but presumes in the spirit of the "Here Comes Everybody" of *Finnegans Wake* that everybody and everyone is the only real actor in a theological voyage. And if that is precisely the identity of a real theological voyage which distinguishes it from every other voyage, then just as "Here Comes Everybody" is the hero of *Finnegans Wake,* the reader is finally the author of this book, or is so at whatever points this book is real. The Christian knows "Here Comes Everybody" as that everybody which is present in Christ, and not only present in Christ but realized only in Christ, and if that realization is an absolutely new realization, it is thereby a realization that is apocalyptically actual in all, and if all and everyone are eternally elected in Christ, "Here Comes Everybody" is each and every one of us.

This book is dedicated to my wife, Barbara Walters Altizer, who has deeply shared in its thinking and writing, and who is a fundamental source of whatever spirit that might here be present. The book is also under the impact of the primal thinking of my colleague, D. G. Leahy, and is particularly indebted to his radically new understanding of novum. A special debt of gratitude is owed Deland Anderson; John B. Cobb, Jr.; Richard Feero; Ray L. Hart; Charles H. Long; Jacob Neusner; Robert P. Scharlemann; Mark C. Taylor; John T. Wilcox; and Charles E. Winquist, who critically responded to portions of the manuscript, and many of their suggestions are incorporated in the book. I am also grateful to John McGuigan of the University Press of Virginia, who initiated the volume published as *Theology at the End of the Century,* for it was the writing of my essay for this project which led to the writing of the present book. This book has also richly benefitted from the extraordinarily able editing of Danielle Alexander. Davis Perkins, the editorial director of Westminster/John Knox Press, has proven to be the ablest and most responsible editor whom I have yet encountered, and this in a fully theological sense.

Prologue

The death of God is at once a primary if not the primary symbol of full or late modernity and also that symbol which most decisively distinguishes Christianity from all the religions of the world. Only Christianity knows that crucifixion which is a unique and actual death, a death occurring in the full actuality of history, and yet a death which Christianity knows as the one source of redemption, for it is a death that is crucifixion and resurrection at once. Therein a full and actual death is realized in Christianity as it is in no other religious tradition, and a death that is an ultimate death, for it is the actual death of Christ or the Son of God or the Word of God. That death occurs as *a once and for all event,* for even if it can be repeated and renewed in Christian faith and worship, it can only be so renewed as an absolutely unique event.

Nothing so effectively annuls or dissolves Christianity than does a dissolution of that event, and yet paradoxically that very atheism which ushered in the fullness of modernity is an atheism revolving about a proclamation and enactment of the death of God, an atheism which first fully appears in the violence of the French Revolution, and most specifically so in the dechristianization of that revolution, a dechristianization embodying that radical secularism which soon was to transform the world as a whole. Hegel understood the death of God as the very center of the French Revolution, and just as Hegel was the first philosophical thinker to ground a whole philosophical system in the death or self-negation of God, that self-negation or self-emptying which is the center of Hegelian thinking was understood by Hegel himself to be a purely philosophical realization of what Christianity knows as incarnation, crucifixion, and resurrection.

Nietzsche's proclamation of the death of God is a full realization of that Hegelian ground, and not least so in its realization of that death as a fully historical event, and therefore as an irreversible event, and an irreversible event embodying an ultimate nihilism, a nihilism that is at once an inevitable historical consequence of Christianity, and yet a nihilism that is the very arena of the ecstatic Yes-saying of Eternal Recurrence. While Nietzsche was more isolated and alone than any major thinker except Spinoza, no other thinker more fully embodied the history and consciousness of his own time and world and, if only for that reason, Nietzsche is now inescapable as a seminal source of our own world, and most manifestly so in his very proclamation of the death of God.

Not even a religious fundamentalism can escape that event; indeed, fundamentalism would be inconceivable apart from it, and if what we know as fundamentalism is found only in the world of late modernity, that is a fundamentalism which is itself a primary witness to the death of God, and is so most clearly in its very assault upon secularism, a secularism which it discovers in every dimension of our world.

But Nietzsche was not only a precursor of the twentieth century; his thinking was a fulfillment of the dominant historical currents of the West, and most manifestly so of those currents which inaugurated the full birth of modernity in the seventeenth century, a century which above all others was the century of revolution, and most clearly so in the poetic, scientific, and philosophical revolutions of that century, revolutions which finally ended the whole horizon of medieval thinking, and therein initially brought to an end everything that had once been manifest as a religious and metaphysical transcendence. That transcendence has never subsequently been recovered in our history, or not recovered in the dominant expressions of our thinking and consciousness, and these are the very expressions which finally issued in a uniquely modern atheism, and uniquely modern if only because of the comprehensiveness of our atheism. Yet, as Nietzsche knew so deeply, our atheism is also and necessarily so a uniquely modern nihilism, and one that is not only present in the historical horrors of our century but also in the most creative expressions of the twentieth-century mind and imagination.

Nietzsche was not alone in identifying our nihilism as a historical consequence of Christianity, for even if a Hegelian idealism is seemingly the very opposite of our nihilism, it is no less grounded in the death of God, a death of God which is a dissolution of both a metaphysical and a religious transcen-

dence, and a death of God which is precisely therein a recovery
of the crucifixion, and a recovery of that crucifixion which is
finally and ultimately the ending of pure transcendence itself,
or the ending of that transcendence which cannot finally and
wholly become incarnate. Christian kenosis, or self-emptying,
and the self-emptying of God in Christ, are realized in Hegelian
thinking as the self-negation of absolute spirit, a self-negation
which is the source of all life and activity, and a self-negation or
kenosis apart from which Godhead itself would be lifeless and
alone, as Hegel declares at the conclusion of the *Phenomenology
of Spirit*. Hegel's whole philosophical opus may be understood as
a continual conflict with an inactive, inactual, and undifferentiated Godhead or Totality, a totality he deeply understood as the
very opposite of the Christian God, and it is the kenosis or
self-negation of the uniquely Christian God which Hegel understood as the "labor of the negative," a labor which is actuality
itself, and therefore a labor which is the pure actuality of history
and consciousness alike. Now it was the symbol of the crucifixion which Hegel seized upon as the primary symbol of the
self-negation of absolute spirit, for he knew the crucifixion as
the final incarnation of pure transcendence, and therefore as
the resurrection of an absolutely new consciousness and world.

That is a resurrection which for Hegel is the birth of
self-consciousness, and the inauguration of an absolute freedom as well, a freedom that realizes itself only in that consciousness and that history which is a consequence of the Incarnation,
and a freedom which he could celebrate as being triumphant in
his own world. And that is also a freedom which in its universal
form is realized for Hegel only in the French Revolution, but
therein it is only a purely abstract freedom, and an abstract
freedom which embodies itself in an orgy of violence and death,
an orgy that is itself the dawning of a uniquely modern atheism.
If the French Revolution is for Hegel the first universal event in
history, it is an event which embodies the ending of all ancient
history, and the initial ending of all consciousness that is
grounded in a transcendent eternity, or grounded in that God
who is God and only God.

So for Hegel, too, modern atheism is a uniquely Christian
atheism, or, at least, it is impossible apart from its Christian
historical ground, and if this is an atheism that after Hegel's
death issues in a uniquely modern nihilism, that is a nihilism
first unveiled by Marx and Kierkegaard, and by Marx and
Kierkegaard as Hegelian thinkers, for even if they are reverse
or inverted Hegelian thinkers they are thinkers who deeply
unveiled the absolute groundlessness of a uniquely modern

consciousness and society. That absolute groundlessness is an
absolute nihilism, and a nihilism that soon was to dominate our
society and consciousness, and if that nihilism is fully present in
every full and pure expression of a post-Hegelian imagination,
it is no less implicitly present in the turbulent currents of our
history and consciousness as a whole. Now even if modern
atheism and modern nihilism are a consequence of Christianity,
we as yet have no real understanding of Christianity as a deep
and ultimate source of our world, and this in large measure
because in defiance of Nietzsche we refuse to understand
Christianity as a nihilistic faith, and therefore refuse to understand Christianity as an embodiment of the death of God.

Kierkegaard, implicitly but decisively, understood Christendom as such an embodiment, but Kierkegaard, even as his
twentieth-century descendents, refused to understand Christian dogma as a nihilistic or atheistic dogma, except for his all
too significant understanding of the Incarnation as that absolute paradox which is an absolute offense to faith. While this is
clearly a uniquely modern understanding of the Incarnation, an
understanding whose historical roots are no earlier than Luther
and whose philosophical foundation is purely Hegelian, this is
nevertheless a Christian understanding of the Incarnation, and
one that would have been impossible in the premodern world.
Hegel believed that Luther inaugurated modernity, and did so
in his realization of faith as infinite subjectivity, an infinite
subjectivity that is the actualization of a uniquely Christian
freedom. As Hegel maintains in his lectures on the philosophy
of history, the essence of the Reformation is that humanity in its
very nature is destined to be free, and historical time, since that
epoch, has no other work to do than the imbuing of the world as
a whole with this principle. But for Hegel that historical
embodiment is a radical and total secularization, a secularization
which Kierkegaard passionately and totally refused, and if
Kierkegaard could know secularization as a pure objectification
of consciousness and society, that is an objectification which is
the pure opposite of the "subjectivity" of faith.

If modern theology was born in the world of German
idealism, it has made no real progress since that era, unless it has
been to radically contract itself and thus to confine itself to a
wholly interior realm, and one that has no point of contact
whatsoever with a world or actuality outside itself. But this all
too modern condition of theology is itself a nihilistic condition,
and a nihilistic condition if only because it is such a pure form of
solipsism, a solipsism knowing and realizing only itself, and
thereby sanctioning the absolute groundlessness of its own time

and world. And if every truly modern theologian has most deeply struggled with pietism, that is a pietism which is nothing more nor less than the actual religion of our world, a pietism that itself is nihilistic in its very flight from the world, and nihilistic in its very exaltation of an unthinkable and unimaginable feeling.

Nietzsche understood such pietism more deeply than did any other thinker, perhaps because he himself had been nurtured by it, so that finally in *The Antichrist* he could identify the Christian God as the deification of nothingness, the will to nothingness pronounced holy. If that is a will which is only manifest as such in a uniquely modern will, that is a will which has its historical origin in Christianity. For Nietzsche, only the Christian God is a pure embodiment of an absolute No-saying, a No-saying which is the absolute sovereignty of the Christian God, and a No-saying which is the origin of that repression which is the real sovereign of our history, a repression that for Nietzsche is nowhere truly manifest or real apart from the presence of the Christian God.

Thus Nietzsche understood the Christian God as omnipresent, and omnipresent in the very negative power of repression, and even if such repression is unknown outside the Christian world, it is nonetheless the hidden and elusive ground of all consciousness whatsoever. For, as Nietzsche discovered in *The Genealogy of Morals,* the origin of consciousness is the origin of the bad conscience.

Nothing is more fundamental for thinking itself than the question of origin or beginning, and if origin is the theological question par excellence, that is the question of genesis, and ultimately the question of absolute genesis. Now even if this must inevitably be a nihilistic question for us, it may nevertheless unveil the ultimate roots of our nihilism, an unveiling that has thus far not even been attempted by theology, and certainly not by a theology that is innocent of an original or primordial nothingness. Barth and Tillich, alone among our theologians, were open to that nothingness, and that is certainly a decisive source of their theological power, but neither of them were able to realize that nothingness dogmatically or systematically, and were unable to do so if only because neither of them could name that nothingness theologically or could grasp it as a ground or a potency that is inseparable from the uniquely Christian God. Now even if the Christian theological tradition has predominantly known creation as creation out of nothing, it has not been able to conceive or even to name that nothingness, and therefore genesis has remained an inexplicable mystery, and even an inexplicable mystery when it is known as the primordial and eternal act of God.

This study has chosen to approach that mystery by way of an exploration of genesis from the perspective of our contemporary nihilism; thereby it will certainly be far distant from our dominant theological traditions, but it nevertheless intends a recovery of a profoundly Christian ground that is alien to those traditions, and most alien to those traditions when they have realized a fully dogmatic or fully systematic form. Yet if we have discovered again and again that the Bible itself cannot pass into those traditions, and is most alien to those traditions precisely when they are most systematic or most dogmatic, so that it is now inconceivable that a biblical theology could be a systematic theology, and was so inconceivable to Barth himself, that is a situation which fully opens the possibility of a radical theology which in some decisive sense could be a biblical theology, and a biblical theology precisely in its distance from our theological traditions. Of course, this is actually little more than a bare possibility, but it is a possibility that is here being prosecuted, and prosecuted with the conviction that this is a way to a genuinely new theology.

As opposed to every other religious tradition, Christianity has celebrated the absolutely new, an absolute novum which it knows to be present in Christ, for even if Christ is the primordial Word, that is the Word which Christianity knows as the incarnate Word, and as that incarnate Word which has come so as to make all things new. Such a celebration of the new, and of the absolutely new, had never occurred in the world before, but that celebration is nonetheless a fulfillment of that prophetic tradition which preceded it, and most clearly so of the ecstatic celebration of Second Isaiah. But Second Isaiah and the Book of Job are the fullest biblical realizations of the creation, a creation which Christianity has known as a new creation, and a new creation precisely when it is known as the creation of Christ, and a new creation which will finally pass into apocalypse.

If a uniquely modern nihilism in its deepest expressions has been a uniquely modern apocalypticism, as most clearly present in Nietzsche, but no less deeply so in that apocalyptic literature inaugurated by Blake, that is an apocalypticism which also knows a new creation, and an absolutely new creation, but a new creation that can only be the consequence of the final ending of an old totality. Now that is an ending which must ultimately be sought in an original creation, and an original creation that is a new creation, and an absolutely new creation, but it is and can be so only by way of the ending of an original totality, an original totality that is a primordial nothingness, and it is precisely as such that it has been unnameable or unrealizable in the Christian theological tradition.

The opening chapters of this book are an attempt at a theological penetration of that nothingness, a nothingness that was negated by the original act of creation, and absolutely negated by that act, and one consequence of that negation is that true or actual images of that nothingness have disappeared from that history and that consciousness which are embodiments of that negation, and disappeared in what is perhaps our deepest and purest iconoclasm. Nevertheless, traces are present of that nothingness, traces which have overwhelmed us in our own world; for if the modern realization of the death of God has issued in a resurrection of nothingness, that is a nothingness which cannot finally be dissociated from an original or primordial nothingness, a primordial nothingness which is a primordial totality. That is a totality which is more fully manifest today than it has ever been manifest before, or historically manifest, and that is just the reason why a uniquely modern voyage is a voyage into nothingness, a voyage epically inaugurated by Dante's *Inferno* and epically consummated in Joyce's *Finnegans Wake*.

That voyage into nothingness which we so deeply know to be our own is a voyage into a totality, a totality manifestly present and real in our great Christian epics, and not only in our epics but throughout the fullest expressions of our imagination. Such a totality is also present in the purest and most comprehensive expressions of our philosophical thinking, as witness Spinoza, Hegel, and Nietzsche. And if both our imaginative and our philosophical voyages have been ever more progressively and ever more necessarily voyages into an empty and ungrounded totality, they have no less so been comprehensive voyages, and voyages evolving ever new worlds and horizons. Remarkably enough, the fullest expressions of both our mind and our imagination, whether implicitly or explicitly, have realized what we can only identify as religious or theological systems, systems which have been impossible for modern theology, as witness the failure in our own time of Barth, Tillich, and Rahner to incorporate the apocalyptic or eschatological ground of an original Christianity. Yet that ground in some decisive sense has been present in our imaginative creations since Dante, and is certainly present in Hegel and Nietzsche, and may well be a deep source of Spinoza's absolute affirmation of the world or nature. If Spinoza is our purest thinker, he is also that thinker who first apprehended an absolute unity between infinity and

finitude, that very unity which Hegel identified as the unique
creation of an original Christianity. Spinoza could know an
absolute necessity that dissolves the very possibility of contingency, and that is a necessity which is a total and totally
comprehensive necessity, but a necessity which is meaningless
and unreal in any thinking which is an unsystematic thinking, or
in any thinking which is not finally and only the thinking of
God.

Spinoza, Hegel, and Nietzsche have been our most God-
obsessed thinkers, just as Dante, Milton, and Blake have been
our most God-obsessed poets. These are the very thinkers and
visionaries who have created our most comprehensive systems,
systems which themselves have been primal embodiments of the
deeper currents of our history. Not since Aquinas has something even remotely comparable to these systems been realized
by theology as such, and if that is a fundamental reason why
Thomism remains even today as the most influential theological
system in our world, no one apart from its contemporary
defenders can know it as a modern system, just as no one
outside of the ever-shrinking world of theology can know any
modern theology as a genuinely modern form of thinking. But
if all too worldly thinkers and poets have realized systems which
are manifestly truly modern systems, and not only modern
systems but religious or theological systems as well, here and
here alone we may discover a full conjunction of the modern
and the theological realms. These theological realms are truly
new and convey a novum that has been absent from our
theological thinking as such, or present only insofar as it
is a theological surd defying systematic or comprehensive
theological understanding. One such surd has been the very
category of emptiness or nothingness, but we cannot unlock or
unveil that surd if we cannot understand it systematically or
comprehensively, and, theologically, that can only mean that we
cannot understand it if we apprehend it only through the act of
creation. We must also apprehend it, and comprehensively
apprehend it, through the acts of revelation, incarnation,
crucifixion, resurrection, and apocalypse. Even if Barth, Tillich,
and Rahner deeply knew the necessity of such a comprehensive
mode of apprehension, this is precisely the unitary mode their
systems failed to realize. But that failure is the failure to realize
a truly modern mode of thinking or vision, and if that mode
now appears to be an impossible theological goal, it may
nonetheless become possible by way of a reversal of our
theological thinking, a reversal already effected by Spinoza,
Hegel, and Nietzsche, and effected by a philosophical thinking

that is simultaneously a theological thinking, and therefore, and necessarily so, a thinking that is *the thinking of totality*.

Virtually all of the great religious thinkers of antiquity centered their thinking upon totality, and this is true of both East and West; and if it is above all true of Hindu and Buddhist thinkers, it is also true of the great medieval Islamic, Jewish, and Confucian thinkers, even as it is true of Aquinas. Nothing is a clearer sign of the advent of modernity than an ever-progressive contraction and disappearance of a theological thinking which is a comprehensive and unitary thinking, and, yet, ironically, it was that very all too modern thinking which most profoundly reversed ancient religious thinking which is so clearly a thinking of totality. So it is that in the modern world a thinking of totality has realized itself as an inversion or reversal of ancient or primordial religious thinking, and if at this point there is a clear continuity between Spinoza, Hegel, and Nietzsche, that is a continuity which culminates in a uniquely modern nihilism which is most clearly nihilistic in its absolute subversion of an ancient or primordial religious world. That is a world which is absolutely reversed in Nietzsche's vision of Eternal Recurrence, but perhaps the deepest ground of that reversal was first established by Spinoza's pure and decisive unification of infinity and finitude, a unification which is comprehensively realized in Hegel's system, with the consequence that a purely philosophical thinking of a religious or metaphysical transcendence has not since been possible in the modern world.

Yet the impossibility of thinking religious transcendence is also and even thereby a nihilistic condition, or is so in terms of the religious traditions of the West, and, all too significantly, the very proliferation of visions of totality in the twentieth century has just therein been a proliferation of nihilistic vision. That nihilistic vision has been most purely nihilistic in precisely those visions which have most genuinely and decisively been visions of totality. Thus *Finnegans Wake* is the supreme epic of the twentieth century, and if therein we may discover a nihilistic vision which is simultaneously an atheistic vision, our atheism is a nihilistic atheism, and one which fully dawns in the dechristianization of the French Revolution. Accordingly, our deepest atheism is an anti-Christian atheism, as most clearly manifest in Nietzsche, and therefore our uniquely modern nihilism is an anti-Christian nihilism, and one, indeed, that would be impossible apart from Christianity. But if Nietzsche and Joyce alike could celebrate that nihilism as a liberating nihilism, and liberating above all in that absolute affirmation or Yes-saying which it alone makes possible, that Yes is the Yes which the Christian knows as the Yes of the gospel, a Yes which faith knows as a total Yes, and a total Yes which is an all comprehending totality. Even if such a totality can only appear and be real to us as a nihilistic totality, both faith and vision finally know totality itself as an absolute Yes and Amen.

1

Genesis as New Creation

At a time of ending, nothing is more overwhelming than the mystery of beginning, just as nothing is more elusive than the deep identity of beginning, for even if our cosmologies now center upon cosmic beginning as they have never done before, we have lost or are losing every sense of a true and actual human beginning, or of a human beginning that now could be actually new. The truly or fully new is that which is most manifestly absent from our world, and this despite the fact that we embody a modernity that has been a passage into and a realization of a new world, a novum that had never been so fully realized in our past, and yet a novum that in our history has never been so interiorly silent or unnameable as it is today.

Nothing is or could be a deeper mystery to us than the novum, and if genesis is the original biblical symbol of novum, nothing is more distant from us than that genesis. Genesis or ultimate beginning is novum, but at a time in which the horizon of a true and actual future is ending, genesis looms before us with an ultimacy that it never had before, and does so because true genesis is absent from our interior world; this absence veils genesis in a seemingly impenetrable darkness, but that very veiling has only deepened the power of the symbol of genesis for us, for even if we can only know genesis as an ultimate mystery, that very mystery is calling us to a quest that otherwise would be absent. That very calling is making possible for us a new naming of beginning, a naming that has occurred in the poetry of the twentieth century just as it has occurred in our cosmologies, and even if such a naming is a naming of darkness, it is naming nonetheless, and therefore it is an evocation, if not an embodiment, of the novum. That novum is genesis for us, and even if it can be named only at the closing time of our history, that closure is making possible an evocation of ultimate beginning, a beginning that is truly and finally beginning itself. Now if the evocation of that beginning is the consequence of an ultimate ending, then so likewise has every such naming in our history been a consequence of deep ending, as witness the wholly new naming of genesis in the first exile of Israel as well as the new naming of fall and darkness by Paul and the Fourth Gospel.

Each of these namings was a consequence of a profound and even an ultimate loss, the loss of an original Israel in Second Isaiah, Job, and the postexilic priestly tradition, and the loss of an original covenant with Yahweh in both the Pauline and the Johannine traditions. Something fully parallel to this is also present in the new naming of genesis in Augustine, Aquinas, and Dante, even as it is also present in Milton, Blake, and Joyce, for only the ending of an old world makes possible a new naming of beginning. If a new naming of beginning is truly a novum, it is realized only in that vacuum or emptiness which is effected by the erosion and erasure of an earlier naming of beginning; and that erasure is the inevitable consequence of the ending of an old world.

The death of God in the modern world is just such an ending, and it, too, has realized a new naming of beginning, and even if that new naming is thus far theologically uncomprehended, it is no less real because of that. Indeed, an all too modern naming of beginning is giving us a truly new apprehension of genesis or ultimate beginning, for now we are offered the possibility of knowing it not only as an absolute origin or source, but also as that event which is absolutely new, and totally new in its very embodiment of a new totality.

That thinking and that vision which has most fully embodied the death of God has given us both conceptions and visions of a new totality, a new totality which is nevertheless totality itself, and thereby a totality which had never previously been fully or comprehensively present in our Western traditions. We will inevitably be closed to such a totality if we bring to it a conception or vision of origin which is not a vision or conception of *total* origin. Accordingly, to the extent that we remain bound to a vision of a pure or unending eternity, we will remain closed to a vision of a new eternity, and an eternity that is not only totally new, but whose novum is all in all. That is a novum which is closed to a conception or vision centered in that God who is simply and only eternal, or whose primordial eternity is simply identical with an apocalyptic eternity, or whose identity and reality as God wholly transcends the novum of an absolute or total beginning. Absolute beginning cannot be a total event if it is not an all-comprehending event; so likewise it cannot be an absolutely new event if it exists in and as the shadow of a preceding eternity, for then its very existence as such would not be absolutely new.

Only the modern realization of the death of God has opened us to the possibility of the absolutely new, and if that novum is now being comprehensively realized in our history, and realized so as to bring to an end the future possibility of an actually new, it may nevertheless open us to our origin in the absolutely new. If absolute beginning is the absolutely new, then to be open to that beginning is to be open to novum itself, a novum which is novum and only novum, and therefore a novum which is totality, which is to say that it is all in all. Visions of totality are inevitably present in pure or total vision, and such visions are present throughout the history of religions, and may even be found in pure negations of vision, as occurred not only in Buddhism but also in that radically iconoclastic Israel which is a primal even if elusive source of Western visions of totality. While Hinduism and Buddhism are centered in totality, and Sufism and the Kabbalah are as well, the dominant expressions of a postbiblical Christianity have profoundly opposed and resisted the call of totality, or, at least, have done so in Western if not in Eastern Christianity, and this despite the origin of Christianity in apocalypticism, and despite the innumerable visions of totality which have been realized in Christian apocalypticism and Christian mysticism, and realized in Western thinking from Meister Eckhart and Spinoza through Hegel and Nietzsche and beyond.

Western Christian theological thinking (and at no other point has there been such a gulf between Christianity East and West) has known visions of totality as assaults upon the Godhead of God, and thus that thinking has centered upon that God who is God and only God, and thereby created a theology of the God who is eternally and only God. Such an apprehension of God led Augustine to affirm that creation is not a new act, and there is no new will in the creation, for God wills all that He wills simultaneously, in one act, and eternally (*Confessions* XII, 15). But if the act of God is one act, and an act which is eternally the same, then not only is creation not a new act, but world itself is not finally or even actually new. At no other point did Aquinas more deeply differ from Augustine, and not only from Augustine but also from Aristotle and Islamic Aristotelianism, and he did so by calling forth a new conception of being, as being is now named as the act of existence itself (*ipsum esse*).

Now world itself stands forth as a new world, and even if the *novitas mundi* or the newness of the world is known only by revelation (*Summa Theologica*, I, 46, 2), existence itself can now be known, and actually known, as the creation of existence itself, and the act of creation is the act of pure actuality or pure act. While the act of creation is an act which is God's alone, it is nevertheless and even thereby the act of existence itself (*ipsum esse*), an act that is the "act of being" lying at the heart of the real, and thus it is identical with actual or real or pure existence. Aquinas can now say what Aristotle could never say: that God is the pure Act-of-Being, and this "act of being" is the actuality of being as being, so that now, and for the first time, existence itself can both be celebrated and be known as God's creation, and therefore known as the very "newness" of the world. If Aquinas thereby became the founder of modern thinking, even as Dante became the founder of modern poetry by realizing a total embodiment of the *novitas mundi* in the *Commedia*, or as Giotto became the founder of modern or even Western painting by realizing such an embodiment in his work, that thinking and that imagination are grounded in the newness of the world, a novum that became ever more fully and finally present in our consciousness and history, and a novum that even now is ending in our own time and world.

But with that ending has come a reversal of our history and consciousness, a reversal wherein the novum has not only ceased to be actually present, thereby ending all we once knew as the horizon of the future, but also a reversal wherein novum itself can now appear and be real only as an absolutely and totally original novum. If that novum is now manifest as the source of all and everything, it is also manifest in an original cosmological moment or instant which in our contemporary cosmologies is so microscopic as to be unimaginable—and yet we know it to be an instant of virtually infinite power, and a power even transcending everything which we can know as the life and power of the macrocosm. Nothing is or could be newer than the first instant of real or actual existence, and if that novum is the newness of world itself, it is also a total novum, and is so because it is totally new. How ironic that we are now being given cosmologies seemingly revolving about a once and for all creation out of nothing, and yet there is no place whatsoever in these cosmologies for that which we once knew as the Creator, and no possibility here of knowing a creation or world with a teleological purpose or goal. Yet this is making possible for us an apprehension of novum itself as totality, a totality transcending any truly knowable or imaginable origin or goal, and thereby transcending anything whatsoever conceivable or imaginable as the Creator.

Is it possible that such a novum is finally the genesis of scripture? Here, novum is far more ultimate than it has ever been in our theological traditions, a novum both absolutely new, and absolutely beginning, and so much so that beginning itself is all in all. In the beginning, God? The act of God as the act of beginning, an absolutely new act, and an act wherein and whereby God begins or dawns as God? If nothing else, such an image evokes the ultimacy of what the biblical tradition alone knows as the ultimacy of revelation, an ultimacy embodying the very speech of God as God, a speech apart from which God would not be and could not be God for us. In the beginning, God "said"; that saying is what Genesis knows as the act of creation, and that saying is repeated and renewed in what the prophetic traditions know and hear as the "I" of God, an "I" which, while wholly invisible, is nonetheless fully present in the speech or revelation of God. Biblically, that speech is the very origin of the world, and even if that origin is initially the once and for all act of beginning, that very origin is repeated in the words of revelation; and this is a repetition apart from which God would not be manifest or actual as God. Therein creation and revelation coincide, and the "word" of revelation is the "word" of creation, for in the beginning was the Word.

If creation is the once and for all act of ultimate beginning, that act is repeated and renewed in the advent of revelation, a revelation that begins with the self-naming of I AM. That self-naming, too, is beginning, and even ultimate beginning, for not only is it the historical or actual beginning of revelation, but therein and thereby it is the embodiment of a total actuality, an actuality which is itself the origin of a full and total releasement. That releasement is what we have known as history, an actuality enacting unique events, events which happen once and no more, and therefore events which as such can never be repeated. Yet having been once, though only once, such events have an actuality that otherwise would be absent, an actuality inseparable from the very ultimacy of their perishing. Only in the wake of the revelation of the divine name have events stood forth and been real in the actuality of their perishing, a perishing fully as actual as is the voice of I AM, and a perishing which is inescapable insofar as it occurs and is internally manifest. The very ultimacy of the revelation of the divine name is a once and for all releasement, a releasement that having occurred can never simply be annulled, and cannot be so annulled because it is an irreversible actuality.

That revelation brings an end to the omnipresent silence of the unsaid; this ending is itself actuality, and an actuality which is the final loss of an original and primordial silence. And that loss and that ending are realized in the self-naming of I AM, a self-naming which is the fullness and finality of speech itself, a finality finally ending an original and total silence. That ending is the beginning of a full and final actuality, an actuality which is perishing itself, and a perishing which we know as history. For the advent of history is the advent of death, and not simply the beginning of a real consciousness of death, but rather the beginning of a consciousness that is inseparable from the full actuality of death, and that not in its periphery but in its center and core.

Such death is not only an inescapable actuality, it is far rather actuality itself, an actuality which is the releasement of once and for all events, events which themselves are actual and real as the embodiment of death, or as the embodiment of a life that is inseparable from the fullness of death. Once the divine name has fully and finally been pronounced, to be open to the hearing of that name is to be open to the fullness of actuality itself, an actuality which is the perishing of all that life which is not an embodiment of death. A hearing of I AM is a hearing of pure actuality, and that hearing itself embodies that actuality, and therefore embodies the full and final presence of perishing and death. History is that presence, a presence which is the consequence of the revelation of I AM, a revelation apart from which neither history nor death would be fully manifest and real.

Thus the beginning of history is the beginning of fall, a fall from a consciousness that is closed to the full actuality of perishing and death, and a fall from an original or primordial state or condition that is an undifferentiated condition and therefore an original state of serenity and silence. That fall is the inauguration of the revelation of I AM, an inauguration which is not only itself a once and for all and ultimately unique event, but a beginning releasing unique events, and events whose very perishing is their full and final actuality. Such perishing is not only a consequence of the revelation of I AM, it is an embodiment of that revelation, an embodiment of the fullness and the finality of the voice of I AM, a voice whose very actualization releases the fullness of actuality itself. The self-revelation of I AM is the releasement of that actuality, a releasement which is the full and total presence of the voice of I AM, a presence which is therein the actual absence of the unspeakability of I AM, and that absence could only be a fall from an original plenitude. That plenitude, as an absolutely undifferentiated plenitude, could only be an absolutely inactive and therefore absolutely silent plenitude. This silence is broken with the advent of speech, and absolutely broken by the self-revelation of I AM.

Speech itself is inseparable from the loss of silence, and the speech or revelation of I AM is inseparable from the loss of the silence of an original transcendence or plenitude, a silence that is inseparable from an original or primordial totality. Hence that totality perishes when revelation occurs, or when a unique and actual revelation occurs, an occurrence which is a unique and once and for all event. The self-naming of I AM in a unique and actual revelation is inevitably and necessarily the loss of an original and total plenitude, and thus a fall from that plenitude, a fall which is the self-emptying of an original and silent totality. That self-emptying could only be both an actual and a final fall, a fall from the pure and total silence of a wholly inactual totality, and a fall which is itself the irreversible beginning of a full and final actualization.

Nothing is more distant from an irreversible beginning than an eternal cycle of return, and if the myth of eternal return is the paradigmatic center of all archaic and primordial worlds, a once and for all and irreversible beginning is the paradigmatic center of an irreversible historical world, a world that is the consequence of the revelation of I AM. Within no other horizon of consciousness do events stand forth and become manifest as unique and irreversible events—events which happen only once, but whose sheer occurrence is an irreversible finality. That finality is inseparable from an irreversible beginning, a beginning which as beginning can never be annulled, and therefore a beginning whose finality is irrevocable. And it is irrevocable as actual beginning, a beginning which can never simply pass into ending, as beginning does in a cycle or circle of eternal return.

Just as nothing finally distinguishes alpha and omega or beginning and ending in a cycle of eternal return, so a once and for all beginning is *beginning alone*, an absolutely unique beginning, and a unique beginning which is the origin and ground of irreversible and unique events. Apart from that ground, events could be neither final nor unique, and then events could never be events which are fully and only themselves. Only in the wake and in the horizon of the revelation of I AM do events appear and become manifest as events which are individually and uniquely themselves, and that wake and that horizon are the consequence of an irreversible beginning. Once that occurrence has entered the center of consciousness, consciousness itself becomes closed to events which eternally repeat and renew themselves in a cycle of eternal return. But with the closure of the cycle of eternal return, ending becomes manifest and real as an irrevocable perishing, a death that is fully and only itself, and therefore a death that can never pass into life.

The advent of irrevocable death is therewith and thereby the advent of a final actuality, an actuality inseparable from unique and irreversible events, and an actuality bestowing upon life itself the finality of an inescapable and irrevocable death. Consequently, the finalities of life and death are now inseparable, as the advent of irrevocable death bestows upon life itself a new finality, a finality never hitherto present and a finality inescapable for a consciousness knowing the ultimacy of death. Once such life has become manifest and real, nothing is more forbidden than a longing for death, a death that now and for the first time appears and is real through the new portal of the full and actual darkness of chaos. Only now does chaos appear as a chaos that is only itself, an ultimate abyss which can never be sanctified or reversed in a cycle of eternal return, and a final abyss which is eternally closed to the presence of light. Yet the manifestation and realization of that chaos is a decisive sign of the presence of a truly new life, a life liberated from the encompassing power of a primordial abyss that can be the giver of life, as the realization of the final and total darkness of chaos shatters the enticing and beckoning power of every primordial or original source and ground. Now death is otherness itself, a death that is wholly other than life; and with the realization of that life the life-giving power of the call of eternal return is ended.

Not until the self-naming of I AM is the call of eternal return truly challenged and reversed. Now that challenge occurs through a radical iconoclasm, an iconoclasm shattering every image and sign of an original or primordial ground or light. That iconoclasm is not a consequence of an epiphany of I AM, but rather of the very speech of I AM, for that speaking which is the revelation of I AM is speaking and speaking alone, a pure speech foreclosing the very possibility of vision. Thereby speech itself gains an identity that it never had before, as primal speech is not only dissociated from myth and rite, but precisely thereby is liberated from every possibility of eternal repetition or eternal return. The words or speech of I AM can never pass into a cycle of eternal return, and cannot do so because these are words which can only be heard as themselves and no other, just as the very pronunciation of these words established the possibility of hearing a speech which is only itself, a possibility apart from which the words of I AM could not be heard. But those words were heard, and their hearing issued in the ending of eternal return, an ending which is the beginning of the impact of irreversible events upon consciousness, an impact which ever more gradually and more fully called forth the release of individual and unique identities. Thereby and therein a once and for all and irreversible beginning becomes manifest and real, a beginning which is not only the ending of the cycle of eternal return, but is also and even thereby the beginning of all individual and unique identity.

The very speech of I AM is the self-negation of an original transcendence or totality which is itself unspeakable, and unspeakable by virtue of the inevitable silence of an undifferentiated totality, a totality foreclosing the possibility of a voice which could actually and immediately speak. Israel alone is the site of the full advent of a wholly transcendent and eternal voice speaking in and as an individual and unique voice, a voice that is itself wholly other than the total silence of an undifferentiated totality, and therefore is in itself and as itself the pure opposite of that totality. The actual occurrence of that voice is undeniable, or undeniable in terms of the revolutionary transformations which followed in its wake, for therein and thereby an archaic or primordial world is truly ended. That is nothing less than a revolutionary reversal of all archaic and primordial grounds, a revolution occurring within the horizons of the self-naming of I AM, as a wholly new hearing now occurs, negating everything in the hearer which is not attentive and wholly attentive to this pure speech occurring here and now, and occurring in actual and immediate words. Thereby the hearer is hurled out of every center which is not fully present and actual here and now, every center which is not immediately present in a horizon of speech and of speech alone, a speech assaulting that center which is not wholly here and now, and therefore a speech immediately calling forth a hearing which ends every center which is everywhere.

Now it is precisely because the self-naming of I AM is a total voice that it is a total presence; therefore that presence is the self-negation of an original and a total silence, a self-negation occurring here and now, and wholly occurring here and now, and occurring in the pure immediacy of this unique and totally actual voice. If this occurrence initially realizes a unique actuality, it also and thereby releases actuality itself, an actuality which now is immediately and totally present, and totally present in a once and for all and irreversible event. That event is inevitably and necessarily a reversal of an eternal presence that is an *eternal now*, and is so precisely because it is a once and for all and unique event, an event that is the very opposite of an eternal now that is eternal recurrence or return. Consequently, the enactment of a once and for all event is a pure negation of an eternal presence which is an eternal now, and a self-negation of that presence, or a self-negation of its own original or primordial ground. Apart from a pure and total negation of that ground, there could be no actualization of eternity in an irreversible event, a once and for all event which is totally present, and totally present in and as this actual and unique event. Therefore the self-naming of I AM is the self-emptying of an eternal presence that is an eternal now, or an eternal presence that is an eternal recurrence or return, or an eternal presence that is the absolute ubiquity of an eternal now. Now that eternal presence is fully and purely actual here and now, and totally present in the final actuality of an irreversible and once and for all event, an event that is not only an irreversible event but therein and thereby an irrevocable event, and irrevocable in the very finality of its actuality, a finality embodying the ultimacy of eternity itself.

Classical Christian theology from Augustine through Aquinas could know the act of creation and the act of revelation as the one eternal act of God, and if Aquinas could differ from Augustine in knowing creation as a new act, he therein knew it as the act of existence itself (*ipsum esse*), or the act of that pure Act-of-Being which is God alone. Act-of-Being is Aquinas's metaphysical conception of the "I AM" of Exodus, and even if it is an analogical conception it is nevertheless a conception of God, and a conception of that God who is pure actuality or pure act. That act is present and is purely and totally present in the act of revelation, even as it is totally present in the original act of creation; and if those acts are one act, or one eternal "act of being," then that "act of being" is a pure actuality which is only itself, and is only itself in that original beginning which is an eternal beginning, or is eternity itself.

Yet this is an eternity that is wholly other than the eternity which is metaphysically known by a pre-Christian world, and is so because it is a truly new eternity, an eternity wholly absent from the myth or the cycle of eternal return, and wholly absent precisely because this is a new eternity. Indeed, it is a new eternity because it is fully and totally present in the original act of creation, even as it is also so present in the original act of revelation, and even if these acts are one eternal act, that act is a once and for all and irreversible act, and it is precisely as such that it is wholly absent from all nonbiblical or nonrevelatory worlds.

So it is that a new eternity is wholly absent from all such worlds, even as a unique and absolute beginning and a unique and absolute revelation are not present in these worlds, and cannot be so present if only because these worlds inevitably remain bound to an eternal cycle of return. That is the eternity which is reversed by the self-naming of I AM, but so likewise is it reversed by the once and for all and irreversible act of creation, an act not only ending the cycle of eternal return, but thereby ending a primordial or original eternity. That is the eternity which is ended by "God said," an eternity which is an original silence or quiescence, and therefore a non-actual eternity, an eternity which cannot be immediately or actually present. That purely actual presence occurs only through "pure act," a pure act that is a new act or actuality, and it is new just because it is a once and for all and irreversible act, an act that never can be annulled or undone, and therefore an act that can never pass into a cycle of eternal return. If creation is fall in archaic and primordial mythologies, it is inevitably destined therein to undergo regeneration in a cycle of eternal return, but a once and for all and irreversible act of creation cannot undergo such regeneration, and cannot do so if only because it is an irreversible act.

Christianity has inevitably known fall as a *felix culpa*, or fortunate fall, and has known creation as a witness to and even an embodiment of the glory of God, a glory that is present in every act of God, and perhaps most clearly manifest in the original act of God. If the Christian can understand that act as a *felix culpa*, it is therein a fall from a primordial or original eternity, or an eternity that cannot become or be a truly or actually new eternity. A once and for all and irreversible beginning inevitably and necessarily embodies a new creation. This creation could never occur in a cycle of eternal return, and therefore could never occur either by way of or within the horizon of a primordial or original eternity, an eternity that is eternal recurrence, or an eternity that could never be present in actual and therefore irreversible acts. An original or primordial eternity must disappear and be dissolved or annulled in irreversible acts which can never be undone, and disappear or dissolve if only because such acts can never return to an eternal source or ground, because such acts can never be truly or wholly annulled. Act realizes a wholly new identity when it is realized as an irreversible act, and if a once and for all creation is an irreversible creation, it is therefore a new creation, and a creation that is wholly and ultimately new.

Yet a realization of that creation must necessarily and inevitably be a fall from an eternity that could never become new, or an eternity that is always and only itself, or an eternity that is an eternal cycle or circle of return. Hence a once and for all beginning is a violent disruption and annulment of that eternity, a disruption so violent that it ends the cycle of eternal return, and therefore ends an eternity that is eternally and only itself. That eternity ends in a once and for all and irreversible beginning, so that, if that beginning is an ultimate beginning, it is therefore an ultimate ending, and an ending of that eternity which is eternal recurrence or return. If such a beginning is wholly absent from all archaic and primordial worlds, and also so absent from all nonrevelatory or nonbiblical worlds, it is fully and totally present within those worlds which have heard and therein realized the self-naming of I AM, a self-naming which is the unnaming of eternal recurrence.

That unnaming is a repetition and renewal of a once and for all beginning, and not an eternal repetition which reverses the irreversibility of that beginning, but rather a repetition which renews that irreversibility, and renews it so as to give it an ultimate and final identity or name. I AM is the name for us of a once and for all and irreversible beginning, a beginning that is an ultimate and final beginning, and therefore a new creation, and not only a new creation but a new eternity, and an eternity that can only be evoked for us by the name of I AM. The revelation of that name silences and annuls all earlier names of eternity, even as the eternal act of speech brings an end to an original and total silence, but that ending is a repetition and renewal of a once and for all beginning, a beginning shattering and annulling an original quiescence, and thus bringing a final end to an eternity that is and only is itself.

Only the ending of that eternity makes possible and actual a once and for all and irreversible beginning, a beginning that is beginning and only beginning, and a beginning that is a new creation or a new eternity or a new totality, and is a new totality because it is a new actuality, and an actuality that can only be the consequence of ending or death. Eternity itself must die to realize a new eternity, or an old or original eternity must perish to make possible the advent of a new eternity; and if that new eternity is absolutely new, it is a novum whose actualization annuls a nonbeginning or simply eternal eternity, now that eternity becomes unnameable, and becomes unnameable because now it is actually absent or gone. Hence an original or primordial eternity is now unnameable, and is unnameable because it is unmanifest and thereby unreal, or unreal to that hearing which has heard the self-naming of I AM. For the hearing of the self-naming of I AM is the hearing of an absolutely new and an absolute actual totality, an actuality which is the perishing of an original eternal presence or eternal now, a perishing which is the perishing of a center which is everywhere, or a center which cannot be actually and totally present here and now. The beginning of that presence is the ending of eternal return, and therefore the ending of an original or primordial eternity, a primordial eternity that is an eternal now, an eternal now that is an eternal recurrence, but an eternal recurrence which is negated in a once and for all and irreversible beginning. That negation can only be both a total and an actual act, for otherwise eternal recurrence or eternal return would not actually cease to be itself; and this is a perishing which inevitably occurs in a truly new creation, a new creation which is an absolute beginning, and that beginning can only be the ending of an eternity which cannot become "new."

Genesis or absolute beginning is the perishing of that eternity; it is a beginning which is the perishing or death of an original eternity or totality, a perishing which is not only the pure negation of that totality but which finally can be only the self-negation or the self-emptying of that totality. Eternity itself becomes absolutely new in that perishing, an absolute novum that is the absolute ending of an original eternity, an absolute ending which is the self-naming of I AM, a self-naming which is genesis or absolute beginning, a beginning which is itself the actual ending of everything which is not realized or grounded in this absolute and ultimate and final act. Thus absolute beginning is inseparable from absolute ending, and if beginning and ending are finally indistinguishable in a cycle of eternal return, they are one act or event in absolute novum, and if that act is absolute beginning and absolute ending at once, nevertheless that beginning and that ending are not simply and only identical with each other, for each is truly itself in its own beginning and its own ending, a beginning which is totally beginning and an ending that is totally ending, and each can truly and actually be itself only through the actual and final enactment of the other.

If a cycle of eternal return is a cycle foreclosing the possibility of the new, the act of genesis or absolute beginning forecloses the possibility of an eternity which is eternally and only the same, that foreclosure is *an act of pure and total negation*, even if it is simultaneously the total realization of the absolutely new. That simultaneity is absolute negation and absolute affirmation at once, a pure negation which is a pure affirmation, but an affirmation or enactment which is an actual and total perishing, and a perishing which is the reversal and annulment of an eternity which is wholly other than absolute novum, or an eternity which is eternally the same. Now an original or primordial eternity is negated and reversed, and negated and reversed in its realization of itself as a new eternity, so that the annulment of an original eternity is itself the self-realization of a new eternity. Consequently, genesis or absolute novum is the self-negation or self-emptying of an eternity which is eternally and only itself.

2

Genesis and Death

The absolute enactment of genesis is the absolute disenactment of an original silence or plenitude. That disenactment is the perishing of an original plenitude, and not simply the perishing of that plenitude, but its absolute disruption, a disruption wherein and whereby an original or primordial totality becomes the very opposite of itself. And it necessarily becomes the opposite of itself if only because of the very advent of a once and for all and irreversible beginning, a beginning which by necessity is an absolute novum, a novum which is the very opposite of an eternal now, and a novum whose actualization is the absolute emptying or reversal of an eternal now. Now, an original silence is no more, and never again will it be heard within that horizon which is the horizon or the arena of the self-naming of I AM; and nothing more manifestly distinguishes that consciousness which embodies the self-naming of I AM from that consciousness which embodies an eternal return than does the very disappearance or annulment of an original silence in the world or in the worlds of that consciousness which is a consciousness of I AM. But the very disappearance of that silence is the advent of an actual beginning, an actual beginning which is irreversibly beginning, and in that very irreversibility is the annulment of an eternal now which eternally begins, or an eternal now which is beginning and ending simultaneously, or an eternal now which is an eternal return.

Consequently, a once and for all and irreversible beginning is the final ending of eternal return, and the actual ending of that now which is and only is an eternal now, or that eternity in which every moment is finally and only now, or that eternity in which every moment is fully and wholly identical with every other moment. That is the eternity and that is the eternal return which actually ends in the advent of an irreversible beginning, an ending which is the actual ending of an original or primordial eternity, and therefore that advent can be named as the real and actual death of an original totality.

Yet it is precisely the actual death of an original eternity which is the advent of the novum or the absolutely new; so long as every moment is an eternal moment or an eternal now, novum as such is impossible, and with that impossibility beginning cannot actually begin. Novum or the absolutely new is by necessity wholly other than an eternal now, and only the self-negation or the self-emptying of an eternal now can realize the advent of the novum, a novum that can be actual only in the perishing of an eternal now, and only in the actual perishing or death of that original eternity. If I AM is the self-naming of the absolutely new, that self-naming is the self-naming of death, the naming of that death which occurs with the revelation of I AM, and which is enacted with the realization of a once and for all and irreversible beginning. The very actuality of this once and for all event is the actuality of death itself, a death that is the actual ending of eternal silence, and therefore the once and for all and irreversible ending of that silence, an actual ending that occurs when, in the beginning, "God said."

Just as the actual beginning of speech is the actual ending of silence, the absolute beginning of speech is the absolute ending of silence, an actual or absolute ending that can occur only through death, a death that is the actuality of a once and for all beginning. The actuality of that death is ultimately new, and not only ultimately but absolutely new, a novum that is named in the self-naming of I AM. Hence I AM is the name of the final actuality of death itself, a death which enacts, and finally enacts, the absolutely new. Absolute novum is truly new only insofar as it is the other side of the actuality of death. That death is not only an actual death, but is an actually enacted death, and a death that actually enacts itself, and actually enacts itself as the pure and total opposite of an original and total silence. The speech or revelation of I AM is the true opposite of an original totality of silence, and it occurs only by way of the actual death of that silence; thereby that silence becomes the very opposite of itself in the self-naming of I AM, and does so through the actuality of the self-negation or self-emptying of itself. That self-emptying is the actual realization of the pure otherness of an original and total silence, an otherness apart from which speech could not actually occur, and the absolutely new could not actually begin.

Thus it is that absolute novum begins in and as the death of silence, the death of a silence which cannot actually speak, and cannot actually speak because it is a silence that is everywhere. Now silence is nowhere, or nowhere where it is only and simply itself, for its very realization as the pure otherness of itself shatters its original plenitude, and with the actual ending of that plenitude, silence perishes as an encompassing totality. That is the perishing or death which is the advent of a full and total actuality, and if that actuality only begins with genesis, its beginning is a total and irreversible beginning, and a beginning whose ending can never occur by way of a cycle of eternal return, but only by way of a final and total realization of itself. Novum is that actual death which not only ends the cycle of eternal return, but ends it so as to foreclose the very possibility of eternal return; and with that foreclosure the backward movement of eternal recurrence reverses itself, and reverses itself by becoming the very opposite of itself. Now the eternally reversible movement of eternal return becomes an irreversible and therefore forward movement, and forward precisely because of the actual impossibility of return, an impossibility which is the consequence of death, and the consequence of that death which is the death or ending of eternal return. Now beginning is not the beginning of eternal return, but the beginning of the reversal of eternal return, a reversal in which the eternal cycle of return becomes the very opposite of itself as a cycle of return.

Then and only then eternal recurrence is only and wholly the absolutely new, an absolutely new which is the impossibility of eternal return, an impossibility realizing a future that is actually new, and is actually new precisely because of the impossibility of return. A real and actual future is born only by way of the ending of the cycle of eternal return; that ending is the actual death of the reversibility of eternal recurrence, and only that death makes possible the realization of the actuality of the future. Hence the actuality of the future is impossible apart from the impossibility of return, an impossibility realized with the enactment of a once and for all and irreversible beginning, a beginning realizing and necessarily and inevitably realizing a forward movement to the future. History is our name for a forward movement to the future, and even if we are living at the end of history, we are thereby living in the wake of history, and therefore in the wake of an irreversible and forward movement, a movement foreclosing the actual possibility of return. I AM is the name of the impossibility of return, and the revelation of that name is the revelation of the impossibility of return, an impossibility that is realized in the advent of history and therefore realized in the advent of irreversible events, events which happen once and only once; but the ultimacy of that occurrence is the realization of an actual future, and a future that is actual only with the realization of once and for all and irreversible events.

If nothing is more alien to all ancient and primordial worlds than the actuality of the future, nothing is more actual in those worlds which have heard, and have actually heard, the revelation of I AM. The hearing of that revelation is the hearing of an absolute event which is a once and for all and irreversible event, and thus the hearing of that event is the hearing of the foreclosure or death of the possibility of return. That death or foreclosure is simultaneously and even therein the actuality of the future, a future that is manifest and real only with the ending of return. History dawns in that hearing, a history that is the consequence of a once and for all beginning, and therefore the consequence of an irreversible actuality, an actuality that is itself the actuality of the future. An actual future is not only the intrinsic other of eternal return but also of an eternal now; only the disappearance of that now makes possible an intrinsic and actual future, a disappearance which is a reversal of a now which is eternally and only itself. That reversal realizes the actuality of the future, a future that can truly and actually realize itself only with the perishing of the now, and not simply the perishing of a present and immediate now, but also the perishing of that eternal now which is present in every now; only that perishing makes possible a true and ultimate future, or a future which is essentially and intrinsically different from both the present and the past.

Now if it is true that an actual and an ultimate future is alien to or absent from every historical world which is innocent of the self-naming of I AM, that very absence is the absence of the reversal of eternal return, and consequently the absence of the self-emptying or the self-negation of an eternal now. Only that self-emptying gives birth to a real and essential difference between the present and the past, a difference which is an ultimate difference, and only the advent of that ultimate difference makes possible a real and actual future. Hence that future is the consequence of perishing or death, the death of an eternal now comprehending each and every now; and with the realization of that death each and every now passes into the past, and into an actual past, a past that is only actually realized with the perishing of an eternal now.

Therefore the actuality of the future is the other side of the actuality of the past, and it can become manifest and real only with the realization of a past which is truly and actually past, and thus a past which can never actually return. Accordingly, the foreclosure or reversal of eternal return is the advent of the actuality of time itself; therein and thereby the past dawns as a past which is truly and only past, and the future dawns only as the consequence of the full actuality of the past. Now a future is at hand which is actually future, but it is so only with the closure of eternal return, a closure which is a realization of the irreversibility of the past, an irreversibility which is itself the actualization of the future. Once the self-naming of I AM has occurred in a once and for all and irreversible event, the past dawns as a past which is fully and finally past, and that dawning is itself the actualization of a new future, a future that never before was manifest or real, for it can become actual and real only by way of the disappearance of the presence of the past.

That disappearance is a reversal of the past, or a reversal of the eternal return of the past, a reversal that is the inevitable consequence of the enactment of a once and for all and irreversible event. The very irreversibility of that event ends the return of the past, and necessarily ends it in the full and final occurrence of an irreversible event; that once and for all event ends the eternal cycle of return, and therefore brings a final end to a past that could or will return. That ending is the advent of the actuality of the future, an actuality that is possible only by way of the ending of the repetition of the past, an ending which is itself the advent of the actuality of the past. Now the past appears and is real as a past which is truly past, and the future appears and is real as a future which cannot be a repetition of the past. But a future that cannot be a repetition of the past is a future that cannot be the future of eternal return, and therefore cannot be an eternal now, and cannot be an eternal now if only because an eternal now eternally returns. Only the ending, and the full and final ending, of an eternal now releases the actuality of absolute novum; that actuality is the consequence of death, and of an actual death: the death of an eternity that is eternally and only itself. Thus the advent of absolute novum is the advent of death, a death apart from which novum would not be and could not be novum, and could not be novum because, apart from the actuality of the self-emptying or the self-negation of an original eternity, the cycle of eternal return would not be ended. Then neither past nor future would be actually real, but just as the actuality of the future is simultaneously the actuality of the past, the very advent of that actuality is the advent of a truly new opposition between the future and the past, an opposition which is the consequence of the actualization of a new otherness, an otherness here and now realizing itself in an essential and intrinsic difference between the future and the past.

No such difference is possible within the horizon of a cycle of eternal return, nor is it possible within an eternity that is eternally and only itself, or an eternity that is an eternal now. Novum is precisely what is absent in that eternity, a novum that is actually and not eternally new, and thus a novum that must necessarily and actually end an original eternity. Hence the advent of a future which is necessarily other than the past is the advent of difference or otherness itself, an otherness that could not be actual or real in an original eternity, for an original eternity is eternally the same. In the beginning, "God said," and that "said" is the advent of ultimate difference or otherness, an otherness that is absolutely new, and an otherness which is the real and actual ending of an eternal now. If I AM is the name of absolute novum, and therefore the name of the actual ending or death of an eternity which is eternally the same, then I AM could only be silent and unspeakable in an original eternity, an eternity foreclosing the possibility of real and actual difference or otherness.

Nothing is more intrinsically other than the self-naming of I AM, a self-naming whose very speech or revelation makes manifest and real a new and wholly other transcendence, a transcendence not possible within the horizon of eternal return, and not possible within an eternity that is eternally the same. Only the ending of that eternity makes possible the self-naming of I AM, a self-naming which is the advent of a real and actual difference or otherness, and therefore the advent of ultimate opposition, an opposition which actually speaks in the self-naming of I AM. That self-naming is the repetition of a once and for all beginning, an actual beginning which is an actual ending, and the actuality of that beginning and ending is the advent of pure difference or otherness itself—an otherness apart from which beginning could not actually begin. Thus an actual beginning is the beginning of an actual otherness, an otherness that is wholly other than the same, and an otherness that could not be real apart from the loss or dissolution or self-emptying of the same. That loss is the advent of absolute novum, a novum which is pure difference or pure otherness, and pure difference from an eternity which is eternally the same, or from an eternity which is only eternally and never actually new. That difference is new, and is both actually and absolutely new, a difference that is not only different from the same, but is absolutely different from and other than the same. That is the difference which is actualized in "God said," a pure difference and a pure otherness which is unreal apart from "God said," and therefore unreal apart from "God."

In the beginning, "God"? Yes, for in the beginning is pure difference or pure otherness, an otherness which is "God," and an otherness apart from which beginning could not actually begin. That difference is what a postexilic Israel could name as the Creator, a Creator who alone is Creator, and a Creator who alone is finally actor, and who is finally actor only by being finally alone. The God who is God and only God is pure difference or pure otherness itself; that is a difference which is necessarily unreal in an eternity which is eternally the same, and therefore that is a difference which begins, and which actually begins, in "God said." If "God said" is the self-naming of I AM, that is a self-naming which is the actualization of pure difference or pure otherness, and therefore the actualization of "God." If "God" is the God who is God and only God, God is the consequence of death, and the actual consequence of an actual death. Only the final ending of eternal recurrence or eternal return makes possible a once and for all and irreversible beginning, an actual beginning which is absolutely new, and is absolutely new only by way of the absolute ending of an eternity which is eternally the same.

Consequently, God is the self-emptying or the self-negation of that eternity, a self-negation which is a once and for all and irreversible event, and therefore is the actual event of death, the actual and irreversible death of that eternity which is eternally the same. A once and for all and irreversible beginning is the beginning of "God," the beginning of that God who is absolutely new, and the beginning thereby and therein of actuality itself, an actuality which is absolutely new, and is absolutely new only by being wholly different from or wholly other than an eternity which is the eternity of an eternal now. If that actuality is inseparable from God, or inseparable from the act or enactment of God, it is unmanifest and unreal apart from God, or apart from the self-naming of I AM, a self-naming which is once and for all and irreversible beginning itself. Yet that beginning is itself the actuality of death, a death realizing itself as pure otherness itself, an otherness which is itself the enactment of the full and final perishing of an eternity which is eternally the same.

Hence the beginning or origin of God is the beginning or origin of death, and not a death which returns as life in a cycle of eternal return, or an eternal death which is finally and only an eternal life, but rather an actual death, and the actual death of that eternal now which is an original eternity. Only that death makes possible a pure difference or pure otherness; indeed, that death is the embodiment of pure otherness, a pure otherness which ends and finally ends the eternal cycle of return. If such pure difference or pure otherness is unmanifest and unreal in all ancient or primordial worlds, that absence is the absence of the actuality of both the future and the past, an absence which alone makes possible an eternal cycle of return. The advent of pure otherness ends that cycle, and irreversibly ends it, for the actualization of pure otherness brings a final and definitive end to every now which is an eternal now, to every now which is simply and only identical with its own future and its own past.

Now, the present moment is the very opposite of an eternal now, and is so by virtue of the absolutely new presence of death or perishing itself, a perishing which is the present moment, and that perishing is irreversibly real. But that is the perishing which realizes the actuality of the future and the past. Only that perishing establishes a true and actual difference between the present and the past, a difference apart from which every moment would eternally be the same. An actual otherness is an alien and opposing otherness, and nowhere is that otherness more fully manifest than in the actuality of the present moment, a moment that in being actually present is actually absent, and absent by virtue of its immediate passage into the past, a passage apart from which a present moment would not be actually present. But simultaneously an actual present immediately passes into the future, and that passage is indistinguishable from its passage into the past, so that an actually present moment is simultaneously an immediate transition into the future and the past, a transition which is a double negation, and a double negation occurring simultaneously. Such a double negation is inherent in actuality itself, and it is inseparable from pure otherness itself, an otherness that is essentially and inherently other than itself, so that the actualization of that otherness can only be a self-negation or a self-emptying, and a self-emptying which is a real and actual emptying of itself. That is the self-emptying which is a once and for all and irreversible beginning, a beginning which is self-negation or self-annihilation itself, and is so if only because it is the self-embodiment of pure otherness itself, an otherness that only now is purely actual, and is actual as the actuality of itself. So it is that pure actuality is pure otherness, and an otherness that is the otherness of itself, and the origin of that actuality is the beginning of pure otherness itself, an origin that is present and actually present wherever actuality is itself.

Death is our name for pure otherness itself, an otherness that is present in every actual moment, and present as the actuality of perishing itself. Even if such perishing makes possible the actuality of the future and the past, it does so precisely as perishing itself, a perishing which is not only pure otherness, but an otherness that is the otherness of itself. That is an otherness that we can name only as death, a death which is an absolutely alien and opposing otherness, and a death that is inevitably and necessarily realized in actuality itself. Thus the presence of actuality is the presence of an abyss, an abyss that is darkness incarnate, and is darkness incarnate because it is a darkness which is actual as itself. Only the presence of that abyss releases actuality, an actuality that is actual only as the otherness of itself; that pure otherness is an embodiment of abyss, and not the embodiment of a silent and unspeakable abyss, but rather an embodiment of an abyss which actually realizes itself as abyss. If that realization is the enactment of an irreversible beginning, that enactment is the inversion and reversal of the eternal cycle of return and that enactment is the embodiment of the very opposite of an eternal now. And it is the opposite of an eternal now by being the embodiment of death, a death which is a pure and an actual otherness, and therefore an otherness which is the full realization of abyss.

Nothing is more distinctive in the hearing of I AM than the hearing of abyss, and if the actual hearing of abyss occurs only in the horizon of the self-naming of I AM, that is a horizon grounded in abyss, and grounded in an actually heard abyss, an abyss that here and here alone is fully and actually spoken. Thereby a hearing occurs that is hearing and hearing alone, as an actually spoken abyss uproots every ground which is not present and actual here and now, thereby releasing a wholly new attention to a present and actual moment, a moment that here and now is an absolute abysmal moment, and an absolutely abysmal moment because it is a purely actual moment, and therefore a moment which is absolute perishing itself. If that perishing is death, it is a fully actual death, and thus a death that is only present as itself, and thus is actual as a pure difference or a pure otherness, an otherness that is the very otherness of itself. That is the pure otherness which is heard in the voice of I AM; now abyss speaks, and fully speaks as itself, and if this is a speech which is speech and only speech, it is so as the voice of a totally actual abyss, an abyss that here and here alone is fully incarnate only as itself. That incarnation is the incarnation of pure voice, a voice shattering every ground that is not open and fully open to itself, and therein and thereby it is the voice of abyss, and the voice of a totally actual abyss, an abyss that here and here alone is fully actual as itself. The self-naming of I AM names itself in and as that abyss, an abyss which here and here alone is fully heard, and fully heard because it is fully spoken, and fully spoken in an actual repetition of a once and for all and irreversible beginning. Abyss speaks in that repetition, and speaks in and as that abyss which is actualized in an irreversible beginning, an abyss that is pure otherness, and a pure otherness whose actualization alone makes possible the final ending of an eternity that is eternally the same. Thereby death itself is manifest and real, a pure death that is a pure otherness, and a pure otherness that is the actual otherness of itself.

Festivals celebrating a primordial beginning are found throughout the archaic world, and such festivals commonly revolve about a ritual and mythical enactment of sacrifice, a sacrifice which is a repetition and reenactment of an original sacrifice, and an original sacrifice which is universally celebrated as a primordial beginning. That beginning is repeated and renewed in archaic rites as the inauguration of a cycle of eternal return, and hence is repeated as a primordial beginning, or as a beginning which eternally returns in a cycle of eternal return. But that is precisely the cycle which is shattered by the self-naming of I AM, and shattered by the embodiment of an abyss which wholly transcends every chaos which is known and named by an archaic world, and it wholly transcends that chaos because here an abyss is present which cannot be repeated in a cycle of eternal return, and cannot be so repeated if only because it is an irreversible abyss. While an archaic or primordial chaos can be repeated in a cycle of eternal return, and thereby can continually pass into its own polar contrary, a once and for all and irreversible abyss cannot cease as such to be only abyss, and therefore it cannot be reversed without wholly and finally ceasing to be itself. And once that abyss has fully spoken or revealed itself, then an archaic chaos disappears from view, and abyss can never again be manifest as an abyss which passes into its own polar contrary in a movement of eternal return. No longer is it possible to know either a primordial chaos or a primordial sacrifice as a death that eternally passes into life, or not within that horizon realized by the hearing of the voice of I AM, a horizon realized by the full and final advent of an irreversible death or abyss.

Now, there can be no awareness of or attention to an eternal circle of return, for the hearing of pure otherness, which is the hearing of the voice of I AM, is the hearing of that otherness which can never undergo an eternal reversal of itself, and thus can never be realized as a life which is the other side of death. Death then ceases to be a death which is life and death at once, and chaos ceases to be a chaos which eternally passes into cosmos, for now death is fully and finally actual as itself, and abyss is that abyss which can never cease to be abyss. Nothing less than this ultimate transformation is at hand in the advent of a pure and final irreversibility, an irreversibility embodying pure difference, and a pure difference which is the very otherness of itself. Not until the self-naming of I AM does an actual death fully enter the center of consciousness, then immortality or eternal life becomes absolutely forbidden to that consciousness, or forbidden so long as the echoes of that self-naming continue to reverberate, and then eternal return in any form is absolutely condemned as idolatry, an idolatry that is a flight from the self-naming of I AM. Only then does an absolute apostasy appear and become real, an apostasy which is the refusal of the voice of I AM, and hence the refusal of a once and for all and irreversible abyss.

Nowhere is death so actual as it is in that hearing which hears the voice of I AM. Simply to hear that voice is to hear the actuality of death, and the actuality of that death which is fully and immediately at hand. Therein an abyss is present, and an actual abyss of death itself, a pure otherness assaulting its hearer, and assaulting its hearer so as to erase every trace of an eternity that is an eternal now. Once this hearing has occurred, an original silence is interiorly ended, and the ending of that silence is the ending of every silence which does not embody the actuality of abyss. That actuality is embodied in pure hearing, a hearing which hears pure otherness or pure difference itself, and does so if only because it fully and actually hears, and therefore it cannot hear silence, or cannot hear a silence which is only itself. Hence that silence ends in such hearing, and it does so if only because of the actuality of pure hearing, an actuality that is irreversible, and therefore an actuality that can never recover an original silence. Now, the possibility of return is fully ended, and is ended in this very hearing, and this is an ending forever erasing an original silence, and with that erasure an original silence is no more.

The disappearance of that silence is the disappearance of every origin which is not the origin of an abyss. Now origin itself can only be the origin of pure otherness, a pure otherness that can never pass into a pure silence, and this because it can never be annulled or erased as otherness itself. Such otherness is irreversible, and it is irreversible as the otherness of itself, an otherness embodying the finality of death, and embodying the finality of an actual and irreversible death, a death that is inseparable from the very enactment of an irreversible act, and therefore a death that is not only present in but is present *as* that act. Consequently, the very enactment of a once and for all and irreversible act is the enactment of death itself, a death that is a pure death because it is irreversible, and that irreversibility is now manifest and real in every actual moment, and is so in the very perishing of that moment, a perishing that can never be annulled, and can never be annulled so long as actuality is immediately at hand. If that actuality is the actuality of death, it is a death that is not only a consequence of a once and for all and irreversible event, but it is also a death that is the embodiment of that event, and therefore the embodiment of an act that can never be annulled. That is the act which is fully and wholly present in the voice of I AM, and totally present as the voice of I AM, so that the hearing of that voice is the hearing of the actuality of death itself, an actuality that now can never be erased. Now actuality realizes itself as an actuality that is all in all, but it does so only by virtue of its origin in a once and for all and irreversible act, an act whose enactment ends every presence which is not the presence of death.

Now death realizes an ultimacy that is absolutely new, and it is new not only as an irreversible presence, a presence which now and only now can never cease to be itself, but also as a presence which is everywhere, or everywhere within the horizon of irreversible events. If irreversible events themselves embody a new world, a world which never could be present or real within a cycle or a circle of eternal return, and never could be actual apart from an ending of the cycle of eternal return, such events are not only new in their very occurrence, but new in their actuality as well, an actuality realizing the ultimacy of death, and realizing that ultimacy in every actual moment. Such a moment is impossible apart from a once and for all and irreversible beginning, if only because only such a beginning could end the cycle of eternal return, a cycle within which no actual moment could ever occur, because here no moment could be present which does not eternally reverse itself, and eternally reverse itself in an eternal now. Now that eternal now is ended, and its ending releases actuality itself, an actuality that is only itself, and therefore an actuality that is irreversible. That is an irreversibility which is the irreversibility of death, and the irreversibility of an actual and final death, a death that can never be reversed as death, and therefore a death that is ultimately new, and ultimately new in its very occurrence. So it is that novum itself is not only inseparable from death, but is the very embodiment of death, and the embodiment of an actual and final death, the death of every moment that is eternally the same, and thus the death of that eternity which is and only is eternity, or that eternity which is an eternal now, or that eternity which is not the self-negation or the self-emptying of itself.

3

The Birth of History

If the advent of history is the advent of once and for all and irreversible events, that advent embodies its own ending, a final ending which is inseparable from an irreversible beginning, if only because such a beginning is not and cannot be an eternal beginning. Now acts have an actuality that they never had before, and that actuality itself is perishing, the perishing of a present that can eternally return, and with that perishing every present moment becomes more precarious than it had ever been before, and so much so that only now does the present moment become manifest as a moment that can never return. Therein the present moment ever more fully becomes manifest as a groundless moment, a moment without a real or actual ground in a past that could encompass it, and with that loss a present moment is alienated and estranged from its own past occurrence, and so much so that the past is ever more fully and finally manifest as an irrecoverable past.

That irrecoverability is a deep and profound loss, and even if that loss is an opening to a new future, a future that was never manifest before, it nevertheless is an ultimate disruption, for it is the disappearance of a past that could ever occur again. That disappearance is an annulment, and an ultimate annulment, for it is the ending of an eternal ground, or the ending of that ground which is eternally present in every moment. Only the loss of an eternal presence or an eternal now makes possible the real and actual manifestation of an irreversible event, and if nothing is more threatening to an archaic or primordial consciousness than an irreversible event, nothing is more manifest in archaic myths and rituals than a continual and ever repeated annulment and reversal of apparently or initially irreversible events. Not only do such events cease to be irreversible when they pass into ritual and myth, but the very movement of archaic ritual action and mythical recitation is the movement of eternal return, a return inevitably reversing irreversibility, and with that reversal irreversible events are renewed as archetypal events and consciousness itself is therein delivered from the profound threat of absolute contingency or perishability.

It is all too significant that the very revelation of the name of I AM is inseparable from an absolute condemnation of idolatry, an idolatry which quite simply is a participation in the movement of eternal return, a movement which is the movement of archaic or primordial myth and rite, and a movement which is the eternal repetition of an eternal now. That is the repetition which is absolutely disrupted by the self-naming of I AM, and even if that repetition is continually renewed in rebellions against the ultimacy and finality of the name of I AM, rebellions which can be understood as compulsive attempts to recover or renew a primordial consciousness and world, those rebellions themselves are continually assaulted in every actual naming of I AM, and necessarily so, for the very revelation of that name is an absolute reversal of the movement of eternal return. That reversal is inevitably manifest and real in an alienation and estrangement of consciousness itself, for the very utterance of the name of I AM is an evocation of a once and for all and irreversible event, and an irreversible event that is an absolutely irrevocable event, so that the very pronunciation of that name is an assault upon the movement of eternal return, and hence an alienation and estrangement of its speaker from every ground in an eternal now. Only now does consciousness become open to a truly groundless present, an absolutely contingent or perishing present dissolving every possibility of the actual presence of an eternal now. That dissolution is the dissolution of primordial ground, and thus the dissolution of every ground annulling the irreversibility of time itself.

If this is the advent of history, it is the advent of a fall from an eternal now, a fall disrupting the consciousness that embodies it, and disrupting that consciousness by ending every source in an eternal now. Now and for the first time consciousness is manifest and real as an absolutely contingent consciousness, and therefore a consciousness that is alienated and estranged, and alienated and estranged from every ground or horizon that annuls or reverses that very contingency. For only such an alienated and estranged consciousness could know an ultimate and final irreversibility, an irreversibility that is manifest in the very symbol of a once and for all beginning, a beginning that is the beginning of alienation and estrangement. So it is that the birth of history is a fall from all identity which is eternally itself, or from all identity which is eternally the same, and that fall is an irretrievable loss of all such identity, and is so in the very manifestation of irreversible events whose actualization forecloses the possibility of recurrence or return. That foreclosure and that foreclosure alone makes possible the manifestation or unveiling of a once and for all and irreversible beginning; that beginning is the beginning of irreversible events, but that beginning is unknown and unreal apart from the self-naming of I AM.

Thus the self-naming of I AM is the inauguration of what we know as history, or the inauguration of the manifestation of irreversible events, events which have never been manifest as such apart from the revelation of I AM, and therefore events which are invisible and silent apart from that revelation. Only that revelation makes manifest and real the ultimacy of perishing, an ultimacy that is manifest and spoken in the self-naming of I AM, for only that self-naming reveals or unveils ultimate difference itself, a difference that now realizes itself in the manifestation of irreversible events. That difference is present and real in irreversible events, events which are different and other than themselves, and other than themselves precisely in their irreversibility, an irreversibility in which they can never be themselves again, and cannot do so if only because they can never again return as themselves.

Irreversibility is perishing, for it is the perishing of reversibility, and therefore the perishing of each event in its very occurrence, an occurrence in which each and every event passes into an irrecoverable past. The dawning of that past is the advent of history, an advent which is the inescapable consequence of the self-naming of I AM, for it is the inevitable consequence of the manifestation or realization of ultimate difference, an essential and intrinsic otherness which now is manifest and real in the very manifestation of irreversible events. That manifestation establishes the horizon of history, a horizon inseparable from the irrecoverability of the past, but the realization of that irrecoverability is simultaneously the realization of the actuality of the future. If the advent of the actuality of the future is inseparable from the actuality of the past, that advent is not fully realized immediately or at once but only in the course of centuries of historical evolution, an evolution that is inaugurated with the self-naming of I AM. Only that self-naming makes manifest the forward movement of history, a forward movement which is the consequence of the ending of the cycle of eternal recurrence or return, and hence a movement which is a reversal of the cycle of eternal return, a movement which is the forward movement of evolution rather than the backward movement of involution or return.

Israel and Israel alone is the site of the dawning realization of the forward or evolutionary movement of history. Here lies the beginning of a real and actual historical consciousness, and the real beginning of historical writing and memory as well. Now acts are ever more fully manifest as singular and unique acts, as acts that happen only once, and therefore as acts which so far from being archetypal or eternal acts are acts which are only themselves. While such acts are only gradually realized as such in the consciousness and the society which enact and embody them, that embodiment is ever more fully realized in the historical evolution of Israel, and that realization enacts a history which for the first time is a real and forward movement into the full actuality of the future. Now a future dawns that is a wholly other future, a future that is wholly other than the past, and with that dawning time itself becomes manifest and real as a time whose very actuality is ultimately and finally a wholly future actuality. This occurs in the prophetic revolution of Israel, a revolution revolving about pure hearing, a hearing which for the first time hears and only hears the words of I AM, and when those words are heard only as pure and actual words, they are heard as words coming from the future and not from the past. The very hearing of the pure and actual words of I AM is a hearing which is a closure of the past, for the actuality of an ultimate and final speech is inevitably a shattering of the past, and a shattering of every past in which such hearing is absent.

Nietzsche was the first thinker to understand the prophetic movement of Israel as a revolutionary event, and for Nietzsche not only a revolutionary event but *the* revolutionary event, and if he could identify it as the "slave revolt of morality," that is the revolt which is the first true or actual reversal of high and low, and a reversal not only reversing an original or primordial morality, which is the morality of the will to power, but thereby exalting for the first time the weak and the humble, and thus a reversal which reversed every value which is upon the horizon of both an archaic and an ancient consciousness. Accordingly, Nietzsche could understand prophetic Israel as a nihilistic Israel, an Israel that negated and reversed its own noble and heroic past, and therein reversed not only a natural morality, but nature or reality itself, a reality which is the will to power. Nietzsche, of course, was also the first truly modern thinker to discover the eternal recurrence of the same, and while Nietzsche's vision of eternal recurrence is a universe apart from the primordial vision of eternal return, it is Nietzsche and Nietzsche alone who is the one philosopher of eternal recurrence. Thus it was Nietzsche who most fully understood prophetic Israel as the most revolutionary movement in history. For this was that time in history when the name of I AM was first fully and purely heard, and if that time is the time of the full dawning or birth of history itself, that time is a time of reversal of thousands of years of a given and established consciousness and society, and an axial reversal that occurred not only in Israel but also in India, China, and Greece.

If that axial reversal established a wholly new center of consciousness, and a center of consciousness that was an interiorization or individualization of an archaic or primordial consciousness, it is manifest in Israel in a new individual faith, a faith that is possible only by stepping outside of a wholly encompassing society and world, a world which here and now is known to be under a total and catastrophic judgment. All of the pre-exilic prophetic oracles are oracles of total judgment, and a total judgment upon the totality of history, or the totality of that history which Israel knew, a history occurring between covenant and exile, and a history which now is known as a history of apostasy and idolatry.

That knowledge is the consequence of a new hearing of I AM, a hearing which now is realized in a wholly individual hearing, and an individual hearing that as such is a new hearing, for it hears with a total attention that was never present before, a total attention demanding a shattering or dissolution of all visions of I AM, and with that dissolution a withdrawal of all true or full energy from every act which is not an act of obedience to Yahweh or I AM, so that now idolatry is unveiled as every act or moment which is not rooted or grounded in the pure actuality of I AM. That actuality is the judgment of I AM, a judgment occurring in the immediate future, and a judgment that will be not the epiphany but the enactment of I AM, an enactment that will be a total enactment, and an enactment that even now is calling for a total attention and submission, a submission that can be enacted only by dissolving or reversing every ground in a society or a world that now is under total judgment. While that judgment is future, it even now is dawning, and dawning as a totality demanding a total repentance, a repentance that is a turning away and a total turning away from an old world, that very world which now and for the first time is wholly manifest as a world of the past, and is so manifest by the prophetic apprehension of the pure and total act of Yahweh, that absolute act before which all other acts are groundless.

Hearing is now and for the first time a full and actual hearing of the future, and if that hearing realizes a total judgment upon both the present and the past, that judgment and that judgment alone makes manifest and real the final ultimacy of the future, a future that can be actual as itself only with the final perishing of the past. That is a perishing which embodies the actuality of the future, but now the future dawns as that act of Yahweh which is only future, and hence a future before which the past is nameable only as a darkness and abyss. Nothing is more distinctive of the new prophetic oracle than its closure of the past; now the past is speakable as a historical or human past only insofar as it is manifest as darkness, and now and only now does an original covenant disappear into the darkness of judgment, and a history that is the history of the past now and for the first time becomes manifest as the history of darkness. If that darkness is the darkness of judgment, that is a judgment which is dawning here and now, and that dawning is itself a reversal of everything which is now knowable as the past. Only that reversal calls forth a future that is ultimately future, and the dawning of that future is the dawning of an ultimate and a final act, the total enactment of Yahweh or I AM. That enactment is the totality of the future, a future whose very sounding transforms the past into a total abyss, an abyss that now passes into hearing itself, as hearing now realizes itself as self-judgment, a self-judgment which is an interior actualization of abyss. Only that actualization makes a total future hearable, as the hearing of that future itself enacts abyss, an abyss consuming everything whatsoever which is knowable as either the present or the past, and therefore an abyss whose hearing alone makes possible the realization of the pure actuality of time itself.

Apocalypse is the ending of a once and for all and irreversible beginning, and while the pre-exilic prophetic oracles are wholly silent about apocalypse, or about an apocalypse which is nameable as such, they nevertheless evoke and embody the ultimate and final act of Yahweh, an act that is dawning now but will only be consummated in the future. Second Isaiah knows that future as a truly new world or new creation, and only in the perspective of that absolute novum can Second Isaiah name and evoke the original creation, a creation that is unnameable as creation and creation alone apart from the advent of a new creation, and unnameable if only because a truly once and for all and irreversible beginning is unnameable as such apart from the actual advent of its own fulfillment or consummation, a consummation which is apocalypse, and is that apocalypse which is the fulfillment of a once and for all beginning.

Now if even a nonprophetic writing such as the Book of Job can know that beginning, it does so only by realizing an ultimate ending, an ultimate ending which is not only the ending of an original Israel, but the ending of every naming which is not the naming of darkness and abyss. Thereafter even a priestly tradition can evoke a once and for all beginning, and even if it knows it as the origin of a movement of eternal return, and an eternal return occurring through a transfigured archaic myth and rite, it nevertheless thereby knows a once and for all covenant, and an eternal covenant which is the very origin of the world.

Nothing is more characteristic of the prophetic revolution than its realization of total judgment, and the total judgment of Israel, the elect or chosen people of Yahweh. Now catastrophe falls upon that chosen people, and a catastrophe which is heard when the pre-exilic prophetic oracle is proclaimed. And that catastrophe occurs in the actuality of history, an actuality that is an ultimate exile, and an ultimate exile from all the original grace or blessing of the elect. That exile is purely realized in the fourth Servant Song of Second Isaiah (Isa. 52:13–53:17), as here Yahweh brings all of our rebellious acts to bear upon the servant, a servant who is crushed because of our guilt, and so crushed by Yahweh Himself. Now if the servant was wounded for our rebellions, that is a wounding reconciling us, and reconciling us as rebels against Yahweh, a reconciliation which is the enactment of a total future, and a total future which Second Isaiah knows as the advent of apocalypse.

Nowhere in the Hebrew Bible is apocalypse so fully named as it is in Second Isaiah, an apocalypse that is at once a new creation and a final reconciliation, and a final reconciliation of all rebels against Yahweh. But in the fourth Servant Song that reconciliation occurs only through the wounding of the servant, a wounding in which the servant bears our suffering and sorrow, and bears that sorrow in being crushed by Yahweh, a crushing that is the initial enactment of the total enactment of I AM. If the suffering and the death of the servant is inflicted by Yahweh, that is a final act of Yahweh, and an apocalyptic act of Yahweh, for it is a fulfillment of the once and for all event of beginning, and a fulfillment of the self-emptying of that beginning. Even the Book of Job knows such an infliction, and an infliction inflicted by the Creator, but here that infliction evokes an ultimate rebellion, an ultimate rebellion which is a final judgment against the Creator, and a judgment which is most decisively present in the third response of Job to his friends. That response is a violent attack upon the Almighty, an attack inverting everything which the Deuteronomic tradition had known as the providence of Yahweh, and inverting that providence so as to name an absolutely alien Almighty. But that naming parallels the naming of Yahweh in the fourth Servant Song, a Yahweh who crushes His servant, and crushes a servant who is even more innocent than Job, a servant whose very innocence seemingly calls forth the total judgment of Yahweh.

While that crushing may well be a sacrifice, and a sacrifice of the innocent, it is not a sacrifice that could be repeated in a mythical and ritual cycle of eternal return, for it is an actual and wholly individual sacrifice, and therefore a sacrifice occurring in the actuality of history. From its very beginning Christianity has known the fourth Servant Song as the purest prophecy of the crucifixion of God, or the crucifixion of the Son of God, a crucifixion that occurs only once, and occurs as an actual historical event. Nothing so distinguishes Christianity from all the religions of the world than does the primacy which it gives this event, an ultimate and total event which is simultaneously an actual historical event, and an actual historical event which is here the one and only source of salvation or life.

Consequently, Christianity can know the self-naming of I AM as the inauguration of the self-negation or self-emptying of I AM, a self-negation occurring in the actuality of history, and a self-emptying which is consummated in what Christianity knows as the final ultimacy of the crucifixion. Nothing is or could be a greater offense than the crucifixion, and if it was Paul who first truly understood that offense, and did so most deeply by identifying the events of the crucifixion and resurrection, and identifying them as one salvation event, then that offense is identical with the Christian kerygma or proclamation that God is in Christ reconciling the world to I AM. Thus Christianity knows a reconciliation with I AM occurring only by way of the death of God's Son (Rom. 5:10), and that death is not only an actual historical event, but a historical event which is the consummation of the acts of I AM. Therefore it is the consummation of the original self-naming of I AM, a self-naming which is a self-negation, and a self-negation because it occurs in the actuality of history. But it is also a self-negation because it is a real and actual act, an actual act which is an irreversible act, and therefore an act which never can be undone, and not even undone by what both Job and Second Isaiah know as the absolute sovereignty of the Creator.

Thus the crucifixion cannot simply be undone, or not annulled by a movement of resurrection or ascension which reverses it, a reversal which would be a dissolution of crucifixion itself, and therefore a dissolution of the very actuality of death, a dissolution which could only be a renewal of the movement of eternal return, and a movement of eternal return in its very backward movement to eternity.

Nothing is more central or more primal in both Christianity and the Hebrew Bible than a naming of the absolute otherness of I AM, and if such a naming is found in no other horizon of history, then it is also true that no other horizon of history knows absolute otherness itself, an otherness that is an essential and intrinsic otherness, and an otherness that is finally the otherness of itself. But such an otherness is also manifest in irreversible events, and therefore in actual historical events, events which occur only once, and events whose very occurrence as such forecloses the possibility of either their reversal or their return. Accordingly, if Christianity knows the acts of God as historical acts, and thus as ultimate and irreversible acts, it therein and thereby knows the acts of God as acts of self-negation, and as acts of self-negation if only because they can never be undone. Hence the acts of God are kenotic acts, or acts of self-emptying, and real and actual acts of self-emptying, for they not only occur in the actuality of history, but they occur in and as irreversible acts. Yet irreversible acts are acts which annul or negate an eternal now, and do so in their very occurrence, an occurrence which itself is a self-emptying or a self-negation of an eternity which is eternally the same, and therefore the self-emptying of an eternity which is finally and only itself.

Certainly nothing more fully distinguishes both Christianity and the Hebrew Bible from all the religions of the world than does their celebration and enactment of a history of salvation, a history that occurs once and only once, and a history that occurs in actual and irreversible events. That history of salvation is inseparable from what both Christianity and the Hebrew Bible know as both the actuality and the ultimacy of revelation, a revelation that is not found apart from these traditions, and a revelation that is both fully and actually a historical revelation. Such a revelation would not only be unmanifest apart from history, it would also thereby be unreal, and thus unreal apart from the self-naming of I AM. But if that self-naming is a self-negation, and a self-negation which is a self-emptying of an original eternity, it is so in its very occurrence, and in its very occurrence as a historical revelation. Nothing is more radical or revolutionary in the Bible than its celebration and enactment of a history of revelation, a history that is inevitably and necessarily the loss of an original or an eternal transcendence that could never speak or act, and hence the loss of an original eternity that is eternally and only itself. That loss is not only actual in a fully and truly historical revelation, it is inevitable in that revelation, and inevitable if only because a historical revelation is irreversibly present, and that very actuality forecloses the possibility of the presence here of an eternity that is an eternal now.

A historical revelation could never be the revelation of a primordial or an eternal now, and could never be so if only because the actuality of history brings an end to an eternal recurrence or an eternal return, an ending which is the end of all return. Thus it is that a historical revelation is necessarily the revelation of the future, an actual future which only dawns with the ending of eternal return, and a future which can only be enacted or revealed by way of an annulment or disruption of the past, or a disruption of all that past which could ever return or recur as itself. But a historical revelation is nevertheless revelation, and is fully revelation; hence it is the revelation not only of an actual future, but of a total future, or a future totality that will be all in all. So it is that in the prophetic revolution time itself is finally and ultimately the time of the future, a time that will not only actually come, but a time that even now is totally present in the voice of I AM, and the absolute difference of that voice is an assault upon its hearer, so that the hearing of that voice is itself an act of self-negation, and a self-negation making actually present both the ultimacy and the finality of the future. That is the future which Christianity knows as apocalypse, and an apocalypse released by the full and total actuality of the crucifixion, a crucifixion which can never be reversed, and can never be reversed because it is the total act of I AM, a total act which is the consummation of the acts of God, and that is the consummation which Christianity finally and ultimately knows as apocalypse.

One decisive sign of the actual presence of that apocalypse which is the center of an original Christianity is the very violence with which Christianity initially realized itself. While that is wholly an internal and interior violence, never before or since has a historical movement occurred which initially realizes itself with such interior violence and disruption. That violence is most clearly manifest in the genuine letters of Paul, and most decisively so in that wholly new "I" or self-consciousness which is first recorded in these letters, a self-consciousness which is internally divided against itself, so that its very own "I" is the dichotomous other of that resurrection or apocalypse which it proclaims and enacts. Never before had a purely internal otherness or guilt been actual and real at the center of consciousness, a center which itself is a new self-consciousness, and a center of consciousness which goes beyond its prophetic roots by actually knowing and speaking a totally negative "I." For this is a new self-consciousness which is the intrinsic otherness of itself, and if a purely internal otherness now speaks for the first time in history, it also releases a new and internal energy, an energy which is the very otherness of itself, and an energy that is manifest and real in the violent turbulence of primitive Christianity, a turbulence that almost immediately realizes the most total transformation of a historical movement which has ever occurred in history.

That transformation itself is a clear and decisive sign of the absolute historical transformation now released in the world, a transformation that is interior and exterior at once, and a transformation with both an apocalyptic beginning and an apocalyptic goal, as a new history is now inaugurated which is an actual process of total transformation. Nothing like this is present elsewhere in the history of the world, unless it is present in those world-transforming movements which are surely its apocalyptic descendents, and apocalyptic descendents if only because they are directed to the absolute transformation of the world.

Primitive Christianity is the inauguration of such transformations, transformations which have evolved historically, and have evolved in forward movements of transformation, and forward movements ever more fully embodying a totally apocalyptic goal. Now even if the evolution of Christianity occurred by way of a progressive reversal of its original apocalyptic ground and source, that progressive reversal occurs in a finally forward historical movement, a movement that soon conquers the most powerful empire in world history. That victory was both a reversal and a realization of primitive Christianity, a reversal of the kenotic or self-emptying ground of that original Christianity, but a fulfillment of an original Christian universalism, a universalism that is now dedicated to conquering the world. And conquer the world it did, even if it only did so by way of the end of Christendom, for Christianity is itself the birth of that new Western society and consciousness which finally realized itself in a universal consciousness and society, a universal consciousness and society that is apocalyptic in its very center, an apocalypticism that was first fully realized in the birth of Christianity, and an apocalypticism that embodied itself in a forward-moving historical evolution that would not be ended until it had wholly transformed the world. A conscious realization of both a forward and a total historical movement first occurs in ancient Jewish apocalypticism, and here it is accompanied, and necessarily accompanied, by a ground in an absolute and total ending, the ending of world itself, a world that only now can be named as old creation, an old creation which is the intrinsic opposite of new creation, and an old creation which must wholly and finally perish if the new creation or the Kingdom of God is truly and fully actualized.

If Jesus was the first prophet to proclaim the full and actual advent of the Kingdom of God, and if that actual advent is the very center of his parabolic enactment and eschatological proclamation, then that advent could only be heard as an absolute and final assault upon both the present and the past, an assault which renews the prophetic revolution, but now and only now a future or apocalyptic totality is actually enacted which is both fully and finally present. The actual advent of that future is the actual advent of the Kingdom of God; that is the advent which now releases an absolutely and totally forward movement of history, a forward movement not only directed to but realizing itself in the totality of history, a totality which does not truly dawn in history until this advent, and if that dawning is the dawning of the end of history, that dawning is the dawning of a total apocalypse. Apocalypticism is at the very center of Western history, a center which is historically actual with the birth of Christianity, and a center which thereafter is ever more fully realized throughout the multiple expressions of Western consciousness and society, for this is that center which is the primal ground of historical revolution, a revolution which becomes global and universal in the twentieth century.

While Islam is that one faith which from its very beginning embodied itself in a total historical transformation, and an immediate historical transformation that has no parallel in history, something of the order of that transformation was born in the Christian Middle Ages, a birth which is a rebirth of an original Christian apocalypticism, but a rebirth which now and for the first time in the postapostolic Christian world knows and celebrates an absolute historical transformation. That is the transformation which ever more fully realized itself in the advent of modern history, a history which was fully born in the scientific, imaginative, and political revolutions of the seventeenth century, each one of which was a rebirth of an original apocalypticism, for each one of them was a real and actual realization of totality, and of an apocalyptic totality, for each realized a truly new world, a world that had never existed before, and yet a world that here and now is the realization of a future totality. It is the very essence of historical revolution that it intends and wills an absolute transformation of history; hence it must give itself to an absolute negation of the past, a negation which can only be an apocalyptic negation, and a negation realizing itself in the advent of a new creation or a new world.

Consequently, historical revolution is the renewal of the original self-naming of I AM, a self-naming which ends an original eternity, and ends an original eternity in the advent of absolute novum, a novum which is an absolutely new totality but a new totality which is a future totality in the prophetic revolution of Israel, and a new totality which is actually at hand with the birth of Christianity. While that totality was negated and reversed in the full advent of the Catholic Church, a negation which is the most radical transformation of a historical movement which has ever occurred in history, that very negation was itself negated in the birth of modern apocalypticism, and that apocalypticism has ever more fully and more finally been a universal apocalypticism, and a universal apocalypticism which is the realization of a new eternity or a new totality. That new eternity is novum, and even absolute novum; hence it is not simply an eternity made possible by the self-naming of I AM, it is an apocalypse which is the realization of that self-naming, and therefore an apocalypse which is the consummation of a once and for all and irreversible beginning. Now alpha is omega, or genesis is apocalypse, but it is so only as an absolutely new actuality, and an absolutely new actuality realizing itself in history or world, and therefore realizing itself in absolute perishing or death, a perishing which is the final realization of the self-naming of I AM, and therefore the final realization of the self-emptying of an original eternity.

4

The Crucifixion of God

If the crucifixion is that symbol which most decisively distinguishes Christianity from all the religions of the world, and above all so when the crucifixion is realized both as an actual historical event and as that ultimate event which is the center of history, then the crucifixion is the decisive key for unlocking the mystery of Christianity. At no point is that mystery deeper than in a Christian affirmation of the absolute mystery of God, an absolute mystery that is the absolute transcendence of God, and thus a transcendence that is finally unspeakable and unnameable. Now even if that transcendence is named as the Kingdom of God, this cannot be an actual naming of transcendence if transcendence is ultimately a mystery, and cannot be if only because a pure and ultimate transcendence can neither be spoken nor named. Indeed, it was the progressive disappearance of the eschatological proclamation of the Kingdom of God which most clearly records the radical transformation of early Christianity, so that with the victory of the Catholic Church or the Great Church in the second century that proclamation had virtually come to an end. Thereafter it primarily appears in heretical Christian movements, and even if such movements have occurred throughout the history of Christianity, they have invariably engendered violent assaults upon orthodox or Catholic Christianity, just as they have also commonly engendered such assaults upon all political and social establishments. If the history of apocalyptic Christianity is the history of Christian heresy, that history is no less heretical when it is sanctioned by the authority of the Church, as in the case of Dante's *Commedia*, for heresy itself can pass into orthodoxy, a process that begins already with Paul.

Indeed, it is the conjunction of heresy and orthodoxy that has been the most manifest source for the forward movement of Christianity, a forward movement that is an evolutionary historical movement, and a Christian evolutionary historical movement without parallel in the history of religions. Nothing so clearly illustrates this movement as does the history of the symbol of the cross, for if it is virtually absent from Christian iconography in patristic Christianity, it decisively appears in the Dark Ages, and then becomes a major presence in Gothic painting and sculpture, until with the fifteenth century it wholly replaces all Western images of the Pantocrator. Thereafter, the symbol of the cross is the primary symbol of Christ in Western Christianity, and even if this would appear to be an inversion and reversal of the exalted Christ of ancient and patristic Christianity, it is precisely as such that Christ has been most manifest and real in the Western Christian world. Thus the crucifixion and not the resurrection has been the primary Christian symbol in the Western world, and if this clearly distinguishes Eastern and Western Christianity, it is also true that images of the resurrection gradually but decisively disappear from Western Christianity, so that with the advent of the modern world the Western Christian can no longer envision the resurrection.

A parallel process occurs in Western poetry, and above all so in epic poetry, as can most clearly be seen in the contrast between the Christ of the *Commedia* and the Christ of *Paradise Lost*, the one an absolutely exalted and transcendent figure whom even a transfigured Dante cannot see, and the other a Christ both of majesty and of passion, but it is wholly the Christ of passion who is the redemptive Christ of *Paradise Lost*. With the full advent of the modern world, as epically enacted by Blake, the Christ of majesty has wholly disappeared, only to be replaced by the Christ who is wholly the Christ of passion, and thereafter the Christ of majesty is absent from modern Western poetry, and even absent from modern Catholic poetry. Thus it is that the Christ of majesty or the Christ of glory is unspeakable in modern Christianity, or imaginatively unspeakable, and this is just as true of modern painting and of modern music as it is of modern poetry. Therein a chasm is established between modern culture and a new sectarian Christianity, and such a chasm had never previously occurred in the history of Christianity. For only with the dawning of the modern world does the Christian church become ever more fully and ever more finally sectarian, and even if this would seem to be true in the very beginning of Christianity, it is not actually true of primitive Christianity, as witness the dynamism of the Pauline, the synoptic, and the Johannine traditions, a dynamism that is not only a forward-moving dynamism, but a dynamism realizing itself in the most vital forces of Hellenistic culture and society.

But nowhere is such a paradoxical transformation of Christianity more deeply present than it is in Western or Western Christian philosophy, a philosophy that begins with Augustine, and therein begins with the subject of consciousness as the sole ground for a universal horizon and world, a truly new subject of consciousness that had never previously been realized in philosophical thinking, but that thereafter was progressively realized as the primal center and ground of philosophical thinking in the West. With Descartes that subject is wholly and purely subject, and therein a new thinking occurs, a thinking that is ontologically groundless, but therein and thereby philosophical thinking becomes ever more gradually and ever more finally a purely epistemological thinking, until it is reversed in both German idealism and in modern materialism so as to become a total thinking, and a total thinking comprehending everything whatsoever which is manifest upon the horizon of thinking. If that total thinking occurs most purely and most comprehensively in Hegel, this is a thinking in full continuity with Augustine, and above all so because of the primacy of the subject of consciousness in Hegel and Augustine alike, a primacy wherein and whereby consciousness itself is finally and fully self-consciousness, and here self-consciousness is an immanent reflection of the transcendence of God.

But in Hegelian thinking self-consciousness passes through the death of God, and it is only thereby and therein that it realizes itself as the pure subject of consciousness, and if *The Phenomenology of Spirit* realizes the history of that subject, this is a history culminating with the Calvary of absolute Spirit, a Calvary which is the actuality, truth, and certainty of the throne or kingdom of absolute Spirit or the Godhead of God.

Not until Hegel does the very center of Christianity pass into the center of philosophical thinking, and yet that center is realized only through a philosophical realization of the death of God, a death that actually occurs in the subject of consciousness, and therein and thereafter occurs in a total philosophical thinking which is the first such comprehensive thinking in the Western world. But just such a realization of the death of God simultaneously occurs in the epic poetry of Blake, and if both Blake and Hegel were initially inspired by the French Revolution, they both understood that revolution as a historical realization of the death of God, and a historical realization effecting both an actual and a final end of the premodern world. That ending realizes the birth of a pure and total self-consciousness, a self-consciousness whose initial advent is the advent of Christianity itself, and therein is realized a consciousness which is the pure otherness of itself, an actually alien and dichotomous consciousness which realizes itself only by a negation of itself, a progressive and forward-moving negation of itself which finally explodes with the birth of modernity. That explosion occurs in the actual realization of the death of God in the modern world, but that explosion had always been the destiny of a purely negative or Christian consciousness, a self-consciousness which is the essential and intrinsic otherness of itself, and a self-consciousness which is an interior realization of the crucifixion.

Already in Paul the "I" of self-consciousness is a doubled and self-alienated "I," an "I" that is the otherness of itself, and intrinsically is the otherness of itself in a new and wholly interior guilt and self-judgment. That guilt is inseparable from the actuality of the crucifixion, for even if the crucifixion had been foreseen by the fourth Servant Song, and by the crushing of an innocent Job, or even by the destruction of an original Israel in the first exile, that prophetic and redemptive history is not yet a full and final self-negation of I AM, a self-negation that occurs only in the crucifixion. So it is that the crucifixion releases a wholly new guilt in the world, a guilt that had never been historically actual before, or historically actual as a wholly interior guilt, a guilt that is inseparable from the new "I" of self-consciousness. That "I" is the consequence of the crucifixion, or the consequence of a resurrection that is crucifixion and resurrection at once, and if self-consciousness is actually realized by an interior repetition of crucifixion and resurrection, that is a repetition which is a self-negation, and a self-negation which is an interior actualization of an otherness that is the otherness of itself. But that otherness of itself was only finally actualized in the once and for all event of crucifixion and resurrection, and if baptism into Christ Jesus is a baptism into his death (Rom. 6:3), that baptism is a burial with Christ, a burial that alone makes possible a resurrection from the dead (Rom. 6:4).

So it is that resurrection is resurrection from death, and resurrection from the ultimacy of that death which is realized only in the crucifixion, a crucifixion which is not simply the actual realization of death, but the actual realization of the death of death, a death and an actual death that is resurrection. Consequently, resurrection is the death of death or the negation of negation, and not only a negation of negation but a self-negation of self-negation, or a final self-negation of that original self-negation which is the self-naming of I AM. If the passion of Christ is the resurrection of Christ, or the crucifixion of Christ is the glorification of Christ, a dialectical identity which is both proclaimed by Paul and enacted in the Fourth Gospel, then that crucifixion or passion is not an antechamber or prelude to resurrection, but is resurrection itself, a resurrection which is the negation of negation, but is so only as the total enactment of negation. Such a total enactment of negation can only be the act of God, and the total act of God, an act that here and here alone is both an actual and a final act, and a final act fulfilling or finally realizing the original self-naming of I AM. That self-naming is repeated in the "I am" statements of the Fourth Gospel, but here Jesus can pronounce this "It is I" absolutely, and so absolutely that this is a pronunciation without any real interior subject, for this is the voice of the resurrected Christ, and therefore the voice of the crucified Christ, the voice of that Christ who is the crucified God.

The identification of Jesus and God in the Fourth Gospel can mean no less than this, and if such an identification occurs nowhere else in the New Testament, it is also true that only in the Fourth Gospel do we find an actual repetition of the self-naming of I AM. That repetition is an enactment of the crucifixion, or an enactment of that crucifixion which is resurrection, for, unlike the synoptic Gospels, in the Fourth Gospel there is no real distinction between the proclaiming Christ and the crucified and resurrected Christ, as can most clearly be seen in the "I am" statements of the Fourth Gospel. Nevertheless, there is a clear parallel to this identification in the eschatological proclamation of the synoptic Gospels, a proclamation which inaugurates the ministry of Jesus, and a proclamation which is the real source of that ultimate offense which is here enacted, and enacted in the very proclamation that the Kingdom of God is at hand. For if the Kingdom of God is truly and actually at hand, then it cannot be present and real in heaven or the beyond, or not actually so, and cannot be if only because its actual advent can only be a transformation of itself, and a transformation of itself as a kingdom which is only transcendent and beyond.

Now that kingdom is no more, or is no more actual as that which it once was, and cannot be if only because of its actual advent, an advent which is first proclaimed by Jesus, and at no other point is Jesus more distinguishable from the earlier prophets of Israel. This is the proclamation which makes

possible the parables of Jesus, parables which are parables of the
Kingdom of God, but these parables are wholly enacted in the
actuality of a present moment of time, and are enacted in
common and worldly events, and even enacted in a common or
vernacular language which is the language of everybody or
everyone. Nothing more distinguishes Jesus from every other
prophet or seer in the history of religions than does his
parabolic language, and if that language is the most common or
vernacular language which has ever been employed by a
prophet or a seer, it is most paradoxical precisely in that context,
for it can be understood immediately by everyone who hears it,
and yet its resaying by another inevitably induces a deep
mystery, a mystery which is already externally inserted into the
telling of the parables by all three of the synoptic Gospels. While
the insertion of that mystery into the synoptic texts may well be
looked upon as a betrayal of the parabolic Jesus, it can also be
seen to be an inevitable or even necessary betrayal, and is so if
only because those parables can never truly or actually be said
by another. Accordingly, it is quite understandable that the
parables of Jesus were ever more fully annulled and reversed in
the history of Christianity, all too quickly becoming the opposites of themselves when they were interpreted as mystical
allegories, and not coming to be understood as the parables
which they are until the late twentieth century. That Christianity could so forcefully resist the actual words of its founder is
mute testimony to the profound offense which these all too
common words evoke, and even if they may well be the simplest
words in any language, they are words which cannot be heard
without inducing an ultimate offense.

But that offense is an enactment of the dawning of the
Kingdom of God, for not only are the parables parables
of the Kingdom of God, they are parables made possible by the
dawning of the Kingdom of God, and parables which evoke that
actuality in absolutely common events. So likewise the parabolic
language which embodies that actuality is an absolutely common language, and as such it is virtually infinitely distant from
the exalted language of Second Isaiah and Job, and even vastly
distant from the language of the pre-exilic prophetic oracles, so
that in the parabolic language of Jesus the sacred language of
the Bible passes into an everyday and a common prose. Thereby
and therein it can be heard by everyone, and heard by everyone
and everybody as a language evoking common and universal
events, events which are realized and known by everyone, and
thus events which are both actual and universal events. But that
is precisely the realm which is the arena of the actual dawning of

the Kingdom of God, and if Jesus sought out sinners and the
outcast in his ministry, that is a sign of that ultimate reversal
which is here at hand, a reversal in which the Kingdom dawns
where it is least expected, and dawns as a reversal of every hope
in heaven or a beyond. Thus nothing could be more offensive
than a proclamation of the actual dawning of the Kingdom of
God, just as nothing is more offensive than a truly and a purely
parabolic language, a language evoking an absolute and ultimate transformation in the common language of everyone.

Yet if a purely parabolic language is a language that can be
heard by everyone and everybody, it is a language that was
actually spoken by Jesus alone. No real parallel to that language
can be found anywhere in the world, and there is no real
evidence that it has ever been present in the language of the
Church. True, fragments of that language are present in the
synoptic Gospels, but there they are a disruptive and deconstructive presence, and certainly disruptive of the grammatical
and syntactical structure of the synoptic texts, just as they
disrupt every attempt by the Gospels to retell the parables in
linear narratives or plots. Such a deconstructive presence is a
decisive source of the power of the parables of Jesus as they are
now present in the synoptic texts, but there is no real sign or
evidence that the parables were present as such in the life and
witness of the primitive Church. Moreover, one can only look
with irony upon the synoptic claim that the disciples have been
given the secret of the Kingdom of God but for those outside
everything is in parables (Matt. 13:11, Mark 4:11, Luke 8:10).
Yes, everything is in parables for those outside the Church, and
if the secret of the Kingdom is present within the Church, that
is a secret dissolving the Kingdom that Jesus proclaimed, and
ever more fully dissolving it as the power and the authority of
the Church expanded.

However, if the primitive Church was the first religious
community to begin with a violent internal and interior conflict,
the parabolic language of Jesus might well have been a decisive
source of that conflict, and most particularly so if that language
was remembered and recalled as a language which once was
meaningful and real to all but which now no longer can be
recovered or recalled as such.

Nothing is more paradoxical about Jesus than his enormous
and even absolute impact upon a history and a world that so
rapidly forgot the eschatological and parabolic language that he
spoke. Nothing like this is present in either the classical or the
biblical worlds, and even if Buddhism did not record the words
of Siddartha Gautama in writing until hundreds of years after

his death, there is no good reason to suspect that Buddhism sustained such a loss, or that a loss of this kind occurred in any tradition with a historical founder. In the aphoristic words of Nietzsche, Christianity is the stone upon the grave of Jesus, and that is an imprisonment or dissolution of Jesus that deepened as Christianity historically evolved, except insofar as it was loosened by assaults upon Christianity, and above all by internal and interior assaults. For such assaults may be understood as reversals of reversals of Jesus, and therefore as assaults which recover an eschatological reversal, and an eschatological reversal that is actual in Jesus' proclamation of the dawning of the Kingdom of God. Such an eschatological reversal was reborn again and again in the history of Christianity, but in so occurring it always recurred as a profound offense, and an offense most clearly present in the very Christian symbol of the cross, for the cross is nothing less than the Christian symbol of the crucified God. No other religious tradition has known or embodied a symbol which in itself is a profound offense, and an offense above all to that tradition which embodies it, for it is an offense which assaults and reverses the deepest mystery of God, and does so both by witnessing to and calling forth the actual death of God.

When the death of God is both known and proclaimed as an actual historical event, it is therein realized as an irreversible event, and even if crucifixion is resurrection it is no less an irreversible event, and an irreversible event which is a total event, for it is the total act of God. That Jesus could proclaim and enact the actual advent of the Kingdom of God is itself the realization of the advent of a total and irreversible act, an irreversible act that is not only the act of God, but the total act of God, and therefore a final and ultimate and eschatological act. Accordingly, that proclamation itself is a profound offense, an offense assaulting the absolute transcendence of God, and not only assaulting but reversing it, and reversing it in its very announcement that the Kingdom of God is at hand. Nothing is or could be a greater assault upon the absolute mystery of God, for now that mystery is apprehended and enacted as a mystery which is coming to an end, and coming to an end in the very dawning of the Kingdom, a dawning which is a dawning of the depths of God, and a dawning of those depths in the actuality of the present moment.

Now even if that actuality is a perishing actuality, and inevitably a perishing actuality if only because of the perishing of actual and irreversible events, that is the actuality which now embodies the advent of the Kingdom of God, an advent which is the advent of an ultimate and final reversal, and a reversal which is the reversal of everything which previously could be named as either world or God. Both God and world disappear in the parabolic language of Jesus, or disappear as all that which was once named and evoked as either God or world, and hence that parabolic language is a cipher or secret, and above all so to all those who know either God or the world. Such knowing is now unveiled as unknowing, and it is unveiled in an absolutely common language, the most common or prosaic language which has ever been spoken, a language which can immediately be understood, but a language which disrupts or deconstructs every other language with which it is conjoined.

Thus parabolic language is itself a parable of the Kingdom of God, a parable embodying that Kingdom in the immediate and the everyday; then it is understood by everyone and everybody, but understood by no one when it is understood as a parable of "God." Here, that God disappears, and disappears in the very advent of the Kingdom of God, an advent which is the ending of "God," and not simply the advent of the ending of every name of God, but the advent of the ending of everything which revelation itself has named as God, and thus the ending of the self-naming of I AM. That ending can be named as crucifixion, a crucifixion which is the consummation of the parabolic language of Jesus, and which is not simply foreshadowed but which already occurs in that language, and certainly so if that language ends the revelation of "God." Thereby we can understand that even the synoptic Gospels conjoin crucifixion and revelation, and do so in the very eschatological and parabolic language which they preserve, and thus we can see that the passion story is the very center of the Gospels, and a center which speaks in every actual word and act of Jesus.

Yet to understand the passion as the actual word and act of Jesus is to understand Jesus as the crucified Word, a Word which is fully and actually present in his eschatological proclamation and parabolic enactment, but only consummated in the "blood" of the cross, and if that blood is the source of what the Christian knows as redemption, it is a blood which is present throughout the actual words and acts of Jesus. Then the Christ of glory is the Christ of passion, or resurrection is identical with crucifixion, and even if that identity is not fully or finally manifest historically until the full advent of the modern world, that is an advent which is a realization of the historical evolution of Christianity, and hence a realization occurring in actual and irreversible events. If those events are themselves a realization of the history of salvation, or of what the Bible alone knows as an

actual and irreversible history of salvation, they are events
which are embodiments or actualizations of the self-naming of
I AM, a self-naming which begins in a once and for all and
irreversible beginning, and a self-naming which is consummated in a once and for all and irreversible ending of that
beginning. That consummation is initially realized in Jesus or
the crucified Word, and therein is realized a self-negation of
God, and if that self-negation is a negation of negation, it is a
negation of an absolute otherness, a negation of the Godhead of
God.

Nothing less than this self-negation is evoked in the Christian
symbol of the cross, so that it is all too understandable that only
in the course of many centuries of historical evolution did the
cross become hearable and seeable as such, for even if the cross
was heard in primitive Christianity, and is present and actual in
the New Testament, it was progressively reversed in the history
of the Church, and does not become fully manifest in history
until the disintegration of medieval Christendom. Nothing else
is such a deep source of the Reformation, or such a deep source
of the advent of modernity, and if that advent ends a Church
which is Christendom, it also progressively ends the actual
presence of the God who is God and only God, and with the
historical realization of the death of that God, the crucifixion
itself is realized in the very center of self-consciousness. If
self-consciousness was born with the advent of Christianity, it
ends in and with the full realization of the modern world, a
realization which is a self-realization, and a self-realization of
the self-negation of God. That self-realization is first actually
realized in the crucified Jesus, and if Blake could choose "Jesus
alone" as the motto of his greatest epic, *Jerusalem*, that is because
this epic enacts the destiny of the modern world, a destiny that
is the actual enactment of what Blake envisioned as "Self-
Annihilation," and that "Self-Annihilation" is the self-negation
or self-emptying of Jesus or the crucified God.

Sacrifice is both the most primal and the most primordial rite
throughout the history of religions, and if that sacrifice is
ultimately the sacrifice of deity, historically it has occurred only
once, and only Christianity among the world religions knows
that sacrifice as an actual and historical event. Yet Christianity
knows this sacrifice as both an actual and a total event, and even
if sacrifice is known throughout the world as the source of life
and salvation, it is Christianity and Christianity alone which
knows sacrifice as the sacrifice of God. That is the sacrifice
which is re-presented or renewed in the liturgical action of the
eucharist or the mass, and that is the sacrifice which is pro-

claimed in authentic Christian preaching. If the Christ of glory is alien both to liturgical enactment and to evangelical preaching, that is because the Christ of glory can only actually be present as the Christ of passion, and above all so in the historical actuality of the modern world. Thus all real images of the resurrection have disappeared in that world, and disappeared as a consequence of faith, and of faith in that crucified God who even now is being realized as being all in all.

Already Paul could know that God will be all in all, but he could know that all in all as an absolute sovereignty to which everything will be subjected, and then the Son will be subjected to the One who has subjected everything to Him (1 Cor. 15:28). Here, as elsewhere in the conclusion of this letter, Paul has reversed the crucified God, and reversed that Son of God so as to glorify the Father or the Creator; thereby the Creator is given the same identity which is given Him by the voice from the whirlwind at the conclusion of the Book of Job, with the clear and necessary implication that the ultimate event of crucifixion and resurrection could have had no real effect or impact upon the identity of God as God. That is precisely the path that Christianity followed in the first fifteen centuries of its development, and at no other point did it so profoundly betray its origin in the eschatological proclamation and parabolic enactment of Jesus himself, an enactment and proclamation in which the kingdom or the glory of God is dawning here and now, and dawning in the full and final actualization of common and universal events. Just as the fifteenth chapter of First Corinthians is a full reversion to the Christ of glory, the absolutely sovereign and triumphant Christ of ancient and medieval Christianity is a reversion to the Christ of glory who is not and cannot be the Christ of passion, and if the Franciscan movement and other heresies challenged that Christ of glory, this was a challenge which was triumphant in the Reformation, or in its most radical and consistent expressions, and even a challenge which is now manifest and real in the new body of Catholicism. At no other point is Catholicism today more distant from its ancient and medieval counterparts, and if that is a consequence of the consistent, organic, and necessary development or evolution of Catholicism in Newman's sense, then the Christ of glory and only glory must be confined to the fossils of an irrecoverable past.

Newman knew such fossils as the dead deposits of Christian heresy, and if such deposits are a consequence of the forward or evolutionary movement of Christianity, they are no less present in an orthodox Christianity that can neither truly move nor evolve, and nowhere is that Christianity more fully present than in the Christian dogma of the God who is God and only God, the God who is and only is an absolutely sovereign and transcendent God.

It is the glory of that God which is annulled and reversed in the crucifixion, and if that crucifixion is the sacrifice of the Son of God, it is the sacrifice of that God who is fully God in kenosis or self-emptying, and fully God in this actual and ultimate act. But the God who is fully God in the ultimate act of self-negation or self-emptying cannot be the God who is and only is the God of glory, or the absolutely sovereign and transcendent Lord, unless that God of glory is finally realized and actualized in the kenotic act of self-negation, a self-negation which is an ultimately sacrificial act, for God so loved the world that He gave His only Son (John 3:16), that Son who in the beginning was the Word, and the Word was with God, and the Word was God (John 1:1). If that Word is the Word of glory, that is a glory that is truly and fully realized only in crucifixion, so that the crucifixion of Christ is the glorification of Christ, a glorification that is a total and absolute act of sacrifice, and the sacrifice of that God who is love (1 John 4:8).

While that sacrifice is the sacrifice of Christ, "I" have been crucified with Christ, and it is no longer "I" who live, but Christ who lives in me (Gal. 2:20). Thus "I" am dead and buried with Christ, and if that death is resurrection or redemption, it is nevertheless a real and actual death, and a once and for all and irreversible death, and consequently not a death that is reversed in resurrection, but far rather a death that is fully and finally actual in resurrection.

It was Christian Gnosticism that transformed that death and resurrection into glory, and if both the Pauline and the Johannine traditions evolved by reversing Christian Gnosticism, that was above all a reversal of the Christ of glory, and a reversal of the resurrection of glory, a glory that simply is eternal or transcendent life, and hence a glory that could never be actually present here and now. If Christian Gnosticism transforms crucifixion into resurrection, thereby knowing only a Lord of glory, that is a glory which annuls and reverses the crucifixion, so that the crucifixion wholly disappears in Christian Gnosticism, and must disappear if only to realize an absolute glory. Such absolute glory is the full and actual antithesis of the crucified Christ, and the antithesis of that "I" who is crucified in Christ, an "I" that is the very opposite of absolute glory, and the opposite of that glory if only because it is dead and buried with Christ.

Now even if that death and burial is resurrection, it is not a resurrection into anything that Gnosticism knows as eternal life, and thus not a resurrection into glory, but rather a resurrection into "life." And not a life which is mine, but a life which is Christ's, and not a life which is Christ's glory, but far rather a life which is Christ's passion, and is Christ's passion insofar as Christ is actually present. Thus the Christ who is present in Christian life is not the Christ of glory but the Christ of passion, the Christ who is the crucified God, or the Christ who is the full and actual embodiment of the self-negation and the self-emptying of God. For the Son of God is the God who is love, a love which is enacted in an ultimate sacrifice, and an ultimate sacrifice of death. That is the death which Christianity knows as life, and that is the death which is annulled and reversed in a Christian celebration of glory, and even annulled in a Christian celebration of the glory of God, for such a celebration cannot be and could not be a celebration of Christ. Or, rather, it could only be a celebration of the Christ of glory, and if the pure Christ of glory is the Gnostic or perennial Christ, then a Christian celebration of the glory of God is a celebration of that purely spiritual Christ, and thus a pure reversal of the Christ who is the crucified God.

Nowhere else in the history of religions may we discover such a deep and pure antithesis at the very center of a religious body or world, and if that center is a purely dichotomous center it is present not only throughout the body of Christianity but also in that new "I" or self-consciousness which is born with the advent of Christianity, a self-consciousness which is not comprehensively manifest and real until the birth of the modern world, and a self-consciousness which finally ends or reverses itself with the full realization of the modern world. If that is the "I" which is crucified with Christ, it is also an "I" that is only born in that crucifixion, an "I" that is a positive and a negative "I" at once, and purely positive and negative at once, for it is that "I" which is the consequence of resurrection and crucifixion, and hence the consequence of that crucifixion which is resurrection. That is a resurrection which ends the pure otherness of I AM, but that ending is the birth of self-consciousness, and the birth of self-consciousness as a pure dichotomy in the center of consciousness itself, a pure dichotomy which is the *coincidentia oppositorum* of its purely positive and negative poles, and thus a *coincidentia oppositorum* of resurrection and crucifixion. That is a *coincidentia oppositorum* which is realized and released in the very advent of Christianity, and that is an advent which simultaneously occurs in the microcosm of self-consciousness

and the macrocosm of a new and total history, and here and
only here microcosm and macrocosm alike are both grounded
and realized in an absolutely dichotomous center, a center
which is both the actualization and the realization of the
crucifixion of God.

5

The Resurrection of God

Christian resurrection is the death of death, a death of death occurring in the full and final actuality of death, and thus a death of death inseparable from the ultimacy of the crucifixion. And as opposed to a Gnostic or spiritual resurrection, such resurrection is not a resurrection of glory, but rather a resurrection which is itself a full realization of the crucifixion, and a realization of the crucifixion in the full actuality of once and for all and irreversible events. Thus Christian resurrection neither occurs in Heaven nor even realizes a destiny in Heaven, for that destiny itself is reversed in the crucifixion, a reversal which itself is a full realization of the original self-naming or self-emptying of I AM, a self-emptying which is the reversal of an eternal now, and therefore the reversal of everything whatsoever which is manifest as Heaven and as Heaven alone. Just as immortality or Heaven is alien to an original Israel, and alien precisely because Israel is in an eternal covenant with I AM, prophetic iconoclasm is a violent assault upon the quest for immortality or Heaven, a quest which itself is apostasy from Yahweh or I AM, and an apostasy if only because it is a refusal of the total presence of I AM.

Accordingly, a true or faithful Israel is closed to an eternal life which is a heavenly immortality, just as a true or faithful Christianity is closed to an eternal life that is not an eternal death, or a resurrection which is not crucifixion, or a Christ of glory who is not the Christ of passion. If a Gnostic and spiritual resurrection is a pure reversal of Christian resurrection, it is all too significant that it is first proclaimed and enacted in primitive Christianity, an enactment and proclamation which is as early as Paul, for its celebrants were, indeed, the foremost opponents of Paul, and not only of Paul but of the Johannine tradition as well.

There is no actual evidence of a pre-Christian Gnosticism, just as there is no genuinely Gnostic text which is a pre-Christian text, and if Gnosticism is born not without but within Christianity, and deeply within it, that birth is not only an assault upon the actuality of the crucifixion, but a flight from the crucifixion itself, a flight occurring throughout the history of Christianity, and most deeply occurring in a flight to an absolutely transcendent God. But just as Gnosticism is a reversal of the crucifixion, it is also and even thereby a reversal and annulment of actual and irreversible events, for Gnostic celebration is a purely spiritual celebration, and therefore it is an annulment and reversal of historical actuality itself.

That annulment occurs more fully in Christianity than it does in any other religious tradition, for no other religious tradition is so deeply and so comprehensively a consequence of an irreversible historical actuality, an actuality continually inducing compulsive attempts to annul and reverse that very irreversibility. Yet these attempts were and are only attempts; never do they succeed in realizing their goal, or not within the historical body of Christianity, and that very failure is itself a decisive witness of the actuality of a resurrection which is crucifixion and resurrection at once.

If Gnosticism is a compulsive attempt to return to a pre-Christian and prebiblical world, it is nowhere found outside of Christianity, unless it is found in the purely mystical expressions of Judaism and Islam. Certainly it is not found in the religious traditions of the Oriental world, and above all not in Buddhism, where one might most expect to discover it. Buddhism knows and celebrates an absolute silence or selflessness which is the pure antithesis of Gnosticism, and the antithesis of Gnosticism if only because of its very "soullessness," a soullessness in which there is no ego or self which could be fulfilled by resurrection or redemption. Nothing so characterizes Gnosticism as does its striving for glorification, a glorification that is not simply and only glorification, but a glorification which is a reversal of actuality, and that is a reversal which can only occur within those worlds which are a consequence of the self-naming of I AM.

But the finality of that revelation can be observed in the inevitable failures of Gnosticism, or, at least, the inevitable failures of Christian Gnosticism, and if those failures are a consequence of a compulsive striving, they are never open to or within the horizon of that peace and serenity which are so characteristic of the Buddhist tradition. Gnosticism may also be understood to be a will to glorification, and a will that struggles against that bondage of the will discovered by Paul, a bondage that is the bondage of sin, and a bondage that ever deepens with the struggling and the striving of the individual will. This is the bondage that was philosophically discovered by Augustine, and Augustine's realization of the total bondage of the will was simultaneously a realization of the freedom of the will. This was the realization that made possible Augustine's conversion, for it was a discovery that the will itself is the source of its own bondage or slavery. Already that discovery is present in Paul, although it would be forgotten by the Church until Augustine, and if it was known and proclaimed by Paul, it was surely known by those Corinthian Gnostics who opposed Paul, Gnostics who believed that even now they were living in the full glory of a spiritual resurrection, a glory transcending both a future resurrection and the passion of the crucifixion.

The "spiritual men" of Corinth professed to live in a Lord of glory who delivers them from the tribulations of the flesh; therein and thereby they have wholly transcended the bondage of the will, and that transcendence is even now a life of glory. Now Paul's assault upon the Gnostics of his world was not simply an assault upon an illusory glorification; it was also an assault upon the claim that the bondage of the will can even now wholly be transcended, and wholly transcended by a new life in the Spirit. That is just what is impossible in what for Paul is the hither side of a future resurrection, and the very will to realize even now that future resurrection is a denial of authentic resurrection, and a denial of that resurrection if only because it is a refusal of the Christ of passion. A Gnostic quest for present glory can be understood as a compulsive quest not simply to reverse the bondage of the will, but to annul and erase the very will of will, and thus to dissolve that will which is the source of the bondage of the will, a will which now and for the first time is internally manifest as the "I" of self-consciousness. Accordingly, a Gnostic will to glorification is a will to unwill, a will to unwill itself, and to unwill itself as a free and an active will, a will whose very actuality freely enacts a continual enslavement of itself. Yet a will to glorification can never realize itself precisely because it is an act of the will, and even if it wills to unwill itself, that very will to unwill remains a will, and its very presence and activity foreclose the possibility of the realization of its intended goal.

So it is that Gnosticism is only born with the birth of Christianity, for only the advent of self-consciousness makes possible a will to unwill or to dissolve that very self-consciousness, and if that self-consciousness is a doubled and purely negative consciousness, or a self-alienated and self-

estranged consciousness, a consciousness wholly divided between the "I" of sin and the "I" of grace, that very division and
discord impels its own negation, and impels that negation as the
very reversal of itself. Hence the Gnostic seeks an absolutely
glorious "I," an "I" that is the "I" of pure Spirit, and an "I" that
is absolutely dissociated and distant from that new "I" which is
simultaneously the "I" of sin and grace. Thereby is born a new
and absolute dualism, a dualism that never previously existed,
for it is a dualism which is the consequence of a new interior "I,"
an interior "I" that can know an absolutely interior otherness,
an otherness impelling the very reversal of that "I," and a
reversal of that doubled and divided "I" in a new "I" of the
Spirit, an "I" that is total in its very enactment, and therefore an
"I" that is infinitely removed from body or flesh.

Unlike that Orphic tradition which appears to be its counterpart, this is a dualism inaugurated by and revolving about the
"I" of self-consciousness, an "I" which now wills to be a purely
spiritual "I," but that will can only occur by way of a total will to
annul and reverse its own interior otherness or guilt. That total
will is a new will to absolute glorification, yet that intended
totality of will remains an interior and individual will, and
thereby an actively striving will, a will which wills its own
glorification, and wills its own absolute glorification, a glorification which is a reversal of a total and interior guilt, and
therefore the reversal of that purely negative "I" which is first
recorded in the letters of Paul. Gnostic glorification intends a
pure reversal of the self-alienation of self-consciousness, and
Gnostic glorification is manifest as a glorification of a new
internal and interior "I," but precisely for this reason it is a
reversal which can never realize or fulfill itself, and cannot do so
if only because it is an intended glorification of a purely negative
"I," an "I" whose very actuality is a self-alienated actuality, and
is so if only because of the full presence here of an interior and
individual will, and an individual and interior will that can will
only by willing against itself. Nevertheless, that will to glorification does realize a pure and total dualism, a dualism only
possible within the world and the horizon of self-consciousness,
and a dualism that ever recurs within that world, and ever
recurring therein by way of an interior and violent opposition to
both a will and an actuality which is the very otherness of itself.

Nothing is more alien to that dualistic opposition than a
celebration of a resurrection which is crucifixion. That *coincidentia oppositorum* ends any possible dualism, and ends it by ending
any real or final distinction between life and death. Indeed, the
actualization of the death of death is the actualization of that

death in life itself, and as opposed to a Gnostic glorification which both intends and claims to be an eternal life which is eternal or heavenly life alone, *a Christian resurrection is the resurrection of death itself*, and a resurrection of that ultimate and final death which occurs in the crucifixion. If a Gnostic resurrection is a dissolution of death and crucifixion, the actualization of the death of death is not a dissolution of death but rather a realization of the ownmost actuality of death itself, and a realization of that actuality at the very center of life and history. So, as opposed to a wholly otherworldly and purely spiritual Gnosticism, a Gnosticism which is an absolute flight from actuality, a resurrection which is a resurrection of the actuality of death is a resurrection occurring at the center of actuality. That is a center whose own actuality is death, a death which is life and death at once, for it is precisely that *coincidentia oppositorum* which is the resurrection of the crucified God.

Christian resurrection is the resurrection of crucifixion; hence it cannot be a flight to the beyond, or even a transition or voyage to the beyond, for it is beyondness which perishes in crucifixion, and perishes so as finally to end the beyondness of the beyond. If the advent of that perishing is announced in Jesus' eschatological proclamation and parabolic enactment, it is fully realized in the crucifixion, and finally realized in that resurrection which is crucifixion and resurrection at once and altogether. Here, nothing whatsoever finally distinguishes death and life or crucifixion and resurrection, for crucifixion and resurrection are one event, and are that one event which is the full and final incarnation of I AM.

Now I AM perishes as absolute otherness, and perishes as such in that final and total act which is the ultimate actualization of the eternal act of God, an actualization which is the ultimate actualization of life and death, and thus an eschatological actualization of the life and death of God. Now the life of God is the death of God, for resurrection is crucifixion, just as crucifixion is resurrection, and as opposed to every other ultimate world or horizon, this is a once and for all and irreversible event occurring at the very center of actuality. Moreover, it is precisely that center which is fully and finally realized in this *coincidentia oppositorum*, and realized by this absolute and apocalyptic actualization of the eternal act of God. Consequently, resurrection is apocalypse, and is the apocalypse of the eternal act of God, an apocalypse which is the apocalypse of God, but nevertheless and even thereby the apocalypse of act or actuality, and thus an apocalypse which is all in all. Only the ultimate actuality of death realizes that apocalypse, but it realizes it in an absolutely new life, a life that is life and death at once, and if that life is the death of death, it is a death of death which is only finally actual through death itself, and through the ownmost actuality of that death which is an ultimate and a final death. If that death is life, it is a life inseparable from death; indeed, it is a life identical with death, and identical with that death which is absolute death, and therefore that death which is absolute life and death at once.

That is the apocalypse which is the center of Christianity, a center which is the one event of crucifixion and resurrection, and if that event is the center of history, it is the center of an apocalyptic history. So it is that a Christian apocalypse is not a heavenly apocalypse, it is a historical apocalypse, and therefore a real and actual apocalypse, an apocalypse occurring both in and as history, and occurring in and as that history which embodies it, a history which now and for the first time is a totally apocalyptic history. That is the apocalypse which is realized in the full and final advent of an absolutely forward movement of history, a forward movement which fully and finally dawns in the very birth of Christianity, a forward movement progressively but nevertheless totally negating the past, and even if it is met with innumerable reversals of itself such as the reversal of Gnosticism, reversals generated by the very power of an apocalyptic negation, those reversals finally only deepen the forward movement of history, and do so if only because they can never finally succeed in realizing their own reversals.

Now, an original self-naming of I AM is fully realized in history, and realized in a total and apocalyptic history which is a full and actual reversal of an original eternal recurrence or an original eternal now, and if that eternal now is now apocalyptically realized as a totally historical and a totally cosmic now, that now is not simply a new world, but is novum itself, an absolute novum which is all in all. If absolute novum is that Kingdom of God which Jesus parabolically enacted and eschatologically proclaimed, it is an apocalyptic self-negation and an apocalyptic self-emptying of the absolute otherness of I AM, a self-emptying and a self-negation which are realized in the crucifixion and resurrection of I AM, and if the crucified and resurrected Jesus is the crucified and resurrected I AM, the Word of revelation is the Word of crucifixion and resurrection, and that is the Word which originally speaks in the self-naming of I AM. Even if that voice was an absolutely other voice, it was nevertheless and even thereby an absolutely actual voice, and an absolutely actual voice that reverses its own otherness in the crucifixion and resurrection of itself, so that that very otherness itself then passes into an irrecoverable past, and does so as a necessary and inevitable consequence of the apocalyptic events of crucifixion and resurrection.

Resurrection is a hearing of the death of death, a hearing which hears death as the very otherness of itself, and thus hears death as the full otherness of itself, an otherness that now is the very reversal of itself, and if Jesus first heard that otherness, that is the otherness which is the full and final advent of the Kingdom of God. That is the apocalyptic triumph of a final self-emptying and self-negation, a kenosis which is the kenosis of the pleroma of the Godhead of God, and thus a kenosis which is the fullness in emptiness of the Kingdom of God. That emptiness releases the pleroma of history, a pleroma which is the actualization of an absolute self-emptying and self-negation, a self-emptying which is the "othering" of pure otherness itself, so that the death of death is the death of otherness itself, a death which is the pleroma of life or history or world.

Now, history realizes an absolute dynamism which it had never known before, and if such dynamism is present in the very beginning of Christianity, that is a dynamism progressively negating or emptying itself, and progressively negating itself in the evolution of history, an evolution which never before had occurred in a full and total historical process, and an evolution realizing itself in both an internal and an external violence, a violence itself without parallel in history, and a violence which is most openly and most immediately manifest in the self-alienation and the self-lacerations of a new self-consciousness. But that alienation and these lacerations are not only internally manifest and real, they realize themselves externally in a new historical will, a will that is present in a wholly new historical process, a historical process realizing itself in a pleroma of historical actuality, or in the pleroma of that historical actuality which is now released in the world. Both Augustine and Dante knew the Roman Empire as the primary political consequence of the Incarnation, and it was so both because it was the first truly universal empire in history and the most powerful empire which the world has ever known. *The Aeneid* is a celebration of the universal peace of that empire, just as the *Paradiso* is a celebration of its universal justice, but that peace and that justice were the consequence of a new and a virtually universal violence, and if that violence itself is the expression of a new historical will, that will is a will to power as it had never been present in history before, and as it will never be present again until the full birth of the modern world. This is an empire of violence which became a Christian empire in the Constantinian era, an empire which now claims to be the empire of Christ, a claim first hesitantly made in the *Civitas Dei* and then triumphantly realized in the *Paradiso*.

Dante was the first thinker and the first visionary in history to envision a universal human community, a community which was initially established in the Roman Empire, and a community which Dante believed would soon become apocalyptically triumphant in his own time. That is the apocalyptic faith which was imaginatively realized in the *Commedia*, and that is the apocalyptic faith which gave birth to the English Revolution and to *Paradise Lost*. The English Revolution inaugurated modern political revolution and was itself a revolutionary movement embodying a universal apocalypticism which is itself the embodiment of a Christian apocalypticism. Thus Christianity initiated a historical transformation without parallel in history, and it was not confined to the Christian world, as witness its offshoot in the triumph of Islam, and its parallel in the triumph of Mahayana Buddhism. Now a truly cosmic history is finally born, and if that history initially realized itself in discrete and opposing centers, it is nevertheless a total historical process, and a total historical process ever more gradually and more fully realizing itself throughout the world. Yet this is a historical process of self-negation, as can most clearly be seen in the history of Christianity, a history fulfilling itself in its own self-negation, a self-negation which is not only the end of Christendom, but the end of every manifest presence of the Christian God, an ending which is the full and comprehensive historical actualization of the death of God.

Nevertheless, this historical actualization is a triumph of the Kingdom of God, a triumph of that Kingdom which is the pleroma of kenosis, and the fullness of emptiness in an actual ending, an ending which must finally be known as resurrection, and as the resurrection of the crucified God.

Already there is present in an original Israel a new Torah which ends all human ranks and stations, an ending which in the prophetic revolution becomes an absolute assault upon all worldly power and authority, an assault which Nietzsche truly understood as a reversal of all worldly values, and a reversal which becomes absolute in the advent of Christianity. Now even if that reversal reversed itself in the history of Church and Christendom, that was a reversal that was ever accompanied by its own negation or reversal, as witness the progressive Christian exaltation of poverty and abasement, a poverty and abasement which become total in St. Francis and Meister Eckhart. That self-annihilation or self-emptying which generates historical revolution in the Christian Middle Ages is a revolution which is both a rebirth of an original Christian apocalypticism and a realization of that apocalypticism in a new history and a new world, a world that becomes a universal world in the American and French revolutions. Yet long before the advent of an actual historical revolution in the West, Islam gave the world a new society and a new consciousness that was grounded in a new and even apocalyptic faith, and if that society was the first egalitarian society in the world, or the first one that was a universal society, Islam also generated a new universal consciousness which negated all previous and given divisions of humanity, and realized for the first time in history a community of faith that is the community of the world, thereby decisively ending every real and ultimate division between the sacred and the profane or even Heaven and earth.

And long before the advent of Islam, Mahayana Buddhism had realized a comprehensive and universal process of self-dissolution or self-emptying, a self-emptying not only ending the center of consciousness but thereby and therein ending every division or barrier between any possible poles or polarities of consciousness. While the pure and total emptiness of Mahayana Buddhism may well be a disappearance of actuality, it is also a disappearance of every distance and otherness between all points or moments of consciousness, a disappearance which is the realization of an absolutely original condition, and an original condition in which all difference and otherness are absent. While such difference and otherness have never been more fully present than they are in the Christian and the Western world, and an otherness and difference which progressively and comprehensively enlarge and expand themselves with the historical evolution of that world, there is an absolute assault upon that difference and otherness in the historical revolutions of the West, and these comprehend not only political and religious revolutions, but scientific, imaginative, and philosophical ones as well, all of which are united in negating and reversing every difference which initially presents itself, and every otherness which is here a historical given. If those revolutions are being consummated in our own time in a wholly anonymous consciousness and society, an anonymity in which both an interior and an exterior otherness and difference are wholly groundless and unnameable, that very anonymity is now becoming a full if reverse parallel and embodiment of a Buddhist emptiness.

Yet if we can know our consciousness and society to be a consequence of an apocalyptic historical revolution or revolutions, revolutions which have inverted and reversed all previous moments and movements in our history, and done so even while fulfilling and realizing the deeper dynamism and direction of those movements, then we can understand the absolute will of a total history as a kenotic pleroma, and a kenotic pleroma ever more fully and finally realizing itself, and realizing itself in the full actuality of once and for all events. Thus that kenotic pleroma is not an original state or condition, and certainly not a primordial origin; it is far rather a pleroma that realizes itself in the actualities of history, and realizes itself as and in an absolutely negative energy or power, a power that is the actuality of self-negation or self-emptying, and a power that is seemingly culminating in the realization of an actually empty society and consciousness. If we now truly stand at the end of history, or at the end of everything that our world has known as history, we therein know our history as a total history, a totality that has enacted itself in historical actuality, and enacted itself in that historical actuality that was released by the crucifixion and the resurrection of God. Nothing is more important than understanding and celebrating that actuality as a forward movement of history, a forward movement released by the full and final advent of a new and absolute future, and while that future was initially proclaimed and enacted by the prophetic revolution of Israel, it was apocalyptically consummated in crucifixion and resurrection. That ultimate event is itself an absolute and final movement to a total future, a future which is celebrated in the celebration of resurrection.

This celebration of resurrection as an actual resurrection is not a celebration of Heaven, but far rather a celebration of that Kingdom of God which even now is becoming all in all, and not all in all as an absolutely sovereign and majestic Lordship, but all in all in a kenotic pleroma, a pleroma which itself is the fullness of historical actuality. That is the fullness in emptiness which is a historical totality, and a totality actually realizing itself in once and for all events, and while those events occur once and only once, they therein realize and embody an actuality which is a final and ultimate actuality. That is the actuality which is the triumph of the Kingdom of God, an actuality which itself is the negation of absolute otherness, and a self-negation of that otherness, a self-negation which can be celebrated as resurrection, but only when it is celebrated as the crucifixion of God. And, as opposed to a Gnostic or spiritual resurrection, Christian resurrection is not a return to a prehistorical and unfallen primordial Heaven, but a release and an actual release of the Godhead of God at the very center of actuality. If the Christian

God is pure actuality or pure act, that is an actuality which fully and finally becomes incarnate in the resurrection of God. That resurrection is the negation of negation, or the death of death, but it is the death of absolute otherness itself, and therefore the negation of that original negation which is the origin of fall, and not a negation which reverses fall in a movement of eternal return, but far rather a negation which is an actual and irreversible negation, and a negation which finally fulfills the original self-negation or self-emptying of I AM.

Consequently, the negation of negation is the self-negation of the self-negation of I AM, and not a negation which is a reversal of that original negation, but rather a negation which is a final realization of negation itself, and a realization of that negation in an ultimate and final death, a death which is resurrection, and is resurrection as the realization of an absolutely future actuality. That future is finally and fully actual in resurrection, and it is actual as a kenotic pleroma, a pleroma which is the very opposite of a primordial or original totality, for it is itself the final negation or emptying of that totality, an emptying which is the advent of the totality of history. If the resurrection of God ends any possible dualism, and ends it because it is the crucifixion of God, then this identity of crucifixion and resurrection is an actual and irreversible *coincidentia oppositorum*, and an apocalyptic *coincidentia oppositorum* ending every chasm between the here and the beyond, an ending which is the ending of every true and final otherness, and thus the ending of everything which is not totally present here and now. That total presence is the actual reversal of every other presence, and if an apocalyptic parousia is a parousia comprehending the totality of time, then time past and time future are now present in a total presence which negates every time which is only past or only future, and that negation is the realization of the totality of history. That is the totality which is the actuality of resurrection, and if now the absolute otherness of God is the absolute self-emptying of God, the self-emptying of that otherness reverses every pure or actual otherness, and otherness now can be present only as a self-negated otherness, and therefore as an otherness which is not and cannot be an actual otherness.

Now absolute difference is absolutely negated, and absolute otherness is wholly reversed; that is the absolute negation and reversal which is resurrection, and is that resurrection whose advent is the advent of a wholly new totality of history, a totality realizing itself in a finally forward and evolutionary movement, and an evolutionary movement which is a continual transfiguration of otherness, a transfiguration in which the very realization of otherness is a transfiguration of otherness, for that transfiguration is a negation and reversal of that very otherness, and if that is the negation which is the historical and actual realization of an absolute self-emptying or self-negation, that is the negation which is the self-emptying and self-negation of the resurrection of God.

6

Emptiness and Self-emptiness

Nothing is or could be more distant from Christianity than is Buddhism, and if Buddhism is the most universal way that has evolved in the Orient, it is also the purest and most total way to an absolute reversal of history, an absolute reversal which it can know and realize as an absolute emptiness, and an absolute emptiness that is infinitely and absolutely distant from a Christian celebration of God, or even from a Christian celebration of the crucifixion and resurrection of God. Yet this absolutely pure reversal of history is not an actual reversal at all, but rather a profound nonrealization or ultimate de-actualization of pure actuality itself. Absolute emptiness or sunyata is the primary Mahayana Buddhist symbol of nirvana, and if this is the purest image in the history of religions, it is finally a nonimage, and a nonimage evoking a pure and total silence, an absolutely primordial silence in which no opposition or differentiation is possible. Now, nirvana is identical with samsara, which is to say that it is identical with its own apparent opposite, and that is a *coincidentia oppositorum* which is the purest possible *coincidentia oppositorum,* for it is, indeed, a *coincidentia* which is not a coincidence or identity as such, but rather the absolute disappearance of the very possibility of either difference or opposition. So it is that in the Buddhist tradition, nirvana is approached through three doors of deliverance: emptiness, the signless, and the wishless. For nirvana has no relationship whatsoever to anything which is given or manifest as actuality, and not even a purely negative relationship, for, indeed, it is precisely the negative as negative which is wholly absent from the Buddhist way. Now even if nirvana is unborn, unbecoming, unmade, and uncompounded, and thereby is absolutely uncon-

ditioned, that unconditionedness has no real or actual relationship to the conditioned, a conditioned which is "dependent
arising," and a dependent arising that, as Nagarjuna declares, is
wholly dependent upon convention, for it quite simply is
"emptiness" (*Mulamadhyamakakarika* XXIV, 18). Thus it is that
the absolutely conditioned and the absolutely unconditioned
are equally empty, and if that emptiness is an absolute peace or
calm, that is a calm that is absolutely other than the pure
actuality of the Christian God, and yet this pure emptiness is not
an otherness at all, but is rather an arising that is not arising, or
a pure origination which is not origination at all.

That realization is an absolute nonrealization, but it is not
thereby a simple inactivity or disengagement; it is far rather a
realization of unbornness, and not an unbornness which is not
being born, but an unbornness which precludes the very
possibility of birth. And if that unbornness is the absolutely
unconditioned, it is not thereby the true or actual opposite of
the conditioned, for its realization ends the possibility of
opposition of any kind, and with that ending origination or
beginning also ends, for even the doctrine of dependent
origination is a way of realizing that there is not and cannot be
an actual beginning of any kind. But if there is not and cannot
be an actual beginning, there is not and cannot be an actual
ending, so that nirvana is not the extinction or the blowing out
of consciousness, for it is not an act of any kind, nor even a
cessation of act or actuality, for here there is no beginning or
actuality to come to an end, for nothing has ever happened, and
nothing has ever begun. Yet that nothing is not a simple or
literal nothingness, for there can be no nothingness that is other
than "is" ness, and this because there cannot be an "other," and
not even an "other" of nirvana, and above all not an "other" of
nirvana if nirvana is absolutely unborn. That unbornness is an
absolute unbornness, and therefore it is not an "un" bornness,
for it is not different from or distinguishable from anything
else, and this because nirvana is absolutely signless, and therefore is absolutely silent. But this is not the silence of death, for
now death is absolutely unreal, but so likewise a life that is other
than death is unreal, and unreal if only because here nothing
whatsoever is "other" than anything else.

Nothing is or could be further from the horizon of Buddhism
than Christianity, and yet from the perspective of Buddhism that very distance is illusory and unreal, and not simply
because Buddhism dissolves otherness, since that dissolution is
not a dissolution of anything, for in Buddhism there is nothing
that is or could be dissolved. Now even as Hinduism can know

Christ as an avatar of Vishnu, Mahayana Buddhism can know Christ as the Buddha, and even if that Buddha is absolutely empty, that is an emptiness which is all in all, and therefore is everything and everyone. Here, a "Here Comes Everybody" is a coming of the Buddha, but that is not the coming of anyone, for here there is no one, and there is no coming or going, hence there is no Buddha who can come, but only the Buddha who is always and already here and now. While that is a here-and-nowness which is everywhere, it is everywhere only by being nowhere, and the Christ who is here the Buddha is the Christ who is nowhere else, and certainly nowhere where hearing is possible, for here there is nothing that can be heard, or nothing that can be heard that is other than anything else. If Buddhism knows a hearing of pure silence, it surely can hear Christ as that silence, and hence as a silence that is not different from anything else.

Now that is a silence that has never been historically present in Christianity, unless it was so present in its very beginning, and, if so, that is a silence that Christianity has wholly lost. Buddhism today is offering Christianity the apparent possibility of a return to such a beginning, but a beginning which cannot be an actual beginning, but far rather a beginning which is no beginning, or a beginning which is unbirth, and the unbirth of the Christ who is all in all in everything and everyone. Buddhism, too, has embodied a kenotic pleroma, but a pleroma which is a full and total pleroma precisely in its emptiness, and in its absolute emptiness, an emptiness which is not "other" than anything else, for this is an emptiness which is the emptiness of fullness or totality itself. Buddhism knows and realizes that totality as the emptiness of the Buddha, a Buddha who is an absolute and total compassion, and is total compassion just because the Buddha is total emptiness, an emptiness foreclosing the very possibility of distance, or of otherness, or of isolation. No religious traditions have made such absolute claims for compassion as have Buddhism and Christianity, and if Christianity knows that God who is absolute love, Buddhism knows that Buddha who is absolute compassion, and only Buddhism and Christianity have known their founders as the total fullness of that ultimate reality or that absolute freedom which each has enacted and proclaimed.

Contemporary Buddhists are unveiling that Christ who is identical with the Buddha, a Christ who is absolute emptiness, and therefore is absolute compassion, an absolute compassion which is a realization of an absolute emptiness, and an absolute emptiness which is all in all. In this perspective, the Kingdom of

God which Jesus enacted and proclaimed can be known as an
absolute emptiness, an emptiness which is absolutely unborn,
and therefore an emptiness which is not different or "other"
than anything else. Thereby that Kingdom can be apprehended
as absolute compassion, and absolute compassion just because it
absolutely empties any and every possible otherness, and it is
even because that pure and total dissolution is not an actual
dissolution of anything, that it brings all actual origin or
beginning to an end. That ending is the ending of beginning,
and above all the ending of a once and for all and irreversible
beginning, but also the ending of sin or original sin, for the
annulment of the very possibility of birth is the annulment of
the very possibility of sin, and with that annulment an actual
origin, just as an actual beginning, can finally disappear. But
that annulment is not an actual annulment, for here there is no
real or actual birth which could be annulled, and this because no
real or actual otherness is possible, and impossible because
emptiness is all in all. Now grace is everywhere, and otherness is
nowhere, a regeneration or being born again which is not being
born at all. Now if dualism has plagued the history of Christianity, this is a dualism which is fully absent in Buddhism, and
above all absent in that Buddhism which knows nirvana as
absolute emptiness, an emptiness which brings all otherness to
an end, or, if it does not bring otherness to an end, and cannot
do so if only because nirvana is the causeless, it realizes a
causelessness which is all in all, and that causelessness is the
disappearance of otherness. Of course, that disappearance is
not an actual disappearance, for there is nothing that can
actually disappear if only because there is no distinction between appearance and disappearance, no real distinction or
otherness between anything and anything else. That very
absence of otherness can be named as compassion, a compassion
which is an illusion if anything can be itself and not another, and
above all if anything can be an "I" or center which is wholly and
only itself. If that is the illusion which is the deepest obstacle to
enlightenment, that is also the illusion that precludes the
possibility of compassion, and an illusion that wholly disappears
in the enactment of compassion. But here the enactment of
compassion is not an actual act at all, and cannot be so if only
because it unacts or reverses every center, and reverses every
center so as to realize a center that is everywhere.

A center that is everywhere is indistinguishable from a
circumference that is nowhere, and if only Buddhism has
historically realized that center, this is not to say that Christianity has not forgotten such a center, and certainly not if such a

center has at least partially recurred again and again in Christian mysticism, and surely recurred in an inverse form in all Christian nostalgia for an original state of innocence. Such nostalgia is absent from the Buddhist world, and absent if only because Buddhism cannot know an original condition which is other than a present condition, or a past time which is truly other than a present time, or a primordial state which is temporally or chronologically a primordial state. If Christianity has known an "I" of God that is wholly and simultaneously present, past, and future, Buddhism, and the oriental world as a whole, have known time itself as simultaneous, and thus as present, past, and future at once, a simultaneity of time in which there are not and cannot be any real or actual or final distinctions between present, past, and future, and hence no real awareness of either an actual future or an actual past. And with the absence of that awareness the present moment can be apprehended as a total moment, or a moment comprehending both the future and the past, and hence there cannot be present in that moment an awareness of the pastness of the past, a past which here is truly absent or gone.

If this is an absence which is the absence of the actuality of time, it is also an absence which precludes the possibility of an actual longing for either the past or the future as such, for here neither past nor future are actually other, and thus they are not actually other than the present moment. Accordingly, the emptiness of the future and the past is the emptiness of the present as such, since here there can be no present which is present and only present, for there can be nothing which is only itself, and if the absence of the future and the past is also the absence of the present, that is an absence which is simply the absence of otherness itself. But that is an absence which is the is-notness of isness, or the pure nothingness of pure isness, a *coincidentia oppositorum* in which no opposites are actually present, for here there is no distance or distinction between is and is not. If that is a pure emptiness which is a pure fullness, it is full precisely by being empty, and hence there can be no actualization of emptiness, and no act which enacts anything whatsoever. Nothing happens in enlightenment, just as nothing happens in compassion, and if compassion and enlightenment are one in Buddhism, that is a union which is the realization of unbirth or nonbeginning, a nonbeginning which is the pure simultaneity of time itself, and hence a nonbeginning which is present in every moment.

So likewise that nonbeginning or unbirth is present everywhere, for the pure simultaneity of time is inseparable and indistinguishable from the pure ubiquity of space, a space in which the center is everywhere just as the circumference is nowhere, and that everywhere which is nowhere is indistinguishable from a present moment that is wholly and fully present, past, and future at once. That is an is-notness which is the is-notness of present, past, and future as such, even as it is the is-notness of center and circumference as such, and if this is a pure emptiness it is the emptiness of every other, and the emptiness of every other everywhere. And if this is a pure emptiness which can be realized only by the pure emptiness of the will, that is a will-lessness which is signless, and hence it is the absolute absence of all actual identity, an absence which is the fullness of compassion. Consequently, that compassion is the total absence of the will, so that it is not and cannot be enacted, for it cannot be present here and not there, or now and not then; these are distinctions that are dissolved and erased in the realization of compassion, a realization that also erases and dissolves every distinction between the subject and the object of compassion. So it is that the "I" of compassion is purely a "not I," and not simply because selfhood is dissolved in the realization of compassion, but because every center is erased in that realization, and if now the "I" or the center is everywhere, that is because its circumference is nowhere, for now every distinction between the "I" and the "not I" is erased, and that erasure is the erasure of every distinction whatsoever.

Christians are commonly dumbfounded by the power of Buddhism, and if that power is an empty power, it is all the more fully power precisely because of that, and all the more so from a Christian perspective, for it is seemingly wholly absent from the Christian world. And yet it might appear that this is just the power which Christianity has always most deeply sought, and perhaps it is a power which Christianity itself has realized in its deepest expressions, for even if those expressions have been theologically uncomprehended, they are no less real for that. And if Christianity in its very center knows a life which is death, is that a life which can be distinguished from a Buddhist identification of life and death, an identification ending every opposition between death and life, and ending it in the very realization of an isness which is is-notness, a life without an actual beginning or ending, and therefore a life which is unborn? Surely Christians have commonly experienced rebirth or being born again as a call not to be born at all, and even if they could not and have not named it as such, is not such a call manifest in a Christian nostalgia for the garden of paradise, a nostalgia which is clearly a longing for timelessness, and a longing for spacelessness as well, a spacelessness and a timelessness which are the full opposites of the full actuality of space and time. Such longing is a longing for a reversal of that actuality, and such a reversal is fully and purely present in Buddhism, and historically present in Buddhism as it has never been historically present in Christianity, and never so present if only because dualism has invariably been present in the historical body of Christianity, a dualism both witnessing to and yet itself a barrier to an absolute reversal of both flesh and death.

Dualism has been more fully absent from the Buddhist tradition than it has been from any other tradition, and if that absence is an embodiment of a pure *coincidentia oppositorum*, that is a *coincidentia oppositorum* quite simply ending any possible otherness or opposition, an ending which is the ending of difference itself, and the ending of difference or otherness at the very center of consciousness, so as to realize and to finally realize a center which is everywhere. While that everywhere is emptiness, and is an absolute emptiness, it is so as a nothingness or a void or an is-notness which is isness, and is that isness which is absolutely indistinguishable from is-notness. Thus a Buddhist void or unbornness is itself its own opposite, for it is an absolute fullness or totality, but, as opposed to Hindu visions of totality, this is a totality that is absolutely empty or void, and as such is wholly devoid of otherness, and so much so that here all echoes or traces of otherness wholly disappear. While that disappearance is the appearance of absolute totality, it is the appearance of that totality which is absolutely unborn, and therefore a totality which at once is and is not, but that *coincidentia* is not an actual *coincidentia*, for here there is no distinction whatsoever between is and is not, and therefore no distinction whatsoever between absolute totality and absolute void or emptiness.

While the Western world has an irresistible temptation to apprehend the Buddhist way as a way of absolute return, such apprehension does violence to Buddhism, and does so if only because in Buddhism there is no distinction whatsoever between forward and backward, and thus no distinction between evolution and involution, or between a forward and a backward movement of cosmos and history. If everything that the West has known as temporality and history is absent in Buddhism, that is also and even thereby an absence of selfhood and will, and thus the absence of a center or point which is the axis of consciousness and experience, a center apart from which there can be neither forward and backward nor up and down. So likewise Buddhism knows a pure reversibility of both space and time that is simply inconceivable in the Western world, a reversibility whereby and wherein there are no distinctions at all between points in time and space, and thus no actual or definite spatial or temporal location, or no spatial or temporal location which is individual and unique. We need not hesitate to say that Buddhism knows a pure paradise that is wholly absent from the Western consciousness, and even if that is a paradise of absolute emptiness it can be apprehended from a Western and Christian perspective as a paradise lost, and lost in our very apprehension of the full actuality of spatial and temporal location, an actuality precluding the possibility of an actual reversal of time and space, and therefore precluding the possibility of an ultimate and final movement of return.

Now even if such a movement of return is inconceivable and meaningless in Buddhism, it is all too meaningful to us, and meaningful to us if only because we have known an original or primordial paradise as a paradise lost, and therefore have known an original moment of time as a time that is truly and actually past. Such pastness is truly alien to Buddhism, for Buddhism cannot know a past which is truly other than the present or the future, and thus cannot know a past which is actually past, or a paradise which either is or could be lost. Nevertheless, it would appear that Buddhism does know a past which the Western and Christian world has wholly lost, and that is a past that even now is present, and present so as to be indistinguishable from either a future or a present moment, for it is a past which is truly and actually an eternal now. If the Christian world has known an eternal now as the now of God, it has thereby known it as a now which is wholly other than our now, and a now that itself became invisible and inaudible with the triumph of modernity. But Buddhism has known a purity and totality of an eternal now which has never been manifest in the West, and never manifest in the West if only because the Western and Christian world has been grounded in the subject of consciousness. While that subject has here been the center of consciousness, that is a center which has been inescapably other than its periphery or circumference, and thus inescapably other than its own horizon or world.

If the inescapable otherness of the world is the full actuality of the world as world, that is an actuality that is truly other than an original all in all, an all in all that here and here alone can be truly known as primordial and past, and therefore as truly lost. Christianity and Christianity alone has known an irreversible fall, a fall occurring in a once and for all and irreversible event, and a fall repeated and renewed in the full actuality of once and for all and irreversible events, events which are fully and only themselves and no other, and thus events that are truly other than their own original and primordial ground. Now that ground is manifest as a truly primordial ground, and thus as a ground that is actually distant and apart, and if that distance is the actuality of otherness, that is an actuality that here and here alone is inescapably present. Thus, in a Christian and Western perspective, a Buddhist eternal now is unreal, and not only unreal but wholly and absolutely unreal, and absolutely unreal because it is a dissolution of difference and otherness, a dissolution which from a Western and Christian perspective could only be known as an absolute deactualization of actuality itself. This is a deactualization which from a Western perspective is unbornness, an unbornness which is "un" bornness, and therefore a return to an absolutely irrecoverable origin. Now if that is an origin which has been unnameable in the West, and even unnameable in the Hebrew and Christian Bible, that is an origin which the West has never known, and above all never known if only because it has known the ultimacy and finality of fall.

Not even a trace of such an identity of fall is present in Buddhism, and not even in a Buddhism which knows desire or craving as the primary source of pain and illusion, for that craving is finally unreal, and unreal if only because selfhood is unreal, and not only selfhood but every axis or center is absolutely unreal which is center or axis as such. Yet this is a center which is manifestly present in Christianity, and most clearly and manifestly present in the Christian God, and if that God is pure actuality or pure act, that is an act whose actualization or realization is the very origin of the world. Such an origin is not only absent in Buddhism, it is simply and wholly impossible in that world, an impossibility which is the impossibility of difference and otherness, and thus the impossibility of a center or origin which is truly different from anything else.

If nothing is more distant from the Buddhist world than what Christianity knows as the Godhead of God, that distance is most clearly manifest in what Christianity knows as the act of God, for even if that act is an eternal act, it is also and even thereby an enactment, an enactment which is actually act, and is actually act in its own realization. And that is a realization which is a forward-moving realization, a realization not only moving from genesis to apocalypse, but a realization enacting or realizing itself in that very movement, a realization realizing itself in actual acts, and not only actual acts but new acts, and absolutely new acts, for they are acts of the Godhead of God. Now even if such acts are wholly alien to Buddhism, they are at the very

center of Christianity, and therein is realized that center which
is absolute center, and thus a center which is the very opposite of
a Buddhist emptiness. If that center has been named by
Christians as the "I" of God, that "I" is not only an absolute "I,"
but it is that absolute "I" which is absolute center, and is that
absolute center which has named itself as I AM. But that I AM
is absolutely other, and is even absolutely other in the self-
naming of itself, a self-naming which is the historical source or
origin of absolute otherness, and yet a self-naming which is a
repetition or renewal of a once and for all and irreversible
beginning. That is a beginning which is the true opposite
of Buddhist unbornness, even as I AM is the true opposite of
nirvana, for each are opposites of any possible dissolution
of difference, just as each are opposites of any inactual *coincidentia oppositorum*.

But it is precisely in that arena and that horizon which is the
hearing of I AM that a total energy is released in the world, an
energy that is the full and actual opposite of a Buddhist
dissolution of the will, even as the acts of I AM are an absolute
reversal of a Buddhist quiescence and calm, for now act is
realized and actualized as absolute act, and that absolute act
is the true and total opposite of absolute emptiness. But it is the
opposite of that emptiness only by being the actual and total
"other" of that emptiness, and that otherness is at the very
center of its pure act and actuality, a pure act and actuality
which is the eternal act of God. If that act is the very Godhead
of God, that is a pure actuality or pure energy which is the very
opposite of absolute emptiness, and the opposite of that emptiness in its very center or "I." While absolute emptiness ends or
dissolves all possible difference or opposition, I AM is the pure
embodiment of difference and opposition, and the embodiment
of pure difference and opposition at the very center of itself.

Thus I AM is the self-embodiment of otherness, and the
self-embodiment of otherness in its own act and actuality, an act
and actuality which bring an original plenitude to an end, and if
that actuality is the self-emptying of that plenitude, I AM is the
self-emptying of absolute emptiness, and the self-emptying of
absolute emptiness in the very actualization of itself. Now an
original plenitude is no more, or not within the horizon of the
hearing of I AM, and hence that plenitude is forgotten, and
above all forgotten in the Christian and the Western world.
Nowhere within that world have we been given visions of an
original plenitude or pleroma; here that pleroma is simply
invisible or inaudible, and purely inaudible and invisible, so that
not even an echo or a trace is present here of a total absence of

all difference and opposition. Yet if I AM is the self-emptying of absolute emptiness, and a self-emptying which realizes or enacts I AM as absolute center, that is a center or an "I" which is other than itself, and absolutely other than itself, and absolutely other than itself in its ownmost acts and actuality. If here and here alone we may discover a pure and total opposition, that is an opposition which is in opposition to itself, and in opposition to itself in its inmost center or "I," an "I" that is a pure and absolute activity or act, and precisely in that act or activity it can only be in opposition to itself, for as absolute otherness it could only be the otherness of itself.

That is an absolute otherness which is absolutely other than absolute emptiness, and it is truly and wholly the "other" of that emptiness, so that even as absolute emptiness is a pure inversion of absolute activity and will, I AM is a pure inversion or reversal of absolute emptiness or nirvana. But in being that inversion or reversal it is a self-emptying of pure emptiness, and it is precisely as such that it realizes its actuality or Godhead, a Godhead that is the total inversion of emptiness, and the total inversion of emptiness in the very realization of its center or "I." Consequently, I AM is the self-emptying of absolute emptiness, a self-emptying which actually realizes its own Godhead or "I," and if that "I" is absolute center, it is that absolute center which is in absolute opposition to itself. That is an internal and even interior opposition which can be known and has been known as absolute will, an absolute will which is absolute sovereignty and transcendence, but a sovereignty and transcendence which is finally and ultimately a kenotic transcendence of itself. If only Christianity has known that transcendence, and known it by knowing the crucified God, it is also only Christianity that has known the ultimacy and finality of the fall, a fall that shattered an original harmony and quiescence, and once that fall enters the center of consciousness, that consciousness can never again apprehend or even remember an original quiescence and calm.

But the loss of that calm can also be understood as a hearing of I AM, for that hearing is the hearing of the total actuality of voice and speech, and thus it is the opposite of a Buddhist silence. If pure silence is the realization of absolute calm, that silence is alien to Christianity, and is certainly absent from the Western world. For the loss of that silence is yet another embodiment of the loss of an original plenitude or pleroma, and while a yearning or nostalgia for that pleroma has never been wholly absent in the West, and is above all present in the modern world, that is a nostalgia or yearning which can never be realized, and thus it is wholly absent from the Buddhist world. The very presence of nostalgia is a decisive sign of absence, and it commonly occurs in the deepest yearning for return, and even if return itself is impossible, or impossible in the Christian and the Western world, that is precisely the condition that makes possible a compulsive will to return, and a compulsive will to return to a paradise that has been actually lost. Nothing less than an actual loss of an original paradise can account for a deep or ultimate or even all-consuming nostalgia, a nostalgia which can only be fully discovered in the postmedieval Western world, and a nostalgia which is finally directed against creation or beginning itself. Why is there any being at all; why not far rather nothing? This is the irresistible question of such a nostalgia, and it can even be understood as a Western yearning for nirvana, or for unbeginning or for unbirth. But it is just because it is a yearning that by an irrevocable necessity it must be unfulfilled, and unfulfilled precisely because it is a will to unwill, for the very activity of that will forecloses the possibility of its deactualization. Such a will is a will to reverse the beginning, and therefore to reverse "God said," so that our nostalgia is finally directed against the Creator, for it seeks a plenum which is on the yonder side of creation, and that is the very plenum which perished when "God said." That is the plenum which Buddhism can know as absolute nothingness, a nothingness which is the totality of an isness which is is-notness, and which can only truly be known by being absolutely unborn. That unbornness is absolute emptiness, and it is absolutely real only in its absolute unreality or inactuality, an inactuality which is on the yonder side of "God said," yet an inactuality which is there and only there, all in all. Such an inactuality perishes in the eternal act of God, and thus perishes in the self-emptying of God, and if that self-emptying is the self-emptying of absolute emptiness, that is the emptiness which perishes in and through the pure actuality of God as God. If that actuality is the very Godhead of God, that is an actuality which brings an original emptiness to an end, an ending which is enacted by the Godhead of God, and an ending which is the actual origin of ultimate difference and opposition. That opposition and difference is wholly absent from an original or primordial emptiness, and that very absence is the absence of God, and the absence of God the Creator, an absence which itself becomes absent and actually absent when "God said." Then silence perishes, and that perishing is the act of God, an act which is an absolutely violent act, for it shatters an original silence, a silence which then can be heard no more, or heard no more and never again by that hearing which has heard I AM. Accordingly, the hearing of

I AM is the hearing of the ending of an original calm and quiescence, an absolute peace that perishes when "God said," and perishes in that act which is the act of God.

Yet that act is itself the self-emptying of that calm and quiescence, a self-emptying which is a self-negation, and a self-negation which is the origin and the actual origin of an absolute difference and opposition. Then an absolute emptiness becomes the very opposite of itself, and becomes the opposite of itself in the pure act of God, an act that is an inversion and reversal of an original emptiness, and the reversal of that emptiness in the very realization of absolute act, an absolute act that is absolute opposition to absolute emptiness. Pure act and actuality can only be an absolute opposition to itself, or to itself as absolute emptiness, a pure emptiness that is the yonder side of "In the beginning," and a pure emptiness that becomes absolute difference in and as the act of God.

That is a difference which is a pure difference, and a pure difference from pure emptiness, and if absolute emptiness is wholly and totally empty of difference, the act of God is itself pure difference, and is finally and ultimately pure difference from itself. That is the difference which speaks in the self-naming of I AM, and that is the difference which is actualized in a once and for all and irreversible beginning, a beginning which is pure difference, and is pure difference from pure emptiness. If that beginning is the act of God, and solely and only the act of God, that act is a total reversal of absolute emptiness, a total reversal which is the emptying of emptiness itself.

But that emptying is an actual emptying, and an actual emptying of absolute emptiness, so that it can only be the self-emptying of absolute emptiness, a self-emptying which is absolute origin. Self-emptying is the pure opposite of pure emptiness, and pure opposite if only because it is pure act, an act which itself is absolute opposition to pure emptiness, and an act which enacts the absolute "other" of that emptiness. That act is an absolutely new act, and that novum is the pure opposite of a pure simultaneity of time, now that simultaneity disintegrates, and it disintegrates in the advent of pure difference.

So likewise the pure ubiquity of space disintegrates, a disintegration which is the advent of world as world, but that advent is simultaneously the advent of the Creator as creator, and the Creator who creates out of nothing, a nothingness which Buddhism knows as nirvana. If that nothingness is absolutely unborn, it therefore is absolutely empty, an emptiness which is the pure absence of difference and opposition, and thus an emptiness which is absolute calm. That is the calm which is shattered by the Creator, and shattered by the eternal act of God, an act that is pure difference from that calm, and thus an act that is an absolute reversal of absolute emptiness. Such a reversal could only be an actual reversal, a reversal occurring in pure act, and a reversal which is the pure act of God, and if that act of God is the pure opposite of pure emptiness, then that act is pure and total difference, and finally and ultimately a pure and total difference from itself.

Pure difference can only be a difference from itself, a difference from itself as pure emptiness, or a difference from that which it would be if it were empty of difference. If pure emptiness is absolutely centerless, pure difference is absolutely centered, a center which names itself as I AM, and that absolute center is absolutely other, and absolutely other than itself as an absolutely quiescent totality. For an absolutely quiescent totality can only be an absolute emptiness, an emptiness which is a pure inactuality, and an emptiness that ends with the actualization of the act of God. That act is creation, and it is creation out of pure nothingness, a pure nothingness which is pure emptiness, and an emptiness which is actually reversed in the act of God. But if that act is pure act or pure actuality, that is an actuality which is absolutely other than pure emptiness, and absolutely other in and as that very actuality. So this is a pure otherness that is purely and only itself, and therefore it is absolutely different from itself, and different from itself in its own act and actuality; for if that actuality is pure actuality, it is an actuality that can never cease to enact itself, and to enact itself as the pure otherness of its own emptiness or inactuality. Consequently, pure actuality is the self-emptying of absolute emptiness, a self-emptying realizing itself in absolute act, and realizing itself as absolute act, an absolute act which is the enactment of itself, and the enactment of itself as the absolute opposite of its own original emptiness or calm.

7

Incarnation and Apocalypse

If pure actuality is an absolute act which is the enactment of itself, and the enactment of itself as the absolute opposite of its own original emptiness or calm, then a pure opposition is at the very center of a pure actuality, and a pure opposition which is in absolute opposition to itself, and in absolute opposition to itself as an original or primordial pleroma. That is the pleroma which is disrupted or reversed in the advent of pure actuality or pure act, and if beginning or absolute beginning is pure act, that is an act which is in opposition to itself, and in pure opposition to itself, and in pure opposition to itself as an original plenitude. For an original or a primordial plenitude could only be an inactual plenitude, and an absolute inactual or empty plenitude, a plenitude that is wholly and only inactive, or unmoving, or calm, hence a plenitude that is a pure emptiness or pure nothingness, and even if that nothingness is the fullness of emptiness or a "being" which is being and nonbeing at once, that is a "being" which is an absolutely inactual "being," and thus a "being" that is indistinguishable from pure nothingness.

Now even if a perennial vision and a perennial philosophy can know that pure nothingness, they can never know it as the God who is pure act, or the God who is I AM, for that is the very nothingness which perishes in the act of God, and perishes in the very realization of the absolute otherness of God, an otherness that is the ending, and the final ending, of an absolute emptiness or an absolute inactuality. Just as unbornness or pure or absolute emptiness is our clearest image of an original pleroma or plenitude, a plenitude which is all in all, absolute otherness is our clearest image of the God who is pure act, and if that act is the actualization of world itself, it is also and thereby the actualization of the Creator, and the actualization of the act

of creation which is in absolute opposition to itself, an opposition apart from which actualization itself would be inactual and
therefore unreal. Consequently, actualization itself is in absolute opposition to itself, an opposition or self-negation which is
the source and ground of all life and activity, and an opposition
which is a continual or even eternal opposition to itself. Now
that opposition is an actual opposition, and an absolutely actual
opposition, and therefore an opposition which assaults or
negates itself, and negates itself in its very center, a center which
itself is a self-negation or self-emptying, and therefore a center
which can name itself as I AM.

But I AM is simultaneously I AM NOT, a simultaneity which
is the source of absolute otherness, and the source of an absolute
otherness at the very center of itself, an otherness which is an
essential and intrinsic otherness, and therefore an otherness
which is not and cannot be either open to or an embodiment of
a polar harmony or coinherence. Pure harmony or pure
coinherence is precisely what is absent or missing from the pure
actuality of I AM, an absence that is present in absolute
otherness, and necessarily present in that pure act which is
enactment itself, an enactment apart from which otherness
would not be actually other. So it is that the very actuality of
otherness is a decisive and irrefutable sign of the loss of an
original harmony or coinherence, a loss that is a final loss within
the horizon or world of an actual otherness, and a loss that is
nowhere more fully manifest than in the very self-naming of I
AM. For that self-naming is and only can be an absolute
negation, a negation absolutely negating an undifferentiated
totality, a negation which is the realization and the enactment of
the absolute otherness of I AM, and the absolute otherness of I
AM at the very center of itself, a center which is I AM and I AM
alone, and consequently a center which is absolutely other than
its own periphery or world.

That absolute otherness is truly and essentially an is-notness,
or pure difference, but a pure difference which is finally a pure
difference from itself, and a pure difference from itself as a
totality which is all in all. The very self-naming of I AM is a pure
and total opposition to an original and total silence or calm, that
is the calm which is absolutely shattered when "God said," so
that the beginning of pure otherness or pure difference is the
beginning of a pure and total opposition, and therefore an
opposition that must be and can only be in opposition with itself,
an opposition to itself that is the absolute act of negation. That
act itself can only be an absolutely dichotomous act, an act
negating itself as a quiescent and undifferentiated totality, and

yet an act affirming and realizing itself in its very enactment of absolute act, so that a pure opposition necessarily and inevitably lies at the very center of an absolute act. That pure opposition necessarily realizes itself as pure difference, and pure difference from itself as absolute emptiness or quiescence, a difference apart from which there could be no real or actual difference at all, and a difference apart from which a once and for all and irreversible beginning could never occur. That beginning is the beginning of pure difference, a pure difference which is the origin of the world, and the origin of that world which is wholly different from I AM, but that world itself can only be the consequence of a pure difference at the very center of I AM, a center which is and only could be a center by virtue of that very difference, and a center which is simultaneously absolutely different from an undifferentiated totality and absolutely different from the world as world.

Nevertheless, such difference or otherness is not simply and only otherness, or not an otherness which is simply and only itself, and cannot be so if only because it is finally that otherness which is the otherness of itself, and is so because ultimate difference cannot be itself apart from its own otherness, an otherness which is truly and actually its own, and is its own as its ownmost center or ground. Now if that is the ground which speaks in the voice of I AM, that is a voice that is inseparable from its own other, an other that is itself as an inactual and silent totality, and an other that realizes itself as an other in the very hearing of this voice, a hearing which is itself a self-negation or self-laceration, and a hearing which is an echo or reverberation of that original shattering which occurred in "God said." If that shattering is the inauguration of world itself, that is the inauguration of a forward-moving time and world, and an irreversibly forward-moving time and world, an irreversibility which is the irreversibility of time and history alike, and an irreversibility which is the absolute reversal of an eternal now, or the absolute reversal of an original eternity or totality. That reversal is the very "isness" of I AM, an isness which is absolutely not an isness which is is-notness, and therefore an isness which is the very opposite of an original isness or totality. Consequently, the isness of I AM is the is-notness of that totality, and this absolute opposition between isness and is-notness is the very origin of that pure act which is pure actuality.

Now if an ultimate and purely actual is-notness is at the very center of I AM, that is an is-notness which is in absolute opposition to an "isness" which is "is-notness," an opposition which is the pure actuality of self-negation or self-emptying, and a self-emptying or self-negation which is the full and absolute sacrifice of itself, and the sacrifice of itself as a quiescent or even "blissful" totality. That is the sacrifice which is evoked by the Christian symbol of incarnation, just as that is the sacrifice which is named by the Christian affirmation that God is love, for the love of God is the self-sacrifice or the self-negation or the self-emptying of God, a sacrifice which is the very center and ground of I AM. So it is that the absolute otherness of I AM is an absolute otherness from itself, and an otherness from itself which is a self-negation or self-emptying of itself, and therefore an otherness which is not a simple and above all not a dualistic otherness, but rather an otherness that is an otherness at the very center of itself. That is the otherness that is named in the self-naming of I AM, a naming which itself is the naming of absolute sacrifice, an absolute sacrifice which is only its own, and that is the ownness which is the true ownness of I AM, and an ownness which is the absolute center of I AM, and is that very center in realizing the absolute otherness both of a quiescent and undifferentiated totality and of the actuality of that world which is world and only world. If I AM is its own "other," that otherness is truly and actually its own, an ownness which is the eternal act and actuality of self-negation or self-emptying, and thereby an otherness which is the eternal act of sacrifice. That act is enacted in and by a once and for all and irreversible beginning, a beginning which is the beginning of that sacrifice, and a sacrifice which can be consummated only in what Christianity and Christianity alone knows as apocalypse.

Fall and apocalypse, or ultimate fall and ultimate apocalypse, are uniquely Christian symbols, and even if traces or signs of these symbols may be discovered throughout the history of religions, it is Christianity and Christianity alone that has proclaimed and enacted the actuality of fall and apocalypse, and the actuality of fall and apocalypse in the actuality of a cosmic or universal history, a history that is not only the arena of apocalypse and fall, but a history that is an embodiment or realization of a *felix culpa*, a fortunate fall that finally culminates in apocalypse. If only the actuality of fall makes possible and real the actuality of incarnation, that is an incarnation occurring in a "flesh" that is the opposite of Spirit, and that "flesh" is not simply and only a bodily flesh, but rather a "flesh" that is a fully and finally fallen body or world, and consequently a "flesh" that is the absolute otherness of the "isness" of I AM. That otherness is fully and finally the actuality of death, and if it is the Fourth Gospel which has most purely portrayed the act of incarnation, that is an act inseparable from death or passion, a passion of

God which is the incarnation of God, and a passion of God which is crucifixion and resurrection at once. But the passion of God is the actual passion of God, an actual passion which is an actual and historical act, and therefore an act which is the self-sacrifice of God, a self-negation or self-emptying which is the pure actualization of I AM. That Godhead is finally itself only in the act of incarnation, but therein and thereby it is truly and actually itself, and actually itself in realizing itself as its own "other," an "other" that is fully and finally its own, but that ownness is an actually realized otherness, and therefore an ownness that is realized only through fall and death.

While intimations of incarnation occur throughout history, and perhaps most clearly so in the highest moments of Greek art and literature, such moments are not only epiphanies of a pure present, and a pure present which is and only is itself; such moments are also wholly instantaneous or immediate moments, and never moments which are incarnations of an ultimate or a final ground. So likewise Hindu deities appear through the mask of incarnation, as witness the avatars of Vishnu, but these are never full and actual incarnations, and just as they never occur in an actual moment of time, they never occur so as to realize a center, a center which in Christianity is the absolute center of history itself.

Only Christianity knows a historical incarnation, an incarnation occurring in an actual and irreversible moment of time, and an incarnation which itself is a final and irreversible incarnation, an incarnation that can never be undone, for it is an incarnation which is an absolutely irrevocable act. Here, incarnation is a once and for all act; therefore it is a repetition of the creation, and a repetition of the creation in the full actuality of history, an actuality that is not only the arena of incarnation, but is the very body of incarnation, for history is that body in which the Word became "flesh." But if incarnation is a once and for all and irreversible act, it proceeds out of a once and for all and irreversible beginning, just as it is consummated in a once and for all and irreversible apocalypse. Apocalypse is not simply the destiny of incarnation; it is far rather the full and final realization of incarnation itself, for incarnation is not simply Word becoming "flesh," it is Word or Godhead realizing itself, and realizing itself as the full and final opposite or otherness of itself, an otherness which is its ownmost otherness, but nevertheless an otherness which is truly and finally its own. Now even if that otherness is integrally and essentially its own, it is only actually its own through the labor of the negative, a labor which is the actuality of history, and the actuality of history as a forward-moving process of self-negation. And that self-negation is an actual self-negation, a self-negation occurring in the actuality of history, and a self-negation realizing an initial terminus in the full actuality of death, a death which is the death of God, but nevertheless and even thereby a death of God which is the full and final actualization of the life of God, for it is the final actualization of that absolute opposition which is the very center of I AM.

Thus incarnation is the realization of creation, and if creation is the self-emptying of an original plenitude, incarnation is the full actualization of that self-emptying in a single but nevertheless absolute event, an event which is the repetition of the original creation, but now and only now a repetition in which self-emptying or self-negation is fully and finally manifest and real as itself. Now even as incarnation is inseparable and indistinguishable from crucifixion and resurrection, it is finally inseparable and indistinguishable from creation and apocalypse, for just as incarnation is the realization of creation, apocalypse is the realization of incarnation, and not an apocalypse which is simply a renewal of the creation, but far rather an apocalypse which is finally a new creation, and a new creation which is possible and real only as a consequence of incarnation. So it is that incarnation is not simply and only Word becoming "flesh," but Word or God or I AM fully and finally realizing itself in its ownmost actuality, and if that actuality is in absolute opposition to itself, and in absolute opposition to itself in its very center or ground, that is an opposition which actualizes itself in I AM's becoming its own opposite or "other," an "other" that is not simply and only the "other" of I AM, but an "other" that is the absolute otherness of I AM itself, and therefore an otherness that is I AM's and I AM's alone.

Nothing could be further from the dialectical identity of I AM than a dualistic image or identity of the Godhead, for a dualistic division of the positive and the negative poles of the Godhead is not only a refusal of the oneness or unity of the Godhead, but a refusal of cosmos and history as well, a refusal which is a flight to the Alone, and to an Alone which is an absolutely solitary and inactive Godhead, a Godhead which could never be Creator, and a Godhead which could never actually be present in history or world. Now even if such a flight has occurred throughout the history of Christianity, that is a flight not only from the incarnation but from apocalypse as well, for it is a flight from the world and history, and thus a refusal of the very possibility of an apocalyptic transformation. Yet that is precisely the possibility which becomes actuality in the incarnation, for if the incarnation is Word becoming "flesh," it is an incarnation which ends the very possibility of the actuality of the Alone, and even if that is a possibility which, indeed, is ended in the very advent of a once and for all beginning, that is a possibility which is finally and ultimately ended in incarnation, and ended if only because the incarnation is the incarnation of the pure actuality of the Godhead.

But that incarnation is not a voyage into a "far country"; it is far rather a realization of the very center of the Godhead, and if that center is "I" and "I" alone, it is simultaneously "I AM NOT" and "I AM NOT" alone, a simultaneity which is actually realized in the incarnation, and a simultaneity which Kierkegaard truly named as the absolute paradox. If it was Kierkegaard who most purely understood the absolute offense of the incarnation, that is an offense which is named as early as Paul, and is actually enacted in the eschatological proclamation and the parabolic language of Jesus, just as it is manifest for all to see in the uniquely Christian symbol of the crucifixion. Hence the negative pole of the Godhead is inseparable and finally indistinguishable from its positive pole, and not in the sense of an eternal and unchanging harmony in the Godhead, but rather in the sense that the absolute negation or self-negation in the Godhead is the positive realization of Godhead itself, a positive realization through the very act of negation, as the self-negation or self-emptying of God is finally the realization of apocalypse itself. That apocalypse is not simply the consummation of incarnation; it is released and is actual in the very act of incarnation, and if that act is the eternal act of God, it is an eternal act which is an eternal act of self-negation, and an eternal act of self-negation which is finally an absolute reversal of itself. That reversal is named in the uniquely Christian symbol of apocalypse, just as that reversal is grounded in that absolute opposition which is the very center of the Godhead, and if that opposition is in absolute opposition to itself, that is an opposition which is finally realized in the absolute reversal of apocalypse, a reversal which is the reversal of incarnation, yes, but also and even thereby a reversal which is a fulfillment and consummation of the incarnation. Reversal is our clearest image of the act of incarnation, a reversal in which Word becomes "flesh," even as God becomes "man"; but that reversal is an irrevocable and irreversible act, hence it cannot truly be annulled by the ecclesiastical symbol of ascension, just as it cannot be affected by the archaic and primordial movement of eternal return. Now even if that archaic movement was reborn in the Christian church, as witness the symbols of ascension and assumption, such rebirth is clearly a reversal of the act of incarnation, and nothing could more clearly indicate the radical transformation which occurred in early Christianity, a transformation ending or initially ending the apocalyptic faith of primitive Christianity, and a transformation isolating the act of incarnation from the actuality of history.

Just as the symbol of the cross does not truly enter Christian iconography until the sixth century, and does not become the center of Western Christian art and iconography until the early fourteenth century, the incarnation is not truly or fully apprehended as a historical act and actuality until the high or late Middle Ages, and is not theologically known as an incarnation in the actuality of the "flesh" until Luther. Indeed, there is no real or pure thinking about incarnation until Hegel and Kierkegaard, and if that thinking inaugurated the full modernity of the modern age, that is a decisive sign of the profound estrangement of Christendom from its deepest ground, a ground that could not appear and become manifest and real until the end of Christendom.

At no point is the radicality of the Christian symbol of incarnation more clearly manifest than in its negation and reversal of the archaic and primordial movement of eternal return, and this most openly occurs in its actual reversal of eternal recurrence or eternal return, a reversal in which the backward movement of eternal return passes into an irreversible and irrevocable forward movement, and a forward movement which culminates in apocalypse.

While it is true historically that this reversal initially occurs in the prophetic revolution, and that it is firmly embedded in a postexilic Judaism, just as it is very close to the center of an apocalyptic Judaism, it is wholly absent from all nonbiblical worlds, and even absent from the great body of Christendom until the dawning of the modern world. Nothing was more radical in the radical and heretical movements of the Middle Ages than the apprehension of a forward and total movement in history, and if this gave birth to a revolutionary Western history, this was a consequence of the ultimate event of the incarnation, for only that event makes manifest and real the actual ending of an old world or totality. That event is the inauguration of a totally forward historical movement, and thus the Christian knows it as the center of history, but that is a center which is manifest and real only through the negation and reversal of the eternal movement of return.

So it is that the incarnation itself is a forward movement, and an irreversible and irrevocable forward movement, and even if finally it is a forward movement from genesis to apocalypse, it actually occurs at a singular and a uniquely singular point of time and history, and if that point is the center of the totality of history, that center is manifest and real only through the absolute reversal of eternal return. That reversal occurs through the act of incarnation, an act which is a forward movement, and a totally forward movement, for only in this act is eternal return finally ended, an ending which is the actual advent of the totality of history. But the advent of that totality is inseparable from an absolute movement of reversal, a reversal in which the backward movement of return fully and wholly passes into the forward movement of history, and a reversal in which the beyondness of the Alone passes into the total presence of Godhead, a reversal which the Church knows as a real presence in the eucharist, yes, but a reversal which the world ever more gradually knows and realizes as a real presence in the totality of history. Now even if the Church itself only too gradually realizes the total presence of God in history, that realization is a decisive sign of the transformation of the Church into Christendom, a radical transformation which is clearly apparent in the immense distance between the *Civitas Dei* and the *Commedia*, and a radical transformation which culminates in the full advent of the modern world.

But the reversal of backward into forward and of transcendence into immanence cannot be a total act and actuality apart from a reversal in Godhead itself, a reversal occurring through the absolute opposition at the very center of Godhead, and a reversal realizing itself through the self-negation or self-emptying of the Godhead. Nothing more clearly makes manifest such a reversal in the Godhead than does the decisive correlation between the backward movement of return and the transcendence of transcendence, and the forward movement of history and the immanence of immanence. For it was the rebirth of the archaic movement of eternal return in ancient Christianity, and above all so in Eastern Christianity, which gave birth to the Christian image of the absolute glory of God, an absolute glory of God which is the absolute transcendence of God, and the absolute transcendence of God the Creator, a Creator who is absolutely sovereign and majestic, and whose majesty is the absolute antithesis of body and time. Even Christ can here be known as the Cosmocrator, a cosmocrator who is the pure antithesis of the Christ of passion, and therein known as embodying the very glory of the Creator, a Creator who can be known only as that eternity which is the antithesis of time, and an eternity which is manifest only through the backward movement of return.

So it is that resurrection is here known as ascension, and as an ascension which reverses the movement of incarnation, and reverses it so that Christ can return to the glory of heaven. Clearly this movement of glorification is a reversal of the movement of incarnation, of the Word's becoming "flesh," and as such a movement of reversal it nullifies the event of incarnation, or transforms it, and radically transforms it, into a moment of absolute glory. Then the event of incarnation is an epiphany of absolute glory, and such an epiphany is an epiphany of the Christ who is and only is the Christ of glory, a Christ who is wholly other than the kenotic Christ of passion and death.

Only in the course of many centuries was the Western Church to recover the kenotic Christ, and then decisively so only in the Lutheran Reformation, a reformation at a virtually infinite distance from the Eastern Church, but then so likewise is modern Christianity and the modern world at a virtually infinite distance from ancient Christianity. But if the Christ of glory and the Christian apprehension of the absolute transcendence of God is a consequence of a rebirth of the archaic movement of eternal return, then so likewise is a Christian apprehension of the total presence of God in history a reversal of that very transcendence, and simultaneously a reversal of the rebirth of the movement of eternal return. Indeed, it is the very reversal of eternal return which itself is an absolute negation of the transcendence of transcendence, a reversal which occurs in the incarnation, and occurs as a forward movement, and a totally forward movement whose destiny is apocalypse.

Just as a Christian apprehension of the incarnation as an epiphany of absolute glory is a reversal of the movement of the incarnation, incarnation is a reversal of absolute glory, and a reversal releasing that glory in the actuality of world and history. Even if it was only after over a thousand years of historical evolution that Christianity could know the glory of God as being embodied in the world, that discovery does occur, and it occurs in that Gothic revolution which reversed a millennium of Christianity by actually celebrating the world, a celebration that was a consequence of a discovery of a new glory embodied in the very texture of the world. While that glory is the glory of God, it is not simply a dim reflection or a fragile and fleeting image of an infinitely distant divine majesty and glory, but rather a glory that fully and decisively enters and becomes embodied in the very language of the world, and thus a glory that here and now is immanent and transcendent at once. While ancient Christianity, and above all, Augustine, could know that God is immanent and transcendent at once, it could not know the immanence of God as being truly or fully present in the world, and certainly not as being totally present in the world and history. That is a presence which dawns only in the Western Middle Ages, and most clearly so in the new architecture, sculpture, painting, poetry, philosophy, and mysticism of the Gothic world. But this is also that Christian world which first decisively breaks away from the myth and the movement of eternal return, and if this occurs in Aquinas's new metaphysical understanding of *ipsum esse* or the "act-of-being," it occurs perhaps even more deeply in the imaginative revolutions of Giotto and Dante, and in Eckhart's mystical discovery of that *Istigkeit* or "I" whom God must become. Now, and for the first time in Christian history, God is fully manifest as being immanent and transcendent at once, and if this is a vision which revolutionizes the ancient Christian vision of transcendence, this itself is a vision which is revolutionized in the very advent of the modern world.

Now we can see that modernity is not simply a reversal of the medieval world; it is far rather a deepening or extension of that world, even as the medieval world was a deepening and extension of the ancient Christian world. And nowhere is the modern world more fully itself than in its discovery of history as an irreversible and forward movement, and even if that discovery is an extension of medieval visions of history, it is nonetheless revolutionary, and most revolutionary in apprehending the totality of history as the embodiment of providence or God, a providence or God which is now the total immanence of God, and a total immanence of God reversing the transcendence of God even as ancient Christian visions of the transcendence of transcendence reversed the incarnation of God. If incarnation only fully enters the mind and the imagination with the full advent of the modern world, that is a consequence of a profound historical transformation, a transformation that only gradually evolves in history, and one generating deep regressions and reversals, but nevertheless one proceeding by a forward-moving process of historical evolution, an evolution that is a reversal of the backward movement of return. But if that reversal is ultimately and finally real, it is a reversal grounded in the Godhead, and grounded in a reversal occurring in Godhead itself. Nothing less than such a reversal can be evoked by the symbol of the incarnation, and if historical Christianity has ever attempted a reversal of that symbol, that is a reversal which itself has been reversed by the actuality of history, and most clearly so in Western Christian history, a history that has very nearly completed a movement from the transcendence of transcendence to the immanence of immanence.

If Christianity has most decisively known the transcendence of transcendence as the sovereign majesty of the Creator, it has ever more fully come to know the immanence of immanence as that absolute reversal embodied in apocalypse, a reversal which could only be the consequence of the incarnation, and the consequence of the incarnation as an irreversible and forward-moving process. Yet it is I AM or God who is present in Christ, and fully and totally present in Christ, and if incarnation is an irrevocable and irreversible process, it can only be a process occurring in Godhead itself, and therefore occurring as Godhead itself. And if that is a process occurring in and as the Godhead, and occurring in and as the reverse movement of incarnation, that could only be a transformation of transcendence into immanence, and a transformation of eternity into time. For if the backward movement of eternal return is a transformation of time into eternity, the forward movement of incarnation is a transformation of eternity into time, and that movement is a movement in and of the Godhead itself, a Godhead that becomes "flesh," and a Godhead that dies to realize apocalypse. If this is an ultimate and absolute reversal, then so likewise is incarnation itself an ultimate and absolute reversal, and not a reversal that can be reversed in a movement of eternal return, but a reversal that can only be consummated in apocalypse. And apocalypse cannot be a repetition or a renewal of an original or primordial eternity, an eternity that disappears or perishes with a once and for all beginning; it can rather only be the final opposite of an original plenum or plenitude, and an opposite that itself is realized only by the absolute reversal of incarnation. While that reversal occurs in and through an absolute difference or opposition at the very center of the Godhead, that is a difference and an opposition that is finally actualized in the event of the incarnation, an event reversing Godhead itself, but that reversal is an act of Godhead itself, and is that act wherein and whereby Godhead passes into the very opposite of itself, and that act is not only a transformation of the Godhead, but a transformation of the Godhead through which the Godhead is even more deeply and more finally itself.

Nothing less than this could be a consummation of the forward movement of the incarnation, for that could only be a forward movement of the Godhead itself, a Godhead that is finally itself in its own death and resurrection, and if that resurrection is apocalypse, and the apocalypse of God, that is an apocalypse which is the consequence of the death of God, and thus a consequence of the incarnation. Incarnation is the incarnation of I AM, and the incarnation of I AM in its own inherent "other," an otherness that is the very "other" of I AM, and yet an otherness that is also and even thereby at the very center of I AM. Thereby the center of I AM is a pure and absolute opposition, an opposition which is an opposition to itself, and an opposition which can be known as a purely negative energy, and a purely negative energy realizing itself in real and ultimate acts, acts which would be impossible and unreal for a wholly passive and undifferentiated One, and acts which are actualizations of the self-emptying or self-negation of I AM. Yet that self-emptying or self-negation is a fulfillment of I AM, a fulfillment which is a realization of I AM, and nowhere is that fulfillment and realization so clear and so decisive as it is in the incarnation of I AM. While that incarnation is a repetition of the creation, and repetition of a creation which is itself the self-emptying of an original plenitude of pure emptiness or pure nothingness, incarnation as such is the self-emptying of the Creator, or the self-emptying of absolute otherness, an otherness which is I AM, and yet an otherness which is finally and ultimately itself only in its own self-emptying, a self-emptying finally and actually occurring in the incarnation.

That occurrence is itself apocalypse, an apocalypse which is crucifixion and resurrection at once, but an apocalypse that is apocalypse only because it is the incarnation of I AM, and an irrevocable and irreversible incarnation of I AM, and therefore an incarnation realizing itself in an absolute reversal of the eternal act of I AM. That reversal is apocalypse, so that apocalypse *is* that which I AM *was*, and is so as the full and final incarnation of I AM.

8

The Genesis of the Will

If there is no greater mystery than the mystery of freedom, that is a mystery inseparable from what our history has known as the will. Even if will as such transcends all possibility of definition, and, indeed, disappears as such with every real attempt at definition, that is a disappearance which is continually reenacted in our history, unless we have finally reached the point at which it has simply and wholly disappeared. That would be the end of history, or the end of what we have known as history, for it would be the final disappearance of the individual will, and hence the disappearance of the uniquely singular individual, an individual who is a person or an "I," and an "I" that is only itself, and hence the disappearance of an "I" that is not and cannot be another.

That "I" is the individual will, an individual will that is unmanifest or silent and invisible in all ancient worlds, for it is not recorded in writing until the letters of Paul, and it does not pass into portraiture until the late Hellenistic age, just as it was not discovered philosophically until Augustine. Now even if it would appear to us that there is nothing more obvious than an individual will, there are no classical philosophical texts which speak of such a will, just as there are no appearances of the will as such in classical literature, and not even in Greek tragedy, for the Greek tragic hero or heroine is not a uniquely singular individual, and never does that hero or heroine engage in an interior *agon* or conflict. That is a tragic conflict which is not truly or fully born until Shakespeare and Racine, just as portraits embodying a uniquely singular individual are not fully born until Rembrandt. If such portraits and such tragedy have wholly disappeared from our world, that would be yet another sign of the end of history.

Just as apocalypse is the very arena and ground of an original Christianity, apocalypse in one form or another may be understood to be a primary ground of the great imaginative and historical breakthroughs of the Western and Christian world, but these breakthroughs have realized themselves through an interior and individual will or enactment, and by a will that knows and realizes itself as a free will, even if that very resolution of the will can therein and thereby know its own enactment as an absolute necessity.

But if there is seemingly no awareness of the freedom of the will in the ancient world, there is also no awareness of the impotence or slavery of the will, for it is will as such which is absent from the consciousness of the pre-Christian world, and the discovery of the will is, in fact, the discovery of the absolute impotence of the will, a discovery which does not occur until the advent of Christianity. Paul most deeply records that discovery in his letter to the Romans, and there, when confessing that "I am of the flesh," given into the power of sin, he can declare: "And I have no clear knowledge of what I am doing, for that which I have a will to do, I do not, but what I have hate for that I do" (7:15). Here, the impotence of the will is a reverse or negative impotence of the will, a will which actually does that which "I" hate, and a will which does not do that which "I" will to do. Accordingly, there is a correlation here between inaction and negative action, the inability of the will to fulfill its own will is inseparable from its enactment of that which is loathsome to itself.

These words are extraordinarily important, for they are the first words which we know that actually speak of the will, and they clearly speak of the will as a reverse or negative will, a will that wills or effects the opposite of its own intention. Thus the effect or action of the will is here a wholly negative action, and if that action is the very will of the will, that will is inseparable from its own inability to enact what it wills. So it is that it is a recognition of that inability which is simultaneously a recognition of the will of will, a will which is a negative and an impotent will at once, and therefore a will which is self-alienated and self-estranged, for it is the very opposite of that which it consciously or intentionally wills.

Not until over three hundred years after Paul's letters does the will truly appear again in what remains to us of ancient Christian writing, but then it effects a philosophical, theological, and even literary revolution with the writing of Augustine's *Confessions*, for then self-consciousness or the will of will is realized for the first time since Paul as being the very center of consciousness itself. That is a center which is wholly silent in the ancient world, except insofar as it is initially enacted in the prophetic tradition of Israel, and particularly so in Jeremiah, but that tradition had no impact or effect upon the classical world, and only became known to Augustine himself well after his conversion. If Paul was the primary master of Augustine, or primary master along with Plotinus, Augustine was the first pure or philosophical thinker to be a Pauline thinker, and thereby the first thinker who could know that sin is not only the absence or privation of being but also and even therein the full embodiment or actualization of the wholly fallen or negative will. While the symbol of fall is primary in Paul, it is even more comprehensively present in Augustinian thinking, a thinking that can know the center of consciousness as a *coincidentia oppositorum*, for it is simultaneously the full embodiment of both sin and grace, of grace insofar as that center is the image of God, and even the image of the Trinity itself, and of sin insofar as that center is the fallen will, and a fallen will insofar as it is a rebellious will, a will rebelling against its Creator by willing to be itself its own center or ground. So it is that the "I" or the center of consciousness is free and enslaved at once, free insofar as it is the image of God, and enslaved insofar as it is a self-centered or prideful will.

If this is the first philosophical understanding of the freedom of the will, it is also the first philosophical understanding of the impotence or the slavery of the will, and whereas Augustine initially thinks that if we do anything against our will it seems to be something that happens to us rather than something which we actually do (*Confessions* VII, 3), he gradually comes to realize that it is his own will which enchains him, and that will is a perverse will, a will struggling against a new will that even now is being born, so that his inner self was a house divided against itself, for it was divided against a carnal and a spiritual will. This is a disease of the mind, wherein there are two wills within us, a carnal and a spiritual will; neither by itself is the whole will, and each possesses what the other lacks. What is now required for health or sanity is a full and resolute act of the spiritual will, and one that will realize what it wills, but that is just what is impossible for him in this moment of agony. Whereas the mind can give an order to the body and it is immediately obeyed, when it gives an order to itself it is resisted; then the mind does not carry out its own command, and this because it does not fully will to do this, and insofar as it does not will the order is not carried out. Now the reason the command is not obeyed is that it is not given with the full will, for if the will were full, it would not command itself to be full, since it would be so already (*Confessions* VIII, 9). But it is precisely in this very agony, an agony which is a response to the presence of two wills, a carnal and a spiritual will, neither of which is a whole will, and neither of which can now will so as to enact its will, that Augustine's conversion occurs. That conversion is a deliverance from bondage, but it is a deliverance which could never be effected by our will, divided as it is in its ownmost center, but only by the grace of God, a grace transcending and wholly transcending everything that is present and real as our will, and a grace whose occurrence in us can only be known as a true miracle. That is the miracle of justification, a justification that is wholly by grace, and a justification that is a conversion of the will, a will that now is free as a consequence of that conversion, but a will that never is free apart from grace. Only now can the will will so as to enact its will, or freely to enact it, for even though the fallen will enacts what it wills, it does so wholly involuntarily, an involuntarity which is the bondage of the will, and a bondage that is nowhere so fully apparent as it is in lust.

We know our lust as our innermost delight, a delight that is truly our own, and yet a delight that is fully involuntary, for even when concupiscence is at the very center of the activity of the fallen will, that is a center which is fully and wholly a carnal center, and a center that we know we have not chosen or freely willed, and know so because we realize in being overwhelmed by lust that we are engulfed by a power beyond us. Yet if that power is beyond us, it nevertheless is within us, for the bondage of the will is truly a bondage that is our own. That is the bondage which we will in willing concupiscence, and a bondage which is ever present in the fallen will. So it is that Augustine can know that we are responsible for our every act, for even when our acts are a consequence of the bondage of our wills, that bondage is truly our own, an ownness that is clearly manifest in the delight of lust or concupiscence, and an ownness that is present in every act of the fallen will, and that will now knows a guilt that is inseparable from freedom.

Indeed, it is precisely in knowing that guilt that the fallen will knows its own freedom, for even if that freedom is bondage or impotence, it is freedom nonetheless, and a freedom necessarily calling for its own judgment. Thus it is all too significant that neither a deep interior guilt nor a deep interior freedom are manifest in the pre-Christian world, for only a realization of deep guilt makes possible a realization of deep freedom, for in knowing our guilt to be truly and actually our own, we know our deep and ultimate responsibility, and an awareness of that responsibility is an awareness of the freedom of the will. Now that responsibility inevitably issues in a breaking of the will, for the will now knows that it is fully responsible for its own bondage or impotence, and even if this is a responsibility which cannot actually will its own freedom, it can know its responsibility as its own, which is to say that it can know its will as its own, and therefore know its own will as a guilty will, and as a wholly guilty will, which is to say a will demanding its own eternal judgment or damnation. Only the "I" can be subject to damnation or salvation, an "I" that is the image of God, and an "I" that is free as that image, and is free even in its own bondage, a freedom which we know when we know deep guilt, and a freedom which itself calls for judgment, a judgment that breaks the fallen will; but that breakage is justification or conversion. So it is that the new will is a will of grace, and a will that can only actually enact itself through the breakage or negation of the fallen will, a negation which is a self-negation, but a self-negation which is possible only through grace. Then and only then the fallen will can be known as an empty will, a will that is empty of God but nevertheless a will that is the creation of God, for the fallen will is good and evil simultaneously, good by virtue of its very existence, for existence itself is sheer goodness, a goodness which is the consequence of the creation, but evil by virtue of its free and rebellious choice, a prideful and evil choice proceeding not from nature or being, but rather from a "deficiency of being" deriving from our having been created from nothing (*City of God*, XII, 6).

Ontologically, nothing is more fundamental for Augustine than his continual affirmation that evil is the absence or privation of being, and even if this was a common Neoplatonic thesis, it assumes a whole new meaning in Augustine, and does so because Augustine also understands evil or sin as the sinful will, a will whose emptiness is a real and actual emptiness, and an emptiness that is will itself in the rebellious or fallen will. Thus Augustine's understanding of the emptiness of the will is the full opposite of the Buddhist understanding of the emptiness of the will; for Augustine this is a way of affirming the reality of the will, or of the fallen will, whereas for the Buddhist it is a way of affirming the illusion of the will, and if the Buddhist can unveil that illusion by realizing selflessness, Augustine can affirm the reality of the fallen will precisely by affirming its emptiness. But that emptiness is a real emptiness; hence it proceeds from a deficiency of being itself, a deficiency which is a real deficiency, and a real deficiency having its origin in that nothingness out of which the world was created.

Now this is a real deficiency or an actual nothingness that never was upon the horizon of the pre-Christian world, except insofar as it was present, or implicitly present, in the tradition of Israel. The immense distance between an Augustinian understanding of nothingness and a Buddhist understanding of nothingness is a decisive sign of the gulf between the Eastern and the Western worlds, for just as the pure emptiness of Buddhism is wholly alien to the Western world, the purely negative nothingness or emptiness of the evil or sinful will is likewise alien to the Eastern world, and alien if only because that world cannot or does not know pure dichotomy as an ultimate ground, and therefore cannot know a self-alienated or self-estranged will, and precisely thereby cannot know what the Western Christian world has known as the will. But neither does the pre-Christian Western world know that will, just as it does not know either a negative or an actual nothingness, which is to say a real nothingness, a nothingness which is present in the reality of evil, and that is a nothingness that ontologically unveils the reality of evil as it had never been unveiled before. We need not hesitate to affirm that Christianity ushered in the realization of a whole new horizon of evil, one that had never been present in the world before, and just as Satan does not undergo a full historical epiphany until the advent of Christianity, the deep reality of evil, and the internal and interior reality of evil, was not spoken until Paul, and not philosophically apprehended until Augustine, and Augustine's apprehension is a very discovery or unveiling of the purely negative "I." That "I," or that wholly fallen will, is an embodiment of a real and actual nothingness, but that is a nothingness which is our own, and is our own as a consequence of our own act of will, for that actual nothingness is our own, and is deeply and only our own, as we know through knowing our own will as a wholly guilty will.

In that deep and wholly interior guilt, a guilt which we can decisively and certainly know, and know most deeply in the deepest acts of the will, we know that we will evil, and even if that willing is an absolute impotence, it is willing nonetheless, and a willing which is interiorly manifest to us in the guilty will. Yet both Paul and Augustine could know the guilty will itself as a consequence of grace, a grace whose very interior actualization necessarily breaks the fallen will, and this breakage is interiorly manifest as guilt, but a guilt that would be absent apart from grace, and absent if only because it is grace alone which breaks the fallen will. So that if a deep interior guilt is not present in the world until the advent of Christianity, neither is an interior grace that can be known and realized only as a purely negative grace, and a grace which in breaking the will unveils the fallen and guilty will, and therefore unveils and therein realizes that actual nothingness which is the nothingness of the fallen will. Nevertheless, it is only in knowing our "I" as a purely negative "I," or as a wholly fallen will, that we know the total responsibility of our will, a responsibility that is a real and actual freedom, and a freedom which is our full responsibility for our fallen condition. Nowhere is that freedom more manifest to us than in the guilty will, for even as that guilty will is a will that is only our own, it necessarily embodies a responsibility that is fully our own, and that responsibility is the very freedom of the will.

The guilty or the fallen will is for both Paul and Augustine that will which is most immediately and most interiorly our own, and as such it is a passage to redemption, or a passage to justification by faith alone, a faith that can only be real by way of an interior passage through eternal death or ultimate guilt. And Paul and Augustine alike know the guilty will as a predestined will, a will predestined from all eternity either to eternal life or to eternal death, for apart from predestination there is no hope whatsoever for the fallen will, a will that in its absolute impotence can will only eternal death. Damnation or eternal death is at least in its origin a uniquely Christian symbol, and it is inseparable from a realization of absolute responsibility, a responsibility that is a full responsibility even in impotence and bondage, and a responsibility that is most immediately manifest in a total sense of guilt.

Hence that responsibility is interiorly real in an overwhelming sense of damnation, a damnation wherein I can only actually do that which I hate, and thus a damnation which is an absolutely negative will, and therefore a will which can never liberate itself. Only predestination, and an eternal predestination of God, can liberate the fallen will from such ultimate bondage, and that predestination is the eternal will of God, and an eternal will which is wholly the act of grace. But the will of God is will itself, and even if it is an eternal will, it thereby is an eternal act, an eternal act which is the eternal act of God, and therefore an act which is indistinguishable from the act of creation. That act is purely an act of grace, a grace which is pure freedom, and that is the source of the freedom which God freely gives the justified sinner. But that sinner is justified only by God, and only by the eternal will of God, a will that is God's alone, and a will that is indistinguishable from an infinite grace and love.

Predestination alone is the source of the conversion and transformation of the sinful will, the potentiality for which is in no way whatsoever present in the empty nothingness of the fallen will, just as predestination is the primary sign and symbol of the freedom of the will, for not only does it make possible the actual freedom of the saints, but it overwhelmingly makes manifest the freedom of the damned, who alone are responsible for their eternal judgment (*The Enchiridion*, XCV–CV), a responsibility which could only be theirs by way of the total absence of the grace of God. That is the absence which makes possible an actualization of the deficiency of being, a deficiency of being which is enacted in the origin of sin or original sin, and a deficiency which is repeated and renewed in every act of the sinful will, and if every such act is a freely willed act, every such act is a choice of damnation, and a free choice of damnation. While that freedom is an empty nothingness, and hence an absolute bondage, it is known as freedom in total guilt, a freedom apart from which guilt would not be guilt just as sin would not be sin. But sin is sin and guilt is guilt only because of predestination, for if no one is saved except by undeserved mercy and grace, no one is damned except for those who are unchosen by predestination. If that unchosenness is an eternal death, it is a damnation for which the damned alone are actively or actually responsible, thus demonstrating that even an impotent freedom of the will can realize an eternal destiny.

Nothing in Christianity is or could be more theologically orthodox than the doctrine of predestination, and if it was created by Augustine, it was renewed by Aquinas, Scotus, and Ockham, only to be renewed yet more forcefully by Luther and Calvin, and renewed even in the twentieth century in Barth's doctrine of election.

One of the many ironies of our history is that the symbol and the doctrine of predestination have always appeared in historical moments and epochs of incredible power; thus, that Augustinian thinking which most decisively established a uniquely Western Christendom culminated in a total affirmation of predestination, just as the symbol if not the very doctrine of predestination was at the center of a historically triumphant Islam, and insofar as the birth of the modern world occurred in the Reformation, it therein occurred by way of a realization of the totality of predestination, as affirmed by Luther and Calvin alike. Indeed, even Marxism, the most powerful revolutionary political movement the world has ever known, knows predestination as the absolute necessity of history, and even if that necessity is a Hegelian necessity, and a historical necessity knowing the totality of history as theodicy, a Hegelian theodicy even as a Marxist revolutionary history is an absolutely predestined history, but a predestination that can truly be known only by knowing history itself as the embodiment of an ultimate power, and an ultimate power enacting itself through the full actuality of history. But that actuality may be known not only as a historical actuality but also as a historical will, a historical will which is the embodiment of predestination, and therefore a historical will which is an absolute will, a will which itself was unveiled by the last philosopher of the will, Nietzsche.

Nietzsche most deeply knew the will as the Will to Power, a will which is an absolute will, and a will wholly transcending everything which is manifest as mind and consciousness, for the will of will is absolute power, and that power is only manifest and real to the interiority of consciousness as an absolutely negative power. But if Nietzsche is the last philosopher of the will, he is thereby the successor of the first philosopher of the will, Augustine, and above all so in apprehending the will of will as a wholly negative power, and a purely negative power which is both the consequence and the embodiment of an eternal predestination, a predestination which Nietzsche knew as Eternal Recurrence.

But Nietzsche's vision of Eternal Recurrence is not to be confused with the archaic vision of eternal return; indeed, it is its very reversal, and is its reversal by apprehending eternal recurrence as the absolute ending of eternal return, or the absolute ending of the very possibility of transcendence, or the ending of every moment which is not an immediate and total now. If "Being begins in every Now" (*Thus Spoke Zarathustra* III, "The Convalescent"), that beginning is the ending of transcendence or the death of God, a death which occurs in every full and actual moment, and therefore a death releasing a total immanence, a pure immanence which is an absolute reversal of every moment which is open to transcendence, and therefore a reversal of an eternal return which is a return of a primordial and eternal moment of time. But Nietzsche's vision of Eternal Recurrence is finally identical with his vision of the Will to Power, for here eternal recurrence is actual and real only in a moment of absolute will, and Nietzsche's absolute will is an all too modern image of what Augustine knew as the will of God, a will which is the source of every event whatsoever, and a will which quite simply is absolute power.

The simplest meaning of will is an internal and interior power, and historically both the first and the last naming of that power is as a totally negative power, a power effecting the very opposite of every conscious intention, and a power whose very actualization assaults and negates the center of consciousness, but that negation makes manifest and real the center of consciousness, a center which is first manifest in that purely negative "I" named by Paul, and a center which is last named by Nietzsche as an "I" which is wholly internal and external at once and altogether. The history of the will occurs between Paul and Nietzsche, a history which is the beginning and the ending of a uniquely Christian history, and thus a history which is both the beginning and the ending of a uniquely Christian God.

Augustine could know the will of God as both the source and the ground of every event, and even know that will as the fully actual source of evil itself. If this is a uniquely Christian apprehension of God, it is nowhere more fully present than in Augustine's understanding of predestination, for it is predestination which is the final source of evil or sin, and at no other point did Augustine so passionately give himself to such a bitter and overwhelming theological struggle. For that was a struggle for the ultimate truth and reality of the uniquely Christian God, a struggle that occurred wholly within Christianity, and even as Augustine's assaults upon paganism were never so violent as were his assaults upon Christian heresy, his full and total affirmation of predestination was directed against a Christian refusal of God, and perhaps finally against his own opposition to God, an opposition which he himself knew to be most fully present in his own Manichean roots.

Manicheanism in one form or another has appeared again and again in Christian history, for the Manichean temptation is one of a pure dualism which knows not only good and evil as wholly and only opposite powers, but knows God as being finally two Gods, the God of light and the God of darkness, so that evil has its sole source in the God of darkness, just as good has its sole source in the God of light. If Manicheanism is a reaction to a pure monotheism, it is an all too humanly understandable reaction, for it cannot bear to associate the God of life with the actuality of evil and death; and if it refuses to acknowledge the nothingness of evil, that is not only a refusal of the unreality of evil, but thereby a refusal of that God who is the source of all and everything.

This is the refusal against which the doctrine of predestination is most profoundly directed, and, just as Augustine most fully created the theology of history, a theology which knows the providence of God as the source of every historical event, so Augustine created the doctrine of predestination as perhaps the most decisive way of knowing that uniquely Christian God who eternally wills everything which happens or occurs, so that everything whatsoever is both an act and an embodiment of grace. Even if Augustine could never escape a Neoplatonism which refuses the reality of evil, he transcended it by knowing the full actuality of the fallen will, a fallen will that is an interior actuality, and an actuality that is born by way of a rebellion against the absolutely sovereign will of God. Augustine could know that rebellion as being present in Manicheanism, but so likewise is it present in a Christian refusal of God as the source of evil, for that is a refusal of the absolute sovereignty of God and therefore a refusal of the full and total actuality of the eternal will of God, which wills not only everything which occurs, but also is a "permission of what is evil" (*The Enchiridion* XCVI), a permission which is necessary for the justice of God, for that justice must annihilate evil. It was precisely because Augustine so deeply knew the reality of evil, and most immediately knew it in his own rebellious will, a will that willed every possible evil and willed it at the very center of his will, that he could know God as the God of justice, a God who would not be God if He did not eternally consume evil in the fires of Hell.

Hell is the destiny of every evil, and thus it is the destiny of the fallen will, a destiny which is manifest and real in the full actualization of guilt, and a destiny which is reversed in a predestination to eternal life, but that predestination is wholly undeserved; hence it is a consequence of absolute grace. Accordingly, Augustine could close the *City of God* with the affirmation that the redeemed saints in the heavenly city, while having no recollection of past evils, will nevertheless know the eternal misery of the damned, for how else could they sing the mercies of the Lord? How else, indeed? For to know the love and the mercy of God is to know an absolutely undeserved mercy, and thereby and finally only thereby to know one's own will as a totally fallen will, and thus as a wholly rebellious and negative will, a will which in willing only itself, empties itself of the grace of God, and that emptying is a real and actual emptying, and it can be known as such when confronting the grace of God. That confrontation is a confrontation with total actuality, but it is interiorly manifest as assault and abasement, an assault upon the purely negative will and an assault therein drawing forth an interior actualization of the fallen will. The fallen will now knows itself to be impotent by knowing the absolute sovereignty of God, and by knowing that sovereignty as the eternal will of the justice of God, a justice that must consume all evil, and therefore a justice which is the justice of damnation.

If no other major theologian was so obsessed with damnation as was Augustine, that could only be because Augustine could know damnation as being inseparable from salvation, a salvation whose very advent makes manifest the purely negative will; and to know that salvation is to know the pure negativity of the fallen will, a negativity which is the eternal death of the damned, and a negativity which the will must know in confronting the possibility of salvation. Then and only then the will can rejoice in an eternal predestination, an eternal predestination which is the one and only source of salvation, for only the eternal act of God can reverse the final ultimacy of damnation, a damnation which the fallen will can now and only now know as its ownmost actualization. This is a damnation which is finally refused by a Christian opposition to God as the source of evil, for that opposition is a refusal of our damnation as the damnation of God, a damnation that God effects in His eternal justice, and a damnation that occurs in the eternal act of God. If that act is the act of predestination, that act occurs in the very creation of the world, and just as God wills all that He wills simultaneously, in one act, and eternally (*Confessions* XII, 15), so the acts of predestination and creation are one act, and one act of absolute love and grace.

Finally, to know one's own will as a wholly impotent and negative will is to know the eternal will of God. Only the full and actual advent of that will makes possible a realization of the actuality of the will, and if that will is actual for us as a purely negative will, that negativity is an embodiment of the judgment of God, and of the eternal judgment of God, a judgment which is enacted in an eternal predestination. Predestination is the eternal act of God, and that act is an embodiment of the eternal will of God, a will which is an absolute love and grace but a will which can only be known to the fallen will as absolute judgment, a judgment which is damnation. Yet that damnation is inseparable from that salvation which is eternally willed by God, and eternally willed in the one act of predestination. So it is that predestination is inseparable from the will of will, a will of will that is an eternal will in the eternal act of God, and a will of will that is a purely negative will in that will which rebels against God. If that rebellion is a free act, and a free act of the will of that one creature who was created in the image of the eternal will of God, that is a freedom now issuing in a pure impotence of the will, an impotence which is not only the judgment of God, but therein and thereby is the total opposite of the eternal will of God. Nowhere is that judgment more fully manifest and real than in the pure negativity of the fallen will, and if that is a negativity which knows the judgment of God, and knows it in the very actualization of itself as a fallen will, that is a knowledge which is a knowledge of the eternal will of God, and an eternal will of God which is interiorly manifest and real to us as the eternal act of damnation.

All too naturally, Christianity has ever willed to know God as an absolute and total mystery, a mystery veiling the will of God, and thereby disguising the eternal act of damnation. But that veil is dislodged by the very activity of the fallen will, an activity both calling forth and embodying an interior negativity, a negativity which is the negativity of an empty and impotent will. Yet that is the will which can know the eternal grace of predestination, and even if it knows that grace only by undergoing an ultimate negation of its very center, that is a negation which is a transformation or conversion of the will—a conversion issuing in a new freedom of the will, but that is a freedom simply and only to do the will of God. Moreover, that is a freedom which is possible and real only by way of the absolute negation of the fallen will, a negation wholly beyond the power of that will itself and hence a negation which is an enactment of the predestination of God.

That predestination is a predestination which is simultaneously to eternal life and to eternal death; each is inseparable from the other, and each is willed simultaneously with the other, and so willed in the eternal act and will of God. Nothing less than a doctrine of double predestination can truly give witness to the eternal justice of God, and nothing less than double predestination can make possible a uniquely Christian theodicy, a theodicy which can celebrate every event whatsoever as an embodiment of the love and justice of God.

Predestination is ultimately a Christian affirmation of the absolute grace of God, a grace which is truly everywhere, and is everywhere present as the eternal act of God, an absolute source which is the actual source of every act, and an absolute source which is likewise present in every absence or "privation of being." If the privation of being is a "deficiency of being" deriving from our having been created from nothing, it is nevertheless a consequence of the creation, and therefore it is a consequence of the eternal will of God. Only predestination makes manifest that consequence, and not only predestination but double predestination, for only the eternal judgment of damnation can justify the reality of evil, and if that is the judgment which is known in the bad conscience of the empty and impotent will, that is a judgment which finally sanctions the most terrible evil, and sanctions it by the just judgment of damnation.

No one knew this more deeply than did Dante, and if the *Inferno* is a glorious witness to the absolute justice of God, that is a witness absolutely necessary to the ecstatic celebration of paradise in the *Paradiso*, just as it is equally necessary to that celebration of love as the center of creation which occurs in canto XVIII of the *Purgatorio*. Inevitably, Christian epic poets have been Augustinian poets, and this is just as true of Blake and Joyce as it is of Dante and Milton, so that nowhere is predestination more fully celebrated and envisioned than it is in Christian epic poetry; and necessarily so, because that poetry is both a celebration and an affirmation of the totality of history. Just as Augustine is the philosopher who discovered the will, Augustine is the theologian who discovered the totality of predestination, for nothing more fully makes manifest the will of will than the doctrine of predestination, even as nothing else more fully calls forth a uniquely Christian affirmation of theodicy. That affirmation is quite simply a celebration of the eternal act of God, and a celebration of that eternal act of God which is all in all, and it is all in all not only in the fullness of being but equally so in that "deficiency of being" which is the origin of evil. Even evil is finally a witness both to the glory of God and to the justice of God, for everything whatsoever is an embodiment of the eternal act of God. Augustine is our greatest theologian of grace only by being our greatest theologian of sin. Here sin itself can be known as the consequence of grace, and the origin of sin or original sin can finally be known as having its source in God, and its source in the will of God, a will which is enacted in an eternal predestination.

Predestination is the clearest path to a celebration of the will of God as being all in all, a will which is finally the source of our deepest horrors even as it likewise is the source of our most ecstatic joys. These horrors and joys are the consequence of the eternal act of God, an eternal act which is the act of predestination. Perhaps only Nietzsche, who is the most Augustinian thinker in the modern world, can take us into the center of Augustine's mind, as he does in one of the last entries in his notebook: "To attain a height and a bird's eye view, so one grasps how everything happens as it ought to happen; how every kind of 'imperfection' and the suffering to which it gives rise are part of the highest desirability" (*The Will to Power*, 1004, Kaufmann translation).

9

Predestination as Eternal Recurrence

Perhaps nothing could be more baffling for the Christian than the discovery that Nietzsche, the most profoundly anti-Christian thinker who ever lived, is at bottom a deeply Augustinian thinker, and an Augustinian thinker who decisively and comprehensively carried forward a pure, even if reverse, Augustinian thinking so as to bring to an end the deepest foundations of the Christian consciousness and the Christian world. If Augustine was the true founder of the Western Christian historical world, Nietzsche is that thinker who most decisively brought that world to an end. That ending occurs by way of a negation and reversal of the deepest center of Christianity, and therefore it occurs by way of a reversal of Augustinian thinking.

No thinkers have so deeply centered their thinking upon God as have Augustine and Nietzsche, except for Nietzsche's deepest precursors Spinoza and Hegel, and certainly no other thinkers have been so obsessed with guilt as were Nietzsche and Augustine; and this guilt is one which Nietzsche and Augustine alike correlate with an internal and interior apprehension of pure transcendence, a pure transcendence which is absolutely other than that subject which apprehends it, and a pure transcendence which is the ultimate ground of the interiority of consciousness, a consciousness which realizes or enacts that interiority only by enacting or realizing a pure transcendence. Indeed, both Augustine and Nietzsche only truly or actually know God by knowing guilt, and it is the ultimate depth of guilt which truly and internally makes manifest the ultimate depth of God, a depth that is wholly absent from an apprehension that is not the apprehension of a guilty consciousness and a totally guilty consciousness, so that pure transcendence itself is here manifest only by way of a purely negative consciousness and will. Yet that is the very transcendence which both Augustine and Nietzsche can finally name as an absolutely gracious power, but it is manifest as such only by way of an absolute negation and reversal of the deepest center of consciousness and will.

For Augustine, nothing is closer to us than the presence of God, a presence that for the Christian is closer than the presence of our deeper self; indeed, it is only the divine presence that makes possible and actualizes the fullness of self-presence. Yet self-presence and what Augustine can know as the certainty of self-presence is a negative presence, for it inevitably evokes an awareness of the contingency and mortality of our existence; and this is a mortality or death that is the true otherness of the goodness of existence, and yet a death and an eternal death which is inseparable from everything which we can actually and interiorly know as existence. Thus the existence which we can actually know is wholly other than the existence of God, for that existence is fully and only an absolute and eternal existence, an existence which is the very opposite of that eternal death which we so fully know to be our own. Whereas our will is deeply divided in its very center, God's will and God's act, just as God's will and God's being, are one. In that unity of will and being, or act and will, God is immanent and transcendent at once, so that His immanence is finally indistinguishable from His transcendence. A fully comparable although reverse coincidence is present and real in the depths of our consciousness, for as those depths realize themselves in the fullness of self-consciousness, we realize ourselves to be simultaneously an embodiment of sin and grace, a simultaneous embodiment of the image of God and of an inversion or reversal of that image. We are a consequence of grace by virtue of the very presence of existence itself, an existence which of itself and in itself is only and wholly good, and we are an embodiment of the image of God by virtue of the very freedom of our will, for even if our will is imprisoned by sin, it remains free in that very imprisonment, and so much so that we can only truly know our will by knowing it as the origin and source of our own imprisonment.

But that self-knowledge or that self-consciousness is a realization of our own rebellious will, a perverse and fallen will which at its very center rebels against its Creator. This rebellion is a free rebellion, and can be known to be free precisely by way of a realization of our individual will. A free but fallen will is inevitably present and manifest in the fullness of our self-consciousness, for the fullness of individual selfhood is for us the fullness of our individual will, an individual will that is free and impotent at once and whose freedom is inseparable from its impotence. Therefore our will is the very antithesis of the will of God, for while God's will is one with His being, our will is turned against our true and essential being, and is so because we will to be the sole source and author of our own individual existence and life.

That will is the deepest will of everything that we can know and realize as pure will, and nowhere has that will been more fully manifest than in Nietzsche, and above all so in Nietzsche's willing of the eternal recurrence of the same. Even if that willing is a transformation of the individual will in which the individual will finally becomes every will and every name which has occurred in history, that transformation is a consequence of absolute will, and an absolute will that reverses the individual will so as to realize the return of everything which is the "other" of that will. Nietzsche, even as Augustine, knew a *coincidentia oppositorum* at the very center of the will, a *coincidentia* that is a full coincidence of Yes-saying and No-saying, of absolute affirmation and absolute negation; so that as Nietzsche declares in his reenactment of *Thus Spoke Zarathustra* in *Ecce Homo*: "The psychological problem in the type of Zarathustra is how he that says No and *does* No to an unheard-of degree, to everything to which one has so far said Yes, can nevertheless be the opposite of a No-saying spirit; how the spirit who bears the heaviest fate, a fatality of a task, can nevertheless be the lightest and most transcendent—Zarathustra is a dancer—how he that has the hardest, most terrible insight into reality, that has thought the 'most abysmal idea,' nevertheless does not consider it an objection to existence, not even to its eternal recurrence—but rather one more reason for being himself the eternal Yes to all things, 'the tremendous, unbounded saying Yes and Amen' " (Kaufmann translation). If Zarathustra is "Caesar with the soul of Christ," Zarathustra is also Nietzsche's symbolic name of the very center of the Will to Power, and therefore the very center of the will of will, and even if that will is illusory in every single or singular will, it is all in all in the circle of eternal recurrence, and while that circle is the "innocence of becoming," it is a circle which is the total energy of life itself. Nietzsche's vision of eternal recurrence was the consequence of a conversion; the deepest conversion in our history since the conversion of Augustine himself, and a conversion which reenacted Augustine's insofar as it effected a liberation of the will, and a liberation of the purely negative and impotent will. That negativity is known by Nietzsche as *ressentiment*, and *ressentiment* is embodied in the purely negative will, a wholly broken and empty will which is broken by the very actuality of existence itself and whose only energy is directed to escaping that very existence, a flight which is itself an enactment of *ressentiment*.

That *ressentiment* is the very center of a wholly impotent will, and a *ressentiment* which was only fully born with what Nietzsche historically understood as the slave revolt in morality—a revolt that was the prophetic revolution of Israel, and a revolt that was historically consummated in the advent of Christianity. But Nietzsche, even as Augustine, also knew the origin of *ressentiment* as an original fall, a fall which is the origin of the bad conscience, and an origin occurring in the very advent of history, for as Nietzsche discovered in the *Genealogy of Morals*, the advent of history is the "internalization" of the semi-animal man, an internalization occurring through the most fundamental change that humanity has ever experienced, a transformation deriving from the new necessity of the social contract, when humanity found itself enclosed within the walls of society, so that its former instincts were disvalued and suspended. In this wholly new world, humanity no longer possessed its former guides, its unconscious and infallible drives, but was rather reduced to its "consciousness," its weakest and most fallible organ. Then all instincts which do not discharge themselves outwardly turn inward, and that internalization expanded and extended itself in the same measure as outward discharge was inhibited or repressed, but that internalization is a return of our free and original instincts, yet a return which is now necessarily directed against humanity itself, for that return is the origin of the bad conscience. So the bad conscience in its beginnings is an original freedom pushed back and repressed, incarcerated within, and finally able to discharge itself only on and against itself, for all instinct that does not release itself outwardly turns inward, and thus finally and most deeply turns against itself.

Nothing could be in deeper continuity with Augustine's understanding of original sin than Nietzsche's understanding of the origin of the bad conscience, and each origin is a sudden and immediate origin, even if it expands and extends itself in the actualization of history. If Augustine was our first historical thinker, Nietzsche was our last historical thinker, the last thinker who could think essentially and historically at once, and thus the last thinker who could understand the will, that very will which was first understood by Augustine, and understood as an empty and fallen will, but nevertheless and even thereby a will that is reversed by the conversion of the will. Augustine finally understood that conversion by understanding the eter-

nal predestination of God, but Nietzsche immediately understood his conversion by envisioning the eternal recurrence of
the same, a conversion which enacts itself as an unbounded
saying of Yes and Amen, even as Augustine's conversion
enacted itself by a total affirmation of the grace of God.

Both Nietzsche and Augustine could then affirm even the
most horrible evil as the embodiment of a total grace, and if
Augustine could do so only by knowing both the ultimacy and
the finality of an eternal damnation, Nietzsche could do so by
knowing and willing eternal recurrence, an eternal recurrence
which is an eternal return of an abysmal horror, and a return of
that horror as itself, but a total affirmation of that return is a
transfiguration of that horror and abyss, and a transfiguration
saying Amen, even as Augustine said Amen to the eternal
predestination of God. If evil is the most ultimate problem that
confronts the mind and the imagination, or is that problem
which most forcefully resists and opposes every resolution of its
dark mystery, predestination and eternal recurrence are the
only real resolutions of that mystery in our history. Terrible as
these resolutions are in the deep assaults which they make upon
our most cherished values and beliefs, they would appear to be
inseparable from any full affirmation of the totality of history.
This is just the point at which we can most clearly see that both
predestination and eternal recurrence are wholly other than the
archaic myth of eternal return, for that myth is the embodiment
of a primordial vision that is wholly prehistorical, and wholly
prehistorical in knowing individual events as being wholly
without individuality or uniqueness. It is precisely that absence
of individuality that makes possible the eternal return of events
as themselves; an eternal return of the same, yes, but that is a
return of an identity without difference, or a same which is
simply, and only, and always the same, and hence a same which
is wholly a nonindividual identity.

Nothing is more absent from that vision than individual and
irreversible events, events which are themselves and no other, and
thus events which irrevocably and irreversibly occur. While that
vision of eternal return can be understood as a flight from history,
it can also be understood as a state or condition transcending any
possible historical actuality, and transcending it by ultimately
reversing both spatial location and temporal duration, a reversal
which is a dissolution of concrete or actual points of time and
space, and thus a dissolution of the very possibility of actuality.
Nothing could be further from the archaic myth of eternal return
than Nietzsche's vision of eternal recurrence, and this despite the

fact that their purely circular forms so fully coincide. Nietzsche did not discover eternal recurrence by discovering a prebiblical vision of eternal return. He knew and proclaimed eternal recurrence as a post-Christian vision, and nothing is more revealing about that vision than its post-Christian identity. For this is a historical identity, and if Nietzsche understood historical reality as deeply as any other thinker in history, he nowhere understood it more profoundly than at this point. Here, above all, Nietzsche is an apocalyptic thinker. And he is an apocalyptic thinker by being our only truly post-Christian thinker, for he is that thinker who most purely and most deeply understood the end of history, and most profoundly understood it by envisioning eternal recurrence. Just as Augustine most decisively inaugurated the Christian historical world by envisioning predestination, Nietzsche most decisively ended it by envisioning eternal recurrence, and if each is a vision of total grace, and an eternal grace which is an eternal consumption of evil or sin, each is a vision of a real and actual transfiguration of evil, a transfiguration which would be impossible and unreal apart from the full or interior actualization of evil itself.

So it is that both Nietzsche and Augustine were obsessed with guilt, a guilt that is impossible of forgiveness, or impossible of forgiveness apart from predestination or eternal recurrence, and that impossibility of forgiveness is not at the periphery but rather at the very center of consciousness or will, a will that is a purely empty and impotent will, but that is the will which is the center of both consciousness and history, and a center whose self-negation or self-reversal is the one and only avenue of a transfiguring grace. Now this is a center which is necessarily absent from an archaic vision of eternal return, for that vision can only know a center which is everywhere, and therefore can never know a center which is a unique and actual center, or a center which is the center of consciousness and history, or a center which is either "I" or I AM. And just as Augustine knew self-consciousness only by knowing I AM, Nietzsche finally knew the will only by knowing the Will to Power, and if the Will to Power is without an actual direction, purpose, or goal, but nevertheless is absolute life or energy itself, I AM is that absolute power who is wholly other than any nameable origin or goal, a power whose actualization breaks the fallen will, even as an interior realization of the Will to Power breaks and dissolves the individual will. But that is a breakage which is a transformation of the individual will, a transformation which is truly a conversion of the will, a conversion wherein and whereby the will realizes itself as the Will to Power, but only when it thereby ceases to be individually and interiorly itself.

The cessation of that individuality and uniqueness is the end of history, or, more specifically, the end of Christian history, and if Christian history begins with that unique and interior individuality, it ends with a reversal of that very individuality. Yet that reversal is only possible and real by virtue of the genesis of the individual will. Just as it was Augustine who philosophically discovered that genesis, it was Nietzsche who philosophically discovered its reversal, a reversal which is a reversal of the individual will, yes, but a reversal which occurs and is real only as a consummation of the history of the will. This discovery was simply impossible before the end of Christendom, and even impossible before a full realization of that ending; hence, it is unknown to Hegel, and this despite the fact that Hegel so deeply and so profoundly knew the death of God.

But finally Hegel understood the death of God as the resurrection of God, a resurrection which is a return of the Godhead of God, and the return of the Godhead of God as the center and ground of self-consciousness and history. That is precisely the return which is ended in Nietzsche's vision of eternal recurrence, and it is ended by a new proclamation of the death of God, a death that is now, and for the first time in our history, a full and final death, and thus it can return only as that death, and never as a resurrection of the Godhead. So it is that Nietzsche's vision of the eternal recurrence of the same is a vision of the recurrence of full and actual events, events which are finally actual events only as the consequence of the death of God, for only that death finally releases events from a transcendent ground, so that only now can they be fully and finally manifest and real as events which are only themselves. Such a full and actual correlation between a final and ultimate death of God and the advent of eternal recurrence is yet another sign of the vast and uncrossable gulf between a prehistorical eternal return and a posthistorical eternal recurrence.

If a prehistorical eternal return is innocent of the actuality of the Godhead, a posthistorical eternal recurrence can know a new innocence, and a truly new innocence, an innocence that never occurred or was realized before, for it occurs only after the full and final actualization of the death of God. That death is the center of Nietzsche's vision of eternal recurrence, and it is truly and actually a center, a center apart from which eternal recurrence would be simply and only eternal return, and a center apart from which eternal recurrence would not be the recurrence of full and actual events. Yet that recurrence is not simply the return of such events, it is the eternal recurrence of those events, and it is precisely because it is an eternal recurrence that it is a transfiguration of those events, for now all events are realized in and as an absolute immanence, an immanence that is only possible as a consequence of the death of God, and an immanence that now *is* that which a pure transcendence once *was*, which is to say eternity itself.

That is an eternity in which events are willed to be wholly and only themselves, and if that willing is the Will to Power, that will is an absolute will, and an absolute will that wills everything that occurs. Therefore it is precisely that will which Augustine knew as the will of God, and if Augustine knows the will of God as a totally transcendent and totally immanent will, Nietzsche knows the Will to Power only as a totally immanent will, and a totally immanent will which is a total and absolute will, but a will which can be realized as such only by knowing the finality of the death of God.

Augustine and Nietzsche are the only thinkers who have known a total and absolute will as a comprehensive and universal will. Both understood that will as an eternal will which enacts everything that occurs, and both understood that will as creation and providence at once. Thus Augustine could understand the act of predestination and the act of creation as the one eternal act of God; that is the act which is the source of the "goodness" of existence, a "goodness" that is all in all, and is even all in all in that "privation of being" or "deficiency of being" which is the negative or inverse reality of evil. Thus Augustine's understanding of the eternal act of predestination is a baptism or sanctioning of evil, an evil which is finally and eternally willed by God, and willed by God even if Augustine could only name it as a "permission of evil," for that permission occurs in the eternal will of God, a will whereby and wherein God wills all that He wills, simultaneously, in one act, and eternally.

Yet that is the very act which Nietzsche understands as the Will to Power, and Nietzsche baptized that will in his ecstatic proclamation of eternal recurrence. If that eternal recurrence is the "innocence of becoming," that is an innocence which Augustine understands as the goodness of existence, a goodness which even occurs in the abysmal horror of evil, for that horror is willed in the eternal act of predestination, a predestination which is an act of total justice, and a total justice which is simultaneously the eternal love of God. That love and that justice are just as fully present in a predestination to eternal

death as they are in a predestination to eternal life, and if
damnation is willed in the eternal act of a just and loving God,
that act is inseparable from a predestination to eternal life, even
as the willing of eternal recurrence is the willing of life and
death at once.

Both predestination and eternal recurrence are a transfiguration of the horror of existence; an understanding and realization of each makes possible a liberation from the negative and
abysmal power of evil, now that evil can be known as "nothingness," for it is absent or nothing in the eternal will of God, just
as it is absent as evil in the willing of eternal recurrence, an
absence which is the absence of the negative or impotent will.
But if Nietzsche understands the eternal act of predestination as
the eternal willing of the Will to Power, that is a willing that only
now is manifest as the ultimate willing of every actual will, and
the willing of every actual will in its ownmost actuality, even if
the fullness of that actuality is a reversal of the individual will.
That is a reversal which Augustine understands as the conversion of the empty and fallen will, and if only that conversion
makes possible an understanding and affirmation of predestination, only the reversal of the individual and interior will
makes possible an understanding and affirmation of eternal
recurrence, for only that reversal makes possible a willing of
eternal recurrence, a willing which is the liberation of the
interior and individual will.

Nietzsche's initial proclamation of redemption occurs in the
second part of *Thus Spoke Zarathustra*, and it occurs in response
to the Augustinian question of whether there can be redemption if there is an eternal justice, just as it occurs by way of an
Augustinian apprehension that our existence must eternally
become deed and guilt again, a fallen and impotent existence in
which the stone of *it was* cannot be moved, and cannot be moved
because a fallen existence is the consequence of an eternal
predestination, for this is what is eternal in that "punishment"
which a fallen and impotent will knows as existence. Zarathustra
immediately repudiates a redemption in which willing should
become not willing, and then proclaims a redemption in which
the will is a creator: "All 'it was' is a fragment, a riddle, a
dreadful accident—until the creative will says to it, 'But thus I
willed it' " (Kaufmann translation). This alone is what Zarathustra proclaims as redemption, a liberation which is a deliverance
from the impotence of the will, an impotence of the will which
cannot will backwards, and an impotence that is reversed in thus
"I" will it, and thus "I" shall will it.

But that "I" is not and cannot be an interior and individual

"I"; that is the very "I" which cannot will backwards, and cannot will backwards because it is imprisoned by *it was*, an *it was* whose very finality is the consequence of original sin or the bad conscience, and a bad conscience that is turned against itself in that punishment or revenge which our impotent will knows as existence, an existence which is fallen precisely because it is imprisoned by *it was*. Redemption is a liberation from that *it was*, a liberation effected by a new will that is a "creator," and therefore a will that is not a consequence of *it was*, but rather a will that wills *it was*, and that willing is the very act of creation.

Therefore that "I" which is a creator is the very opposite of the impotent and guilty "I," and its willing is released only by a reversal of our *ressentiment*, a reversal which is a reversal of every apprehension of *it was*, and thus a reversal of that "I" which cannot will backwards, which is to say a reversal of that "I" which is interiorly and individually itself and only itself. That is a reversal which is the willing of eternal recurrence, a will which can will only by willing everything that occurs, but that willing can never be the willing of the unique and individual "I," an "I" that can will only itself, and therefore an "I" that cannot will eternal recurrence, and cannot will the eternal recurrence of everything if only because it can only will itself. Just as Augustine understands the fallen will as a will which wills only itself, and does so precisely in willing to be the source of itself, a will which is the will of original sin, and an original sin which is repeated and renewed in every act of the fallen will, Nietzsche understands *ressentiment* as will willing against itself, a willing which is the stone of *it was*, and is the stone of *it was* because it is wholly imprisoned within itself, and thus is incapable of a full and actual act of the will.

That incapacity is the impotence of the will imprisoned within itself, and imprisoned by its own negative will, a will which can only actually will against itself; and that is the willing which deepens the interiorization of consciousness, an interiorization which finally realizes the interior and individual "I." Now that is the very "I" which Augustine knows as the empty and fallen will; each is an absolutely isolated and absolutely solitary "I," and each can only truly or actually will against itself. Augustine knows that willing as the willing of nothingness, even as Nietzsche knows it as the totally negative and totally self-lacerating will of *ressentiment*, and even as the will of God is the total opposite of the fallen will, the willing of eternal recurrence is the total opposite of *ressentiment*. Now even as the solitary and dichotomous "I" of the fallen will is the very opposite of the will of God, the willing of eternal recurrence is the very opposite of the wholly guilty and self-lacerating "I" of the bad conscience or *ressentiment*, so that the willing of eternal recurrence is just as infinitely distant from an impotent will as is the will of God from a fallen will. Now even as an Augustinian conversion of the will can only be the consequence of predestination, the absolute willing of the will as creator can only be the consequence of eternal recurrence, an eternal recurrence which now *is* that absolute and infinite will which Augustine knew as the will of God. Thus it is the ultimate and final event of the death of God which is the deepest ground of a wholly immanent eternal recurrence, and if that eternal recurrence is the Will to Power, the willing of eternal recurrence is everywhere, even as the will of God is everywhere by willing the eternal act of predestination.

Thus a totally immanent eternal recurrence is a post-Christian willing of predestination, and it is every bit as absolute as is the eternal act of predestination, and is so even as the act of creation, a creation which is a creation from "nothing," for it is a creation arising from the absolute impotence of the bad conscience or *ressentiment*, a *ressentiment* which is simply and only the individual and interior act of No-saying, but a No-saying which becomes Yes-saying in the willing of eternal recurrence. That is a decisive reason why eternal recurrence is circular, and is even circular by being a circle in which the center is everywhere, but as opposed to the circle of eternal return, this is a circle of becoming, and only of becoming, a totally immanent becoming which is the consequence of the death of God. Yet predestination is every bit as real in that becoming as it is in the creation of God, and if the fallen will of that creation is finally willed by the predestination of God, the No-saying of the bad conscience and *ressentiment* is finally willed by the willing of eternal recurrence, and is so because that willing wills everything that occurs, so that everything that occurs can finally be celebrated in an ecstatic act of Yes-saying, a Yes-saying that is a willing of predestination in a world and in a history in which God is dead.

If Nietzsche believed that we can never escape God insofar as we cannot escape the very grammar of our language, we likewise cannot escape God insofar as we live under the impact of our history, for the shadow of God only expands and extends itself as a consequence of the death of God, even as repression becomes ever fuller and more comprehensive as a consequence of the birth of the bad conscience. But even as Christianity knows the fall as a *felix culpa* or fortunate fall, Nietzsche knows the origin of the bad conscience as a fortunate fall, for it is the reversal of that fall which is the willing of eternal recurrence, a reversal that would not be possible apart from the very advent of the inverted and negative will, and that cannot occur apart from a reversal of that will, and if that reversal is a reversal of the interior and individual "I," that is also a reversal that realizes a truly new "I," the "I" that wills eternal recurrence, and therefore an "I" that truly parallels that "I" which wills predestination—and the act of each is the act of creation.

It is not an accident that Nietzsche at the very outset of his madness could claim to be both God and the Crucified, or that he so frequently confessed that he could not bear not to be God, for Nietzsche most deeply embodied that will which Augustine knew as the will of pride, the will to be ourselves our only ground and source, a will which is the interior and individual origin of sin. That is an origin which is reversed in eternal recurrence, but it can only be reversed by a will that is a "creator," and is a creator by willing backwards, and willing eternally backwards to the very creation of the world, so that the world is re-created or created once again in the willing of eternal recurrence. The official bull which condemned Meister Eckhart in 1329 accused Eckhart of asserting that what scripture says of Christ is true of every good and divine man, and that man performs whatever God performs, even including the creation of Heaven and earth. Whether or not Eckhart was guilty of that condemnation, Nietzsche certainly is, and even if it is not possible to see an all too modern rebirth of Eckhart in Nietzsche's willing of eternal recurrence, it is possible to see a consummation of our history in that willing, and it is precisely as such that the symbol of eternal recurrence is overwhelmingly real in a postmodern or post-Christian history. If our symbol of eternal recurrence is the symbol of a pure and total immanence, that immanence is certainly a consequence of the death of God, a death which first fully and actually occurs in the Crucified, and a death which even can be understood to be universalized in the willing of eternal recurrence.

Nietzsche gave us only one concrete portrait of Zarathustra and, ironically, that occurs in Nietzsche's portrait of Jesus in *The Antichrist*, a Jesus who is incapable of *ressentiment*, is free of history, and is himself the exact opposite of Christianity. For Nietzsche understands the proclamation of Jesus as the abolition of sin and guilt, any distance separating God and man is now abolished, and grace or blessedness is now the only reality. That reality is now lived in an absolutely new "practice," and even if Jesus was the only Christian, his life and death was nothing other than this practice, only this practice leads to God:

"indeed, it *is* God" (*Antichrist* 33). We need not wonder that
Nietzsche employed the literary genre of the gospel as his
vehicle for embodying Zarathustra, and if *Thus Spoke Zarathustra*
continues to remain a unique work of literature, that is because
it is the only gospel in our postbiblical literature. Only Nietzsche
dared to write a scripture which is scripture and only scripture,
or a scripture which is wholly and only the consequence of
inspiration. Therein only Blake is Nietzsche's true precursor,
and if Blake and Nietzsche share a common image of Jesus, that
is most clearly so in their common realization that Jesus is the
name of the total forgiveness of sin, a forgiveness of sin which is
an abolition of sin, and therefore an abolition of that Judge
whom Blake knew as Satan and Nietzsche knew as the deification of nothingness or the will to nothingness pronounced holy
(*Antichrist* 18). Nietzsche believed that in *The Antichrist* he told
the genuine history of Christianity, for the original gospel died
on the cross, and what has been called gospel in Christianity is
the exact opposite of the gospel which Jesus lived: "*ill* tidings, a
dysangel" (39). So it is that Nietzsche proclaimed the Yes-saying
of Zarathustra as the very reversal of the No-saying of Christianity; therein it is a rebirth of the "evangelical practice" of Jesus,
and is so because it is a Yes-saying in which guilt passes into
grace, and precisely thereby is a reversal of the bad conscience,
a bad conscience or *ressentiment* which is most purely embodied
in Christianity. Therefore that Yes-saying is a reversal of our
history, and accordingly a reversal of all that history following
the fall into the bad conscience, a history that can only truly or
fully be embodied in the fallen or wholly impotent will, and a
history that is the history of that will.

This is also that history which Augustine enacted in the *City of
God*, but here it is enacted wholly in the city of the "flesh" as
opposed to the city of the Spirit, and whereas each of these cities
is predestined by God from all eternity, it is only the city of
"flesh" that is the full arena of the fallen will, for even if the city
of the Spirit comprehends both saints and sinners, it "even now"
is the Kingdom of Christ (XX, 9). Nietzsche knows that "even
now" as the kingdom of eternal recurrence, a kingdom which
surely comprehends the evangelical practice of Jesus, and does
so if only because eternal recurrence is eternal grace, and is so as
an absolutely total and absolutely eternal will, a will which is that
will that Augustine knew as the will of God. Accordingly,
Nietzsche finally knew but one city, a city that could even be
identified as a *civitas Dei*, for it is a city that is regenerated by
eternal recurrence, and a city that is regenerated by the willing
of eternal recurrence, just as Augustine's *civitas Dei* is regener-

ated by the eternal act of predestination. So it is that the willing of eternal recurrence is the willing of predestination, or that willing of predestination which can occur only after the death of God; nevertheless that willing is virtually indistinguishable from the eternal will of God, a will that remains and enacts itself even after the death of God.

Nothing more clearly witnesses to the presence of such a will than its enactment of a uniquely Christian theodicy, and a theodicy which goes beyond the *City of God* by its full justification of even the most horrible evil, an evil which now can be known and celebrated as the consequence of grace. If such celebration is impossible for Augustine, it is ecstatically embraced by Nietzsche, or by Nietzsche's Zarathustra. And what is to distinguish the totally transcendent will of eternal predestination from the totally immanent will of eternal recurrence? All too clearly, Zarathustra's celebration of eternal recurrence is a celebration of absolute grace, a celebration that sanctions evil by willing that it recur eternally again, for there can be no joy without woe, and even the most horrible woe is inseparable from the deepest joy, for joy wants everything eternally the same. That joy is an absolute affirmation of everything whatsoever, and if such a joy is wholly alien to Augustine, such an absolute affirmation is fully present in a double predestination, a predestination which is simultaneously a predestination to salvation and to damnation, and a predestination which must inevitably be known as an eternal willing of life and death. For even if the will of God cannot will death, it can and does withhold its will so as to make death and an eternal death inevitable, and that withdrawal of the will of God is nevertheless the willing of the will of God, even as the willing of eternal recurrence is the willing of an abysmal evil.

Both Augustine and Nietzsche know a total and an absolute will, a will which is inevitably a willing of evil, and if therein both share a uniquely Christian theodicy, that theodicy is ironically far deeper in Nietzsche than in Augustine, and is so if only because Augustine is incapable of celebrating evil, and even incapable of affirming that God wills evil, and this despite the fact that double predestination is a major theme in the *City of God*, just as a double predestination was fully enacted in that Christian history following and inspired by Augustine, a history which only reaches its terminus in Nietzsche. Nietzsche claimed that all the names of history are his own, but they are "his own" only in the willing of eternal recurrence, and if that willing is finally the willing of every actual will, that actual will is a total immanence, and a pure immanence that *is* that which a pure transcendence *was*. That pure transcendence is what Augustine knows as the will of God, and a will that is most actually itself in the willing of predestination. For even if the act of predestination is identical with the act of creation, it is predestination that the converted or liberated will most deeply knows as the will of God, for our will can only know grace as predestination, and can do so if only because it can never know grace as our own. So likewise eternal recurrence can never be known as our own, and can never be known as our own because that which is our own is the pure negativity of the wholly impotent and self-lacerating will, a will which Augustine knows as the wholly fallen will, and a will which for Augustine and Nietzsche alike is wholly transformed in the liberated will, a will which is a wholly gracious will, and if Augustine knows that will as the will which wills the will of God, Nietzsche knows it as the will which wills eternal recurrence.

Ironically, it is Nietzsche alone among modern thinkers who knows the absolute triumph of grace. Therein, too, Nietzsche is an Augustinian thinker, but he is so only by knowing the death of God. And if Nietzsche knew that death more purely than any other thinker, that is precisely our way to a grace that is all in all. Perhaps Augustine is the deepest ancient name of Nietzsche, just as Nietzsche is the deepest modern name of Augustine; and if those names are one name in the willing of eternal recurrence, that is a name which is a portal to a uniquely Christian grace, a grace that is not only everywhere, but is everywhere as a transfiguring grace.

10

The Apocalyptic Christ

Perhaps the deepest theological response to Nietzsche's vision of eternal recurrence was the *Church Dogmatics* of Karl Barth, the first theology which was a theology of the Church and only of the Church, and thus the first Christian theology which effected or intended a total disjunction or chasm between the Church and history, for it was the first theology created in full response to the historical realization of the death of God. That response occurs at one of its deepest levels in Barth's doctrine of predestination or election, where Barth once again realizes a transformation of theology into Christology, and does so by understanding Jesus Christ as the one Elector and Elect, and again as the one Rejector and Rejected. This is effected by what Barth himself judges to be a total revision of the dogma of predestination, a revision in which Jesus Christ rather than the absolute decree of predestination is regarded as the real basis of the election of each elected individual, so that Christ is simultaneously the electing God and the elected man. But Christ is the elected man only because he is the rejected man. He is the man abandoned to eternal perdition, a perdition or Hell which is the inevitable lot of every single human life, but a perdition which is diverted to Christ alone, a Christ who has challenged and brought upon himself the destructive hostility of God, for God has made him who is uniquely His Son "to be sin." Thus Christ is the Rejected because he is the Elect, and just as he is the only elected one, he is also and thereby the only rejected one: "By permitting the life of a rejected man to be the life of His own Son, God has made such a life objectively impossible for all others" (*Church Dogmatics*, II, 2, 346).

For Barth, the doctrine of predestination or election is the very sum of the gospel, for it is the content of the good news which is

Jesus Christ. If this is that Yes which is the very Yes of God, it cannot be heard unless the No is also heard, but that No is said for the sake of the Yes, and therefore the first and last word is Yes and not No. Thus the free election of grace is the whole of the gospel, and even if to an opposing world the election must of necessity become nonelection or rejection, and for that reason there does exist a definite sphere of damnation ordained by God as the negation of the divine affirmation, that is the work of "the almighty non-willing" (27) which accompanies God's willing. Yet the divine affirmation, the divine willing as such, is salvation and not damnation, for the Yes of God is total and irrevocable. Only in the divine predestination is God self-revealed to us as the God whom He is, and only in that predestination or election can we perceive and understand the totality of God's activities, including providence and creation, for it is the act of predestination which most fully makes manifest to us the eternal act of God. And that eternal act and will is the election of Jesus Christ.

Here, Barth decisively breaks with all previous interpretations of the doctrine of predestination, and he does so by maintaining that in the eternal predestination of God we have to encounter only one name and one person, the same name and the same person, Jesus Christ. Only thereby can we know that all are elected to grace, for the content of the eternal divine predestination is nothing less than the eternal will of God to give Himself for the sake of humanity in the election of Jesus Christ, a will that is realized in the incarnation, crucifixion and resurrection of His Son. Thus it is "God's self-giving" (161) which is the election of grace, and thereby the real content of an eternal predestination.

Barth even retains the doctrine of double predestination, but he revolutionizes it by maintaining that from all eternity the election of Jesus Christ is simultaneously the election of the elected man as well as the electing God, and here God wills to lose in order that man may gain, for humanity gains election, salvation, and life, whereas God ascribes to Himself reprobation, perdition, and death. God's partner in this eternal covenant is a wholly fallen humanity, and if God Himself became man, this man, what else can this mean but that "He declared Himself guilty of the contradiction against Himself in which man was involved" (164), He made it His own, and for the sake of this choice He hazarded Himself wholly and utterly, and elected our suffering as His own suffering. This makes possible a faith in which it is impossible to believe in our rejection, because now we can know that God not only permits but wills evil, but God wills evil only because He wills not to keep to

Himself the light of His glory but to let it shine outside Himself, and it shines outside Himself by God's becoming guilty in His Son, therein and thereby our guilt is wholly born by God in Jesus Christ, and thus the thought of God's double predestination can only awaken a pure joy in us. But that joy is inseparable from God's act of making His only Son "to be sin" (352), an act which is eternally willed in double predestination, and an act which is fully actualized in God's becoming a "curse" for us in Jesus Christ (Gal. 3:13); therein Christ is the only one rejected, the only one who has suffered the damnation of Hell, but that suffering was wholly "for us." Barth's radically new doctrine of election is a profound response to Nietzsche's vision of eternal recurrence, and is so because it so wholly conjoins Yes-saying and No-saying. If here Yes-saying and No-saying are wholly and only the eternal act of God, that is an act in which No-saying becomes Yes-saying, but it does so only in God Himself becoming sin and undergoing damnation or eternal judgment in the incarnation, crucifixion, and resurrection of His Son. That damnation is the realization of salvation for a wholly fallen humanity, which is why it is an eternal Yes and Amen, but it is so only by being the suffering of God, a suffering which is finally damnation, so that double predestination is a predestination of a fallen humanity to life and of a self-giving God to death; each is inseparable from the other, and their full conjunction can only be named as a total and irrevocable Yes. If that is a Yes which Nietzsche knew as the Yes of eternal recurrence, it, too, can only interiorly be manifest and real as No-saying, and as a total and irrevocable No-saying, the No-saying of God becoming sin in Jesus Christ, a No-saying which quite simply is eternal damnation, but a damnation which is an election from all eternity of a fallen humanity to eternal life. Thus that very election is the election of God to suffering and death, so that if it was Nietzsche who most fully proclaimed the death of God in the modern world, it was Barth who most fully proclaimed that death as the very essence of the gospel, for that death is the actualization of an eternal election, and thus for Nietzsche and Barth alike the death of God is an absolute Yes and Amen.

Barth's doctrine of double predestination led him to an ethics whose first principle is that there is no humanity outside the humanity of Jesus Christ, and this, too, parallels Nietzsche's ethics of eternal recurrence, an ethics which is the total willing of eternal recurrence, and therefore an ethics which quite simply is Yes-saying, an ethics which the Christian can know as the willing of the will of God. It is grace, and a free grace, which is triumphant both in Nietzsche's vision of eternal recurrence and in Barth's radically modern Christian dogmatics. And if Barth's dogmatics centers wholly upon Jesus Christ, Nietzsche's radically atheistic vision centers upon the death of God, a death of God which Barth knows as the actual consequence of an eternal and irrevocable election, even as Nietzsche knows it as the consequence of a total Yes-saying, a Yes-saying which Barth can celebrate in a full realization of an eternal and double predestination. In this light we can see that Nietzsche's vision of eternal recurrence is a vision of a double predestination, for here the death of God is inseparable from a total Yes-saying, even as in Barth's dogmatics the total and final Yes of an eternal election is inseparable from the self-giving of God even unto sin and damnation.

Nothing is closer to Barth's dogmatics than Milton's vision of the Son of God's free acceptance of an eternal condemnation in *Paradise Lost*, and if that vision is inseparable from a new and all too modern vision of the totality of a uniquely Satanic energy and power, that is the very power which Nietzsche baptized in his vision of eternal recurrence, even as Barth baptized it in his radically new understanding of God's free and eternal acceptance and willing of damnation itself in the passion and death of His Son. So it is that at this point at least Barth's dogmatics is a profoundly modern dogmatics, and one that here has no parallel or warrant in the confessions of the Church, so that his doctrine of election is not a Church dogmatics, but rather a response to an overwhelming historical reality which is itself an annulment or reversal of the Church. Yet authentic visions of Christ have again and again in Christian history been annulments and reversals of the authority and the dogmas of the Church, a historical process that begins with Paul and it is to be hoped has not ended with Barth. And if it was Barth who founded a truly modern or postmodern theology, that is a theology in full continuity with Christian history, and above all so in its radical understanding of Christ, a Christ who is the full and final embodiment of damnation. If that damnation is the election of all, that is an election which is a full reversal of the God of glory, but a reversal which is thereby and therein a consummation of the eternal and double predestination of God. Now even if Barth resisted and opposed the very possibility of an apocalyptic theology, that is a possibility which becomes actuality in his radical understanding of Christ, for if Christ is the embodiment of that No-saying which is finally Yes-saying, that is a Yes-saying which is an apocalyptic Yes-saying, and is so if only because it is the final ending of damnation, a damnation which ends in its one and only full occurrence, and that ending is the ending of a history which is a rebellion against God.

Apocalyptic vision is inevitably a vision of the end of history, and the apocalyptic Christ is the Christ who ends history, but unlike a Buddhist vision of the end or emptiness of history, Christian apocalyptic vision is a vision of the actual ending of history, an actual ending which is the crucifixion and the resurrection of Christ, and is the crucifixion and the resurrection of Christ as a once and for all and irreversible historical event. If that is an event which is a total event, and for the Christian the one total event which occurs in history, that is an event which is total in its very occurrence, a totality which is the totality of history, and even if that totality is only manifest and real as such in this event, this is that event which is the end of history, and is the end of history because it is the totality of history. Nowhere is this identity of history more fully present than it is in Nietzsche's vision of eternal recurrence and, more specifically, in Nietzsche's vision of the death of God as the full actuality of eternal recurrence, an eternal recurrence that is the ending of *ressentiment* or the bad conscience only insofar as an absolute or total will is present that wills the eternal recurrence of the same, and if that will is a total Yes-saying, that is the will of every full and actual will, and thus it is the will of Here Comes Everybody. Christ is the Christian name of Everybody, an Everybody which is the humanity of Christ, a humanity which is the ending of the city of man, or the ending of the eternal damnation of sin, so that now there is no humanity outside of the humanity of Christ. Christ *is* Here Comes Everybody, an Everybody which is eternally elected to grace, but an election which is only actualized in that damnation which is the crucifixion of God. Thus it is that the apocalyptic Christ is life and death at once, a life which is the new life of humanity and a death which is the death of God, and if it was Nietzsche who first fully understood that death as a total Yes-saying, that is a Yes-saying which is the inauguration of apocalypse, and the inauguration of that apocalypse which is the totality of history. Accordingly, the advent of the totality of history is the ending of a No-saying which is *ressentiment*, and if that is the ending of damnation, that is the ending of every humanity except the humanity of Christ.

The deep cipher or "curse" of Christian theology has always been the doctrine of damnation, and if damnation can be understood as having been realized in Christ alone, then damnation can then be understood to be the center of the gospel or the good news of Jesus Christ, a center which is a real and actual center and a center which is the center of history. At no other point is Christianity so different or so distant from the other religions of the world. If Christianity has centered upon damnation as has no other religious tradition, just as Christianity and a uniquely Western history have realized a depth and power of guilt to be found in no other history or tradition, these are decisive signs of a uniquely Christian apprehension of an ultimate No-saying, a No-saying which is absolutely directed against itself, and a No-saying which is most fully manifest and real in a uniquely Christian God, that very God whom Nietzsche in *The Antichrist* declared to be the deification of nothingness, the will to nothingness pronounced holy. But that is a nothingness which is the very opposite of a Buddhist nothingness, and is so because it is an actually negative power, a negative power that is fully present in an interior realization of damnation, and if that is a unique presence which marks the very advent of Christianity, that is the presence of the Crucified, and the actual presence of that Christ who became a "curse" for us, a curse which we know when we know the crucifixion of God. Nowhere else is such a pure negativity so fully manifest or real, and here that negativity can be understood as a full and actual event, an event which can be named as an absolute act of No-saying, but an act which for us is absolute Yes-saying. And if that Yes-saying is the good news of Jesus Christ, that is a Yes-saying inseparable from the absolute No-saying of damnation, so that a hearing of Yes-saying is not possible without a hearing of No-saying. Christian salvation itself is wholly meaningless and unreal apart from damnation, and if this deep and ultimate truth of Christianity is hidden and disguised in a uniquely modern Christian church, it is at the very center of the epic poetry of Dante, Milton, Blake, and Joyce, just as it is at the very center of the New Testament itself.

Indeed, Jesus was the first prophet, or the first prophet apart from John the Baptist, to proclaim and enact an eternal damnation, and in the Gospels this can most clearly be seen in the Sermon on the Mount, and whereas the Hebrew Bible is silent on the subject of damnation, there is no other theme or motif which more fully dominates the New Testament. At no other point is there such a chasm between the Hebrew Bible and the New Testament, just as at no other point is there such a chasm between Christianity and the other religions of the world, for the uniquely Christian identity of both God and Christ is inseparable from damnation, a damnation which is the deepest interior identity of the triumph of the Kingdom of God. The Christian knows that triumph as occurring in Christ, and occurring in a once and for all and irreversible event. And if the Fourth Gospel can know that event as occurring simultaneously in incarnation, crucifixion, resurrection, and apocalypse, it is nevertheless so manifest as an ultimate event, and an ultimate event which is a final reversal of history. Yet to know damnation as occurring uniquely and only in Christ is to know damnation itself as the final reversal of history, a reversal which is an apocalyptic reversal, and a reversal which is only fully manifest interiorly in Christianity, and there most clearly manifest in the uniquely Christian apprehension of the individual and impotent will. If it was Augustine and Nietzsche who most deeply understood that will, it is in Augustine and Nietzsche that we can apprehend most clearly the absolutely negative will, a will that is the will of an ultimate guilt or *ressentiment*, and therefore a will that knows itself to be damned, and knows that damnation as the deepest interior center of its own individual will.

So it is that Barth can say that, in its true and strict historical sense, "know thyself" can be understood only as a summons to rebellion against the grace of God (*Church Dogmatics*, II, 2, 541), a rebellion which is the rebellion of the guilty will, but a rebellion which is only manifest as such as a consequence of absolute grace. And that absolute grace actually occurs in the damnation of Christ, and if that damnation is a unique damnation, and a unique damnation which is the election of all, that damnation is an apocalyptic reversal, and the apocalyptic reversal of a totally guilty humanity. Then and only then is all humanity the actual humanity of Christ, and if that humanity is the "curse" of damnation in the unique and individual Jesus Christ, it is the grace of election in the new innocence of Here Comes Everybody, an Everybody that is only the consequence of Christ, and only the consequence of the damnation of Christ. Thus the humanity of Christ is salvation and damnation at once, salvation for all humanity, but damnation for the unique and individual Jesus Christ; each is inseparable from the other, just as each is realized only in the realization of the other.

At no other point is Barth's Trinitarianism so profoundly radical, just as at no other point is a uniquely Christian God so manifest and real, and if that God is the will to nothingness pronounced holy, that is a holiness that is the holiness of damnation, and a holiness that can be celebrated precisely thereby as the total Yes and Amen of an absolute grace. Then Yes is Yes and only Yes, but it is so only as the consequence of an absolute No, and if Christianity alone knows that No, it is only Christianity which knows an apocalyptic Yes. This is that Yes which is the apocalyptic Christ, an apocalyptic Christ who is the incarnate Word, and an incarnate Word who is the Crucified, and a Crucified who is resurrected in and as that apocalyptic Yes. If that Yes is all in all, and all in all in the election of all, that all in all is the consequence of damnation, and the damnation of the unique and individual Jesus Christ. But Jesus Christ is the Son of God, and most fully or most actually Son of God in that very damnation, a damnation which is therefore the damnation of God, and a damnation which is eternally elected or predestined by God Himself, even if that predestination is fully and only the election of Christ. Yet that Christ can only be the apocalyptic Christ, the apocalyptic Christ who is the end of history, but that ending is the actualization of the totality of history, a totality in which all are elected, but all are elected only through God's "rejection" or damnation of Christ.

Such a damnation could only be a rejection of God by Himself, or a rejection of the Son of God by the Almighty. If Barth insists that we can only know the Almighty by knowing an absolute grace, that is the grace of God's rejection of Himself, and that absolute No-saying of God is finally an apocalyptic grace. If it is the Christian and the Christian alone who interiorly knows the reality of damnation, that is the reality which is the reality of Christ, and the reality of that unique and individual Christ who is the apocalyptic Christ, an apocalyptic Christ who is the embodiment of the death of God, and therefore the embodiment of absolute grace. Nietzsche was the first to know that death as a triumphant Yes-saying, but it was earlier celebrated by Blake as that "Self-Annihilation of God" which is the source of all life and grace, just as it was first proclaimed by Paul as that crucifixion which is resurrection, and even that proclamation is a reenactment of Jesus' triumphant proclamation of the dawning of the Kingdom of God. This is the gospel or the good news of Jesus Christ, a gospel in which the damnation of one is the salvation of all. That damnation is an absolute act of No-saying, but it realizes itself only as a total Yes-saying, for even if Yes-saying is here inseparable from No-saying, that No-saying can only be pronounced or enacted as Yes-saying, so that if crucifixion is here resurrection, that is because the No-saying of the Almighty is the Yes-saying of the apocalyptic Christ.

Hence the Christian can know God only by knowing Christ, and if the Christian knows God only by knowing an absolute grace, that grace is the rejection or damnation of God by Himself, and if that is a "self-giving" which is all in all, it is all in all in God only by being the damnation of God, and a damnation of God which is the free and eternal act or election of absolute grace. Thus the Christian can know grace only as the rejection of Christ, a rejection which is an absolute rejection or damnation, and a damnation of that Christ who became a "curse" for us, and therefore became guilty for us, and if that guilt is the consequence of the act of God, that act is the eternal act of predestination or election, an act that is the act of the uniquely Christian God, and an act that is enacted only in the unique and individual Jesus Christ. So it is that the act of election is enacted only by Christ, or only by the uniquely Christian God, or only by that God who can be known only through Christ, and only known by knowing predestination or election only as damnation, for only that damnation is the election of all. Alone among the great religions of the world, Christian celebration is primarily a celebration of death, a celebration occurring in a eucharist which is a renewal or re-presentation (*anamnesis*) of the death of Christ, and a celebration occurring in a proclamation of a gospel which is a continual announcement of that crucifixion which is resurrection, or that death which is life, but a death which is life only in the actual occurrence of death, and the actual occurrence of the death of God. That death of God is the damnation of God, but a damnation only actually occurring in Christ, and therefore a damnation which can be interiorly known only by the Christian, an interior realization which is the birth of the unique and individual will.

That birth is the advent of the election of all, an election of all which is the consequence of a unique and individual death or damnation, and a death which is fully manifest in the pure negativity or impotence of the individual will, and if truly to know that will is to know an absolute rebellion against God, that is a rebellion which only fully occurs in that "curse" which Christ became, a rebellion which is the rebellion of God against God, but that rebellion is the eternal sacrifice or self-giving of God. If that is the sacrifice which is renewed or re-presented in the eucharist, and proclaimed in the gospel, that is the sacrifice of an apocalyptic reversal, and an apocalyptic reversal of God, a reversal which is the apocalyptic Christ, and is that apocalyptic Christ who is the free and total grace of God. Now even if it is impossible for us to believe in our own rejection or damnation, that is only because or insofar as we can know the rejection of Christ, and even if Christ is both the Rejector and the Rejected One, just as he is both the Elector and the Elected One, that is an election or predestination which is damnation, or is so for God in Christ, for even if that death or damnation is the election of all, it is so only through the absolute condemnation of Christ, a condemnation which is an eternal damnation, and an eternal damnation which is an absolute act. That act is the eternal act of God, and an act which is the absolute opposition of God, and the absolute opposition of God to Himself, an opposition which can only interiorly be known to us as damnation, and an opposition which we can know only insofar as we know Christ. And it is only insofar as we can know that opposition or damnation as occurring only in Christ that we can know a total grace, a total grace which is the eternal act of damnation, but the actual enactment of that absolute No-saying is the realization of the absolute Yes-saying of an apocalyptic grace, a grace that is all in all, but is all in all only by what we can only know as the eternal damnation of God in Christ.

Thus to know an eternal damnation is to know an absolute and an apocalyptic grace, an apocalyptic grace which is the apocalyptic Christ, and an apocalyptic Christ who is the damnation of God by God, or the damnation of the Son by the Almighty, and an Almighty who is almighty only by the "self-giving" or sacrifice of God. Yet that sacrifice is both a sacrifice of God by God and a sacrifice of God to God, a sacrifice which Christianity in its very beginnings knew as atonement, an atonement occurring through the sacrificial death of the Lamb of God, but only in modernity has Christianity known the guilty and the totally guilty Christ, a modernity launched by Luther and Milton and consummated in Nietzsche and Joyce, and thus a modernity which knows the death of Christ as the death of both the humanity and the divinity of Christ. Barth is the theologian who knows this most deeply; and he knows it most deeply by knowing the damnation of Christ, a damnation that frees humanity, so that now all are actually elected. But this is nevertheless a damnation whereby and wherein God ascribes to Himself reprobation, perdition, and death.

In classical Calvinism, reprobation, or *reprobatio*, is the eternal decree of God according to which He wills to abandon the mass of humanity to their fallen condition, and the source or cause of *reprobatio* is the absolutely sovereign will of God. Barth reversed this classical Calvinism by understanding reprobation as the reprobation of Christ and only of Christ, a reprobation which is a consequence of that sin or guilt which God has ascribed to Himself in Christ, and even if that guilt is the guilt of all humanity, that is a guilt which becomes grace when it is enacted in and upon God. At no other point is Barth such a profoundly modern thinker, and if this is the most deeply modern theology which we have been given, it is nevertheless a theology which is a rebirth of the Bible, and of the Christian Bible or the New Testament. Not even Luther could reach such a deeply Christian understanding of guilt, and even if it was attained by Nietzsche before Barth, it was only Barth who understood it dogmatically, and understood it dogmatically by transforming theology into Christology, and therein and thereby transforming guilt into grace.

Guilt becomes grace when it is the guilt of God, or the guilt which God ascribes to Himself in Christ, and if that ascription occurs in an eternal predestination or election, that is an eternal election which is only actually enacted in the death of Christ, a death of Christ which now can be understood as the damnation of Christ, and therefore the damnation of God in Christ. That is a reprobation effected both by Christ and upon Christ, for Christ is both the Rejector and the Rejected, and is the Rejector and the Rejected because Christ is both the Elector and the Elected, and that is an election which is an election of grace and of grace alone.

Already Augustine knew that predestination is by grace and by grace alone, but only in the modern world has Christianity known a guilt that is grace alone, a guilt that is grace alone in Christ, and is grace alone in the apocalyptic Christ, an apocalyptic Christ who is the end of history by being the totality of history. Only in the death or damnation of that Christ is everyone actually elected to grace, a grace which is inseparable from the total condemnation of Christ, and a grace which is an absolutely new innocence. That condemnation is an apocalyptic act, for it is an act effecting an absolute transformation of history, a transformation in which guilt passes into grace, or a transformation in which a totally fallen humanity passes into the humanity of Christ, an if that is a new humanity, it is an apocalyptic humanity, and an apocalyptic humanity because it is the humanity of Christ. So it is that the apocalyptic Christ is Here Comes Everybody, an Everybody that is totally guilty in its own unique and individual will, but an Everybody that is totally gracious in the humanity of Christ. If that humanity is an apocalyptic Christ, and an apocalyptic Christ that is all in all, that all in all or Everybody is a universal humanity or world, and thus a new world, and a new humanity, a humanity which has realized an actual movement from guilt to grace, but done so only through that apocalyptic damnation which is an apocalypse of grace.

If Buddhism knows a samsara which is nirvana, or an emptiness which is Emptiness, Christianity knows a guilt which is grace, and a fall which is a fortunate fall, but that is a fall and that is a grace which is only fully and actually present in the absolute condemnation of Christ, a condemnation which is an apocalyptic condemnation, and is an apocalyptic condemnation because it is an absolute transformation of history. Accordingly, an apocalyptic condemnation is absolute No-saying and absolute Yes-saying at once, and if it can be known interiorly and individually only as No-saying or guilt, it is known or realized universally only as the Yes-saying of grace, a grace that is an apocalyptic grace, and is an apocalyptic grace because it is all in all. But it is all in all only by being the damnation of God in Christ, a damnation which is an apocalyptic damnation, and is an apocalyptic damnation because it and it alone actualizes the election of all. That election can only be greeted with an ecstatic affirmation, an affirmation which is a Yes-saying and Amen, and an affirmation which is an inevitable response to our election, and if now it is impossible to believe that we are damned, that can only be because God is damned, and only God is damned, a damnation which we can know only as absolute grace, but a damnation which is nevertheless and even thereby the damnation of God. Yet the damnation of God is the salvation of all, a salvation which is only actual through that very damnation, and if this is a salvation which is the consequence of an eternal election or predestination, that is precisely the election which returns in this damnation, and returns again and again thereafter as a consequence of the damnation of God. That return is apocalypse, and is the apocalypse of Christ, an apocalypse in which guilt has wholly passed into grace, and in which the Almighty has wholly passed into Christ.

So it is that the damnation of God is finally the incarnation of God in Christ, an incarnation that only in the modern world has been known as a total and a final act, and even if that act is at the very center of the New Testament, that is a center which is only known as such by knowing the damnation of God in Christ. Thus damnation is finally greeted as grace, a grace that is everywhere, and is in everybody, and thereby a grace that is grace and is grace alone, and if this is that grace which is the Yes of God, this is that Yes which is the apocalyptic Christ, and therefore the Christ who is all in all. But that Yes is Yes and Yes alone only as the consequence of the total enactment of the No of God in Christ, and if that No actually and fully occurs only in Christ, that is a No releasing the apocalyptic Christ, and a No apart from which the apocalyptic Christ would be unmanifest and therefore unreal. Therefore the Yes of Christ is inseparable from the No of God, and if that No is the eternal act of damnation, the grace of Christ is inseparable from the damnation of Christ, just as salvation is inseparable from damnation, and if the Yes of God in Christ is grace and grace alone, that can only be because the No of God is No and No alone, a No which is realized only in Christ, but a No which eternally is only a Yes, and is eternally only a Yes because it is finally realized only in Christ. Only Christ knows damnation, or only God in Christ knows damnation, and if that damnation is salvation, or that No is Yes, then an ultimate and absolute No is finally and only Yes.

11

Christ and Satan

At no point is Christianity more distinctive or unique than in the ultimacy with which it apprehends and enacts an absolute dichotomy between life and death, or salvation and damnation, or Christ and Satan. Such a dichotomy is found nowhere else in the world, and if that dichotomy is interiorly manifest in the Christian consciousness as an absolute opposition between Spirit and "flesh," it is externally present in the Christian world in an absolute opposition both to heresy and to "idolatry," and if those oppositions have withered away in the modern world, that is but another sign of the end of Christendom. Satan does not truly or fully enter scripture of any kind until the New Testament, and if Jesus is unique among the prophets in having centered his prophetic mission in an assault upon Satan, his followers remembered his miracles as being primarily a consequence of his conflict with Satan. Thus a large body of Christian tradition understands the redemption of Christ as a cosmic victory over Satan. Absolute evil or pure negativity has nowhere so fully been envisioned as it has been in Christianity, and that vision deepened and comprehensively extended itself as Christianity historically evolved, a process that is most clearly manifest in the Christian epic tradition, and as that tradition evolved through Dante, Milton, Blake, and Joyce, its vision of Satan became ever more total, until in *Finnegans Wake* that vision is all in all.

The very first page of *Finnegans Wake* records the eternal fall of Satan, and even if that fall is reversed in the final section of the *Wake*, it nevertheless is the center of the great body of the *Wake*, even as it is the center of the epic visions of Milton and Blake. If Satan is only actually present in the *Commedia* in the conclusion of the *Inferno*, and there is present as a wholly silent and passive negativity, that is a presence which inaugurates the Christian epic tradition. But a witness to the presence of a Satanic negativity becomes comprehensively present with the closure of the medieval world, a negativity which is fully actualized with the birth of modernity, and if that birth is epically enacted in *Paradise Lost*, it here occurs through the epiphany of an absolutely majestic Satan, and a Satan who is known and envisioned for the first time as the polar opposite of Christ, and as the full and actual opposite of Christ. Now Satan realizes in a purely reverse and inverted form every act and identity of the Messiah or the Son of God, as the imperial majesty of Satan in Hell is an inverted form of the monarchic majesty of the Son in Heaven, and even as the Son undergoes a kenotic voyage from Heaven to earth to offer himself in sacrifice for a totally guilty humanity, Satan undergoes a kenotic voyage from Hell to earth where he kenotically empties himself into a serpent so as to tempt and ensnare a totally innocent humanity, and if that destruction of humanity is realized by the enticement of a totally exalted and ecstatic consciousness which is a totally negative consciousness, the salvation of humanity is realized by a passion and a death that is an equally negative act and enactment.

Paradise Lost, even as the *Commedia*, is an interior as well as a cosmic epic, and at no other point are our Christian epics more distant from ancient epics; and the dramatic action of the Christian epic is cosmic and interior at once. Yet it is all too significant that in *Paradise Lost*, interior conflict and dialogue occur only in Satan's domain; its true soliloquies always occur either in Hell or under the direct influence of Satan, for Satan's kingdom is the kingdom of the purely negative consciousness, a consciousness whose very activity and life is a negative movement and energy, and negative above all in its pure negation of itself. But whereas the *Paradiso* can only envision an absolutely exalted and purely transcendent Christ, *Paradise Lost* envisions the Christ of passion, a Son of God who truly and actually dies, and does so at the very center of Satan's domain, a domain which is the kingdom of eternal death, and it is precisely here that the Son and Satan become conjoined, a conjunction which is not only the dramatic center of *Paradise Lost*, but is that conjunction which is the symbolic center of a uniquely modern world. *Paradise Lost* imaginatively realizes that absolutely dichotomous center, and if that center is the historical arena for the realization of a truly new individuality and freedom, that freedom itself is a dichotomous freedom, for even if it is the deepest freedom which had thus far been realized in history, it is also and inevitably so the most profound and ultimate internal bondage which had thus far poetically been spoken.

The poetry of *Paradise Lost* is without parallel in the world in terms of its absolutely exalted and yet absolutely negative power, a poetry which clearly bears the impact of the Shakespearean soliloquy, a soliloquy arising out of a profound interior conflict and dichotomy, which is the very conflict that becomes the cosmic conflict of *Paradise Lost*, and a cosmic conflict which is the consequence of the interior epiphany of a purely negative energy and power, an energy and power that is divided and polarized at its very center, thus making possible a truly new naming of both Satan and Christ. But the name of Christ never occurs in Milton's epic poetry; indeed, in the whole of his poetical works it only occurs in the title of *The Nativity Ode* and in the sonnet protesting against forcing consciences "that Christ set free," and this despite the fact that it occurs innumerable times in his prose, and above all so in *De Doctrina Christiana*. Both in *Paradise Lost* and in *Paradise Regained*, Milton speaks of the Son of God, the Son, or the Messiah, but never of Christ, a fact of extraordinary importance for such a profoundly Christian poet.

The truth is that a truly new Christ is present in Milton's epic poetry, and not simply the "Arian" Christ of the *Doctrina*, but rather a Christ who is at once a fully biblical and a fully modern Christ, and precisely thereby a Christ who is inseparable from Satan. While this is a Christ that is truly present in Luther's thinking, and even more comprehensively present in Jacob Boehme's new and radical vision of the dark or negative potency in the Godhead, imaginatively, this new vision of Christ is not fully manifest or real until *Paradise Lost*, but then it dawns with such power as to profoundly question if not to negate all previous images of Christ.

That pure power of the negative which Hegel philosophically discovered, a power wholly absent from the ancient world, except insofar as it occurs in the darkest moments of Greek tragedy, is a power that does not truly dawn as such in the Western world until the waning of the Middle Ages; there it fully appears in the triptychs of Hieronymus Bosch, these truly embody an epiphany of Satan, and a full epiphany of Satan that is a truly new epiphany. The Satan of *Paradise Lost* is in full continuity with that epiphany, and even if there are no true poetic precedents to Milton's Satan, there are certainly poetic descendents of that Satan, and above all so the epic Satan of Blake.

Yet the mature Blake did that which Milton could never do,

and that is to name God as Satan, a naming that transformed Blake's work and vision, a transformation which realized its culmination in the conclusion of *Jerusalem*, which is nothing less than a realization of a *coincidentia oppositorum* between Christ and Satan. This goes far beyond anything that is present in Goethe's vision, even if it is in continuity with a Hegelian *coincidentia oppositorum*, just as Hegel's conceptual understanding of the emptiness of abstract Spirit and the "Bad Infinite" is in full continuity with Blake's vision of Satan. Indeed, both Hegel's understanding of abstract Spirit and Blake's vision of Satan were initially inspired by the French Revolution, a revolution which Hegel knew as precisely the time in which Spirit is first fully manifest and real in its full and final opposition to and alienation from itself, and thus the French Revolution is not only the historical point at which a universal consciousness first fully and finally becomes actual and real, but also that time which is the decisive ending of all ancient and primordial worlds, for that universal consciousness which was fully born in the French Revolution is inseparable from its counterpart in a new "Unhappy Consciousness," a consciousness which realizes itself by interiorly realizing that *God Himself is dead (Phenomenology of Spirit* 785). Now just as Hegel most intimately associated the French Revolution with a wholly new and wholly impersonal actuality of death, nothing is newer in the Protestant Reformation than Luther's discovery of the ultimacy of the crucifixion, and if this is a new unveiling of the death of Christ, although one fully foreshadowed in late medieval painting, it does not truly or fully enter dogmatic theology until Milton's *De Doctrina Christiana*. Here, Milton declares that Christ is the sacrificial lamb of God who is slain for us, and he must be considered as slain in the whole of his nature (I, xvi), so it is that the Son of God is the redeemer who has freely and fully died, and therefore the Son of God cannot be the fullness of the Godhead. Nevertheless, Milton's Son of God is fully and wholly the redeemer, and he is so by an acceptance of death which was freely and individually his own. That death is an ultimate event, but its occurrence is a free and individual act; therefore it can be "communicated" to its recipients, recipients who become free and individual as a consequence of that act.

Paradise Lost is a celebration of that freedom, a freedom inseparable from an ultimate death, a death that is itself a consequence of the victory of Satan in the Fall, a victory wherein the Creator Himself "hath giv'n up both his beloved Man and all his World to Sin and Death" (X, 488). So it is that the redemption of Christ is inseparable from that victory of Satan, just as the "merit" of the Son of God is inseparable from the "merit" of Satan, and if despair itself uplifts Satan high beyond hope, an exaltation realized by "merit," and an exaltation gloriously and dreadfully arising from his very descent and fall (II, 5–16), the Son of God is declared by the Creator to be exalted in his humiliation, and to be by "merit" more than birthright the Son of God, a merit realized by the Son's offering himself as a sacrifice for a wholly fallen world, and a sacrifice wherein "Love hath abounded more than glory abounds" (III, 12). Indeed, it is the downward and self-destructive or self-emptying movement of fall which actualizes the "merit" of both Satan and the Son, a "merit" which would be unactualized and therefore unreal apart from that movement, and a "merit" which is most integral and individual to the identities of both the Son as Son and Satan as Satan.

Thus it is a full apprehension of the totally kenotic or self-emptying act and actuality of the Son which is inseparable from and necessary to a full apprehension of the totally negative power and actuality of Satan. The Son cannot act as the sacrificial and atoning Son apart from the sovereignty of Satan over a wholly fallen world of death, just as the Son's abandonment of the glory of Heaven is a response to that very exaltation of Satan. The purely negative energy of Milton's Satan can be understood as an imaginative embodiment of that revolutionary political power and will which was released in the English Revolution, and even as the causes and origins of that revolution continue to remain historically inexplicable, the historical origin of a uniquely modern Satan would appear to be an unfathomable mystery, and yet it is surely related to what Goethe envisioned as the Faustian will, a will to absolute power which Nietzsche baptized as the Will to Power, and a will which in this perspective can be understood to be the decisive source of that all too modern discovery of the infinity of the universe, a discovery that was quite simply the origin of modern science. That discovery brought to an end every real distinction between the heavens and the earth. Therein perished the finitude of the world, and if that made possible the conceptual apprehension of a united and unified universe, that is a universe which ever more comprehensively is manifest and real as being wholly alien to an interior and individual center. So it is that a Faustian will is a will to damnation, and even if that will released a virtually infinite power, that power is wholly alienated and estranged from anything whatsoever that once could be known as "soul" or spirit. Hence all too inevitably there arose in its wake a uniquely modern naming of Satan. And that naming is not only a response to a new and revolutionary science, but also a response to a revolutionary economic, social, and political transformation, a transformation that was first decisively present in seventeenth-century England, and there most clearly present in our only poet who was a prophetic political actor and thinker, John Milton.

We know far more about Milton than about any previous poet, and not least because of his major political role in the English Revolution. If that revolution was the first revolution with an apocalyptic aspiration and power, just as it marks the first real political recognition of a common or universal humanity, that is a revolution which both Milton and Cromwell knew as a Christian revolution, and a Christian revolution that inevitably inspired the assault of Satan. Only in revolutionary England was there a triumph of the radical Reformation, and even if that triumph was only momentary and soon reversed, it did make possible the birth of a deeply modern apocalyptic hope, a hope which was transplanted to America, and which would soon appear again in a far different form in revolutionary France.

Yet that hope itself made possible a new naming of Satan, for apocalypticism had always known that Satan or darkness will not fully triumph until the very eve of apocalypse, only then will darkness itself be fully visible, and only then will darkness be truly sovereign throughout the world. That is a sovereignty which Milton knew as did no previous poet, and that is a sovereignty which is a consequence of Milton's apocalyptic hope. And even if he wrote *Paradise Lost* while in a state of political despair, that hope is present in his new vision of Christ, and therefore present in his radically new vision of Satan. For Satan and the Messiah are dialectical opposites in *Paradise Lost*, opposites which had never previously been realized as such in the Christian imagination, for never before had each been envisioned as the true opposite of the other, and if Milton's Christocentrism is an authentic expression of the Reformation, his revolutionary enactment of the totality of Satanic energy and power is the first imaginative realization of the totality of a fallen world which can only truly be known as a fallen world by knowing the apocalyptic victory of Christ. The primary movement in *Paradise Lost* is the movement of fall, and if this first occurs in Satan's expulsion and fall from Heaven, that fall is repeated and renewed in a reverse form in the Son's acceptance and willing of humiliation and death. Each fall is a consequence of a free and individual decision and will, and if Lucifer rebels in revulsion against the enthronement of the Son, an enthronement which to Lucifer establishes a new monarchy in Heaven, and a monarchy eclipsing the angels under an anointed Messiah, that is a rebellion in which Lucifer realizes both the name and the identity of Satan. Thus it is that the original fall is the fall of Satan, a fall wholly occurring by way of a rebellion against an anointed king, an anointed king who is the newly exalted Son, and whose "New Laws" Satan knows as the annulment of an original freedom.

All too significantly, Satan's rebellion therein parallels what conservative England knows as the Great Rebellion, and if Milton was a primary actor in that rebellion as its great propagandist and the leading defender of the trial and execution of Charles I, then Milton is also the great apologist for Satan, for it is only in *Paradise Lost* that one can find a true dramatic enactment of the rebellion and fall of Satan, and not simply a dramatic enactment but a glorious enactment, and therefore, inevitably, an exaltation of Satan. But even as Lucifer only becomes Satan by rebelling against a new Messiah, the Son only realizes his "merit" as Son by abasing himself in response to the inevitable victory of Satan over humanity; therein he abandons his kingship and glory in Heaven, an act of humiliation or self-emptying which embodies in a reverse form the purely negative glory and energy of Satan, so that Satan's monarchic sovereignty in Hell is inverted in the Son's free and sacrificial acceptance of incarnation and crucifixion, an incarnation and crucifixion which is a full and total reversal of the Son's rule and glory in Heaven. Nothing like this is present in the Christian tradition, but that tradition as such had never known a Son of God who truly and fully dies, and if Milton was the first dogmatic theologian to know that death, Milton was inevitably the poet who exalted Satan, an exaltation that is a necessary response to a deep and comprehensive realization of the ultimacy of death. For only a fully sovereign Satan could be the ground of that death; that sovereignty is a sovereignty over a wholly fallen world, a world whose very center is eternal death. Moreover, that death alone makes possible the kenotic or self-emptying movement of the Son. Consequently, to know the full actualization of the self-emptying of the Son is to know the sovereignty of Satan, a sovereignty which is first dramatically enacted and imaginatively envisioned in *Paradise Lost*, and a sovereignty apart from which there could be no apocalyptic victory of Christ.

Accordingly, the epic poet Milton cannot pronounce the name of Christ, or cannot pronounce the given and traditional name of Christ, because he knows a truly new Christ, a Christ who fully and wholly died in the crucifixion and therefore a Christ who is truly a victim of Satan's sovereign power, and thereby a Christ who therein is inseparable from that power.

Aquinas could speak for the ancient Christian tradition as a whole in asserting that Christ's passion did not concern or affect his Godhead, for God's nature eternally remains impassible, and can neither be wounded nor suffer any change, so Christ only suffered in his "lower powers"; his "higher reason" did not suffer thereby, and Christ's soul suffered only insofar as it was allied with the body of Jesus (*Summa Theologica* III, 46, 8–12). This was the tradition that Milton revolutionized in *De Doctrina Christiana*; and if Milton, too, could only know an eternally impassive God, that led him to the inevitable conclusion that the Father and the Son differ from each other in essence, and above all so because Christ "totally died," a death that is the consequence of self-emptying, and a self-emptying that would be "impossible" for a God who is only infinite and eternal.

That infinite and eternal God is the absolutely transcendent God, and whereas in the *Doctrina* the Creator produced all things not out of nothing but only out of Himself, and Christ is the beginning of God's creation—which can only mean that he was the first of the things which God created (I, vii)—in *Paradise Lost* the Father retires in the act of creation, a retirement necessitating that the creation be "by" the Word or the temporally generated Son (VII, 163–173). No deeper difference exists between the *Doctrina* and *Paradise Lost*, a difference surely occasioned by a far more profound understanding of the ultimacy of death and the fall, which was possible for the epic poet but not for the dogmatic theologian. It is just because the Father knows the inevitable destiny of the fall that He must retire in the act of creation. If here, too, Milton is a profound theological innovator, that is because Milton knows the totality of death and the fall as did no previous theologian; nor was such a knowledge possible before the full advent of the modern world, an advent which only occurs in the seventeenth century.

Now the heavens themselves have vanished from view, and in *Paradise Lost* only the prefallen universe embodies an integral and harmonious order, for even if this is the universe which is celebrated in the great body of the poem, it is a lost universe, and lost as a consequence of the universal movement of fall. But that loss makes possible the epiphany of a new Christ, a Christ who totally dies and therefore a fully kenotic or self-emptying Christ. While that Christ was known by Luther, it was not dogmatically known by Luther, because at this crucial point Luther could not or would not break away from the dogmatic authority of the ancient Church. Only the radical Reformation did that, a radical Reformation which does not truly realize its theological voice until Milton, and does not fully realize that voice until the prophetic and epic poetry of Blake.

At no point is Blake more fully Miltonic than in his realization of the totality of fall and death, but now that fall and death comprehends Godhead itself, a comprehension impossible in the seventeenth century but all but inevitable by the nineteenth century, a century which was inaugurated by the French Revolution. Blake is the epic poet of both the French and the American revolutions, and thus the epic poet of the death of God, but here that death is an apocalyptic death, and an apocalyptic death culminating in the total realization of Jerusalem or the apocalyptic Christ. Nothing is more decisive in Blake's epic poetry than a full correlation between the death of a purely alien and negative Creator and the "Self-Annihilation" of Jesus the Christ.

> Jesus said: "Wouldest thou love one who never dies
> For thee, or ever die for one who had not died for thee.
> And if God dieth not for Man & giveth not himself
> Eternally for Man Man could not exist; for Man is Love:
> As God is love: every kindness to another is a little Death
> In the Divine Image nor can Man exist but by Brotherhood."
>
> (*Jerusalem* 96:23–28)

Indeed, only the "Self-Annihilation" of Christ makes manifest the Satanic or purely negative identity of the Creator; now an ultimate and absolute passion and life is wholly and only a kenotic or sacrificial passion and life, so that a Godhead which is isolated and apart from that sacrificial passion is finally and only Satan. Yet a Blakean or fully and totally apocalyptic Satan is inseparable from a totally apocalyptic Christ, for Satan is that Godhead which dies or is "Self-Annihilated" in Christ. Only that self-negation or self-emptying makes manifest and real the pure negativity of the Godhead, a negativity that is true negativity only as a consequence of the crucifixion.

Now this is the very identity of the crucifixion that Hegel conceptually realized at the very time when Blake was creating his mature vision, and for Hegel as for Blake, evil is the withdrawal into self-centeredness, a withdrawal which *from the beginning* occurs in the "externalization" and "alienation" of the divine Being, for Absolute Being becomes its own "other," and thereby it withdraws into itself and becomes self-centered or "evil"; but this is that self-alienation which yields to death, a death which is the death of the abstraction or alienation or "evil" of the divine Being (*Phenomenology of Spirit*, 778–780).

Nothing is more revolutionary in Blake and Hegel than their apprehension of the death of God. While this had never previously occurred in either poetic vision or philosophical thinking, it occurs now only by way of an apprehension of the totality of pure negativity, but a totality which is a dialectical totality and therefore a totality in which negativity negates itself. This negation of negation is the negation of Satan or the wholly abstract and self-alienated God. Christ is the Christian name of that self-negation or self-emptying, and therefore the name of Christ is inseparable from the name of Satan, and if this dual naming of Christ and Satan already occurs in *Paradise Lost*, that could only be because *Paradise Lost* embodies the totality of the fall, a fall that finally can be known as the fall or death of God. It was just because Milton could not know that fall that he could not know the Godhead of Christ, and so likewise no modern philosopher earlier than Schelling and Hegel could know that Godhead, for that is a Godhead that only can be known by knowing Satan, and by knowing Satan as the total self-alienation and self-estrangement of God. Yet that Satan is absolutely necessary and essential to the self-emptying of God in Christ, for apart from that Satan there could be no real and actual self-emptying or self-negation of God, and hence no real or actual apocalyptic or self-annihilating Christ.

That Milton could so deeply know Satan is a decisive sign of his knowledge of the apocalyptic or kenotic Christ, and the continuity between the epic poetry of Milton and Blake is a decisive sign of the continuity between the imaginative Satans of the seventeenth and the nineteenth centuries; but these are imaginative Satans which embody the historical worlds of their centuries, and therefore these Satans are both historically and actually real.

If the modern Church cannot know Satan, that is but another sign of the alienation of the modern Church from both history and reality. Only in the twentieth century has there been a truly comprehensive epiphany of Satan, an epiphany realized not only in the horrors of the twentieth century, which are unique horrors in history, but also in the imagination of the twentieth century, and above all so in the twin epics of the twentieth century, *Ulysses* and *Finnegans Wake*. Those epics are in full continuity with their epic predecessors, and most clearly so in their visions of Satan, for even if Satan is as silent and impassive in *Ulysses* as he is in the *Inferno*, *Ulysses* does initiate us into that Christ who is Satan, a Christ who is "God becomes man becomes fish," and who is now a nameless or anonymous Christ.

> Come. I thirst. Clouding over. No black clouds anywhere, are
> there? Thunderstorm. Allbright he falls, proud lightning of the
> intellect, *Lucifer, dico, qui nescit occasum*. No. My cockle hat and
> staff and his my sandal shoon. To evening lands. Evening will
> find itself. (Modern Library edition, 50)

Christ here and now becomes indistinguishable from that Lucifer
who falls and yet knows no fall, and if Joyce's Latin phrase is
borrowed from a phrase in the Roman Catholic liturgy for Holy
Saturday, that is because Joyce wholly knows the fall as a
fortunate fall, a fortunate fall which is the very plot or action of
both *Ulysses* and *Finnegans Wake*. The very first pages to be written
of *Finnegans Wake*, 380 through 382, eventually became the
conclusion of Book II, chapter iii, which is both the central or
axial chapter of the *Wake* and also the most difficult and complex
section of this dream or night epic. But the virtually literal center
of the earliest writing in the *Wake* is a divine acceptance of
death—*I've a terrible errible lot todue todie todue tootorribleday*—a death
which is not only the center of a historically cosmic Holy Week,
but which is reenacted again and again throughout the course of
this epic. A constantly repeated prayer in the *Wake* is a prayer for
sleep—"Grant sleep in hour's time, O Loud!" (259.4)—a sleep
which is the deepest sleep in the "Ainsoph" or En Sof, the mystical
Godhead of this Christian Kabbalah. Yet arising from the center
of this sleeping Godhead is original sin or "original sun," a
"felicitous culpability" or *felix culpa*, and a *felix culpa* which this epic
poet derives from "*Hearsay in paradox lust*" (263). Original sin in
the *Wake* evolves into a full and total linguistic actuality, an
actuality which is cosmic and historical and exterior and interior
at once, and an actuality which is the cosmic sacrifice of the
Godhead. Therein and thereby Godhead itself is the self-
emptying or self-negation of God, a self-emptying which occurs in
every act and voice of this epic, until it is finally consummated in
the resurrection of Anna Livia Plurabelle, a resurrection which
absorbs the power of the Godhead.

> So. Avelaval. My leaves have drifted from me. All. But one clings
> still. I'll bear it on me. To remind me of. Lff! So soft this
> morning, ours. Yes. (628.6–9)

Accordingly, the final "Yes" of *Ulysses* culminates in a "Yes" or
"Lff!" which is all in all, and all in all in a cosmic crucifixion
which is finally a cosmic resurrection, even if inevitably this is a
cosmic act which is a dream act, and therefore an absolute
reversal of the totality of our history.

No writing as such rivals the deep and ultimate authority which is present in true epic, an ultimate authority which is undeniable, or undeniable in terms of the revolutionary historical transformation which it either embodies or effects. The Christian epic alone is exterior and interior at once, and the transformations which are realized in its narrative movement are simultaneously realized in the interior of its reader, so that the reader is called to actually enact that which is read; and that enactment is a primary source of the authority of the epic. So it is that the Christian epic is a form of the eucharist or the mass, and there is a "real presence" in that epic which is a eucharistic presence, and a eucharistic presence which is a eucharist consecration, and a consecration which is most openly and comprehensively present in *Finnegans Wake*. Then the eucharist of the Church becomes the eucharist of the world, or the *missa solemnis* becomes the *missa jubilaea*, and the breaking of the body of Christ becomes the full realization of death and chaos throughout history and the cosmos alike, a chaos which is the totality of eternal death, and therefore the totality of the body of Satan. Now Christ and Satan are fully and wholly one, and if that *coincidentia oppositorum* is initially realized in the final epic poetry of Blake, it is consummated in *Ulysses* and *Finnegans Wake*, and consummated in that final union of Christ and Satan which is the very Godhead of God. Or, rather, it is the apocalyptic Godhead of God, and even if the Creator is now fully and wholly present as Satan, that Satan is the presence of the apocalyptic Christ, and the final and total presence of the apocalyptic Christ.

If Hegel was the first and the last thinker who could truly know history as theodicy, that providential totality has passed into its very opposite in our world. Now a fully visible darkness and an eternal death are all in all, and all in all in that apocalyptic Satan who is the deep sleep of the Godhead, a sleep in which cosmos itself is chaos, and a chaos which is spoken in a uniquely contemporary language, a language which is the language of *Finnegans Wake*. But that language is truly and fully language, therefore it is "Lff," a language which speaks us, and thus a language in which our deep sleep is awake. The first word of the Saviour in *Jerusalem* is "Awake!", and it is addressed to the sleeper in Ulro or Hell, a sleeper who is enslaved to the body of Satan, a body which is now the body of the absolutely alien God. But that alien body of God is the consequence of the crucifixion, and in the last poetry that Blake was to give to the world, contained on the two plates of *The Ghost of Abel*, Satan arises from death and addresses Jehovah: "Thou shalt Thyself be Sacrificed to Me, thy God, on Calvary." To this, Jehovah thunders, and replies:

> "Such is My Will that Thou Thyself go to Eternal Death In Self Annihilation, even till Satan, Self-subdu'd, Put off Satan into the Bottomless Abyss . . ."

Compressed as these lines are, they contain the dual theme that God must be sacrificed to Satan in the crucifixion, and that Satan must therein and thereby be self-annihilated and forever perish as Satan. Nothing could more succinctly state the plot or action of *Finnegans Wake*, and if this is the deepest reality of our history, and a reality that we can know only when we are deeply asleep, that is a reality in which the fall is finally a fortunate fall, and therefore Satan is finally Christ.

12

Apocalypse

The proclamation and enactment of the dawning of the Kingdom of God is the very center of the synoptic Gospels, a center which is present in eschatological and parabolic enactment, and a center which is nothing less than the full and final incarnation of God. That incarnation has always been the deepest scandal of Christianity, a scandal which is not only an ultimate offense, but an ultimate offense which is the absolute paradox. Kierkegaard is the thinker who most purely apprehended that paradox; and even if this is a deeply Lutheran apprehension, it is not until Kierkegaard that an absolute paradox is manifest and real which is a universal paradox, a paradox inevitably and necessarily present in every expression of inwardness or "subjectivity," and necessarily present if only because of the full and total triumph of objectivity in a uniquely modern consciousness and society. At no point was Kierkegaard more Hegelian than in his understanding of objectivity, and if a total objectivity is a consequence of the historical realization of the death of God, it is that objectivity which makes possible a purely "subjective" faith, a faith that then can only be grounded in a pure or absolute paradox. That is the very paradox which is the paradox of the incarnation. A Kierkegaardian contemporaneity is a contemporaneity with that paradox, and if here contemporaneity with Christ demands a leap over two millennia of our history, that is because here our history must necessarily be known and realized as the reversal of the incarnation.

While innumerable forms of sectarian Christianity have always known such a reversal, it is only in the modern world that a historical reversal of the incarnation has become manifest and real as a comprehensive reversal, thus necessitating a purely subjective faith, or a faith that is the faith of the Church alone, and even if a Kierkegaardian faith is a purely individual faith, that faith is a consequence of the end of Christendom. So it is that in his final hour, Kierkegaard could publicly declare that the Christianity of the New Testament no longer exists, for Christianity has become exactly the opposite of what it is in the New Testament. Nevertheless, this was precisely the situation that gave birth to a uniquely modern form of faith, and a faith that could know the totality of the incarnation as it had never been known before, even if that apprehension is inseparable from a realization of either the death of God or the end of Christendom. Only then did historical scholarship unveil the apocalyptic ground of the New Testament in the eschatological proclamation and enactment of the dawning of the Kingdom of God, a Kingdom of God which is all in all, and thus a Kingdom of God which is at an infinite distance from the traditional Christian dogma of the absolute transcendence of God. This is the earthquake that twentieth-century theology has known as the eschatological scandal, the scandal of realizing that Christianity is most distant from its origin precisely in its deepest theological affirmation, an affirmation that is a negation of the deepest ground of the New Testament.

There is a profoundly paradoxical relationship between Hegelian and Kierkegaardian thinking, for even as Hegelian thinking and only Hegelian thinking made Kierkegaardian thinking possible, Kierkegaard profoundly negated that Hegelian ground; this is a truly Hegelian negation that simultaneously occurs in Marx, and a paradoxical negation that is also present in Kierkegaard's radically new understanding of time and history. If Kierkegaard was the first thinker to effect a full dialectical negation of history, that negation is inseparable from a Hegelian understanding of history as the self-embodiment of God. If only Hegelian thinking truly and fully knows history as theodicy, only Kierkegaardian thinking knows history as a reverse or inverted theodicy, for here and here alone history is the real absence and the real negation of God. Such an understanding of history is wholly different from a Gnostic or "spiritual" negation of history, for it apprehends history not simply as the otherness of God or Spirit, but rather as the real and actual negation of God, a negation which is a real negation, and therefore a Hegelian negation, for it is realized in an ultimate act and actuality.

A profoundly self-lacerating Kierkegaard knew that actuality, and knew it at the very center of his own uniquely individual consciousness—a center which is fully manifest both in his journals and in the great bulk of his pseudonymous publications—and that is an individual center which became a universal center in the deepest interior expressions of the world of late modernity. But the darkness of that vision is not a Gnostic or a dualistic darkness, for it is closed to every actual expression of light, and so closed because of the full and final actuality of the darkness which it knows, a darkness which now comprehends everything which was once actually manifest as light.

Yet this new darkness of the center of consciousness is a darkness which ends every real and actual center; now not only has an interior center disappeared or become anonymous, but the very possibility of center as such has ended. With the triumph of twentieth-century physics and astronomy there can no longer be an apprehension of the center of the universe, or even a knowing mind or subject which is truly distinct from the object of knowledge, thus ending that subject which is the subject of an objective consciousness. Thereby the ending of the center of consciousness is a comprehensive ending, and thus an apocalyptic ending, an ending which is the ending of the world or horizon of every center or subject, as an anonymous consciousness is now becoming all in all.

All the great prophetic thinkers and visionaries of the nineteenth century deeply knew and unveiled the necessity and inevitability of that ending, and just as this is true of Kierkegaard, so likewise is it true of Marx and Nietzsche, but it is only in the imaginative expressions of late modernity that an apocalyptic ending fully realizes a reverse or inverted cosmos or world, and so much so that now chaos and cosmos are indistinguishable, and each is itself only insofar as it is the other. So, far from shrinking the cosmos that once was present in the Western imagination, this uniquely modern or postmodern *coincidentia oppositorum* has extended our cosmos into a new infinity in which cosmos and chaos are identical. But that new infinity can perhaps more aptly be named as a *new nothingness*, a nothingness not visible or nameable until Nietzsche, and a nothingness which is the true and actual ending of our cosmos or world, so that what is most distinctive in the imagination of late modernity is not the absence of the name of God but rather the absence of any actual naming of the world as world.

Not only is the twentieth century the site of the end of nature, and the end of nature in a radically new and ever more total technology, but the end of a nature that is present to and in consciousness, and thus the ending of a nature that can be known or envisioned as nature or world. Now even if no such world or nature is present in an archaic or primordial consciousness, such an undifferentiated consciousness could be open to a horizon which is its own horizon or world, whereas it is horizon itself which has ended in our consciousness and society, and ended as a horizon which is the limit of consciousness. That ending is the advent of a new nothingness, a nothingness that is not beyond our horizon but rather *is* our horizon, and is our horizon because horizon has disappeared, and with that disappearance there is no longer a real distinction between the without and the within, or the exterior and the interior, or macrocosm and microcosm.

While it may well be true that all such distinctions wholly disappear in the deepest expressions of mysticism throughout the world, historically those expressions have been confined to a deeply interior realm, whereas we are being initiated into a disappearance of all those distinctions in our everyday realm, a realm in which there is no real distinction between the public and the private, or society and the individual, or the unconscious and consciousness. If a political totalitarianism is unique to the twentieth century, now we are coming to see that such a totalitarianism is only an initial totalitarianism, only the beginning of a far more comprehensive totalitarianism, a totalitarianism so total that it will be invisible and unheard as totalitarian. Consequently, that new infinity or that new nothingness which is being realized in our midst confronts us with a paradox that is an absolute paradox, for every deep and given difference that we have known is all too rapidly withering away, a disappearance wholly coinciding with apocalyptic and mystical visions of the end of every real and intrinsic otherness; and yet the new totality here being born is manifestly the very opposite of an apocalyptic new aeon or a mystical Emptiness or Godhead.

Nietzsche could greet eternal recurrence with an ecstatic Yes and Amen, just as Joyce could pronounce and enact an epic and total Yes to the advent of Here Comes Everybody, but all such ecstatic celebration has disappeared in our time and world, for it is precisely Yes as Yes which no longer can be pronounced. Even if that absence is also the absence of a deep and radical No which is only No, it is naming as such which is now wholly eroding, and a wholly inactive passivity which would appear to be our destiny, a passivity which is a cosmic or even an eternal death. While it is true that apocalyptic and mystical vision have given us our deepest images of the totality of an absolutely alien otherness, an alien otherness that quite simply is identical with all given and manifest forms of consciousness, here that total otherness is inseparable from its absolute reversal, whether by way of an apocalyptic end of the world or a mystical reversal of consciousness. Yet now we are ever more deeply and finally coming to know an alien nothingness that is absolutely irreversible, and irreversible precisely because it is a full and actual nothingness, a nothingness that is not the hither side or pole of a mystical nirvana or an apocalyptic Kingdom of God, but a nothingness that is an actual emptiness, and a fully actual emptiness, with no reverberations whatsoever beyond its immediate sounding.

It is true that an apocalyptic faith knows damnation or the absolutely impotent and negative will only by knowing the triumph of the advent of the Kingdom of God, just as Buddhism knows an absolutely empty and illusory consciousness only by knowing the peace and plenitude of Emptiness, so that here there is a real coincidence of darkness and light, a *coincidentia oppositorum* which is a totality of grace. But that is a *coincidentia oppositorum* which, if present at all for us, can only be so in a wholly inverted or reverse form, for while we are coming to know the depths of chaos and emptiness, peace and joy have wholly disappeared, and disappeared precisely in our realization of our deeper depths, and if that realization is carrying us into a new infinity, that infinity is all too unspeakable to us, and unspeakable just because of its very presence. Nor is ours a silence that is truly comparable to a Buddhist silence; indeed, it is its very opposite, for ours is a silence that is indistinguishable from noise, and unlike that chaos which is the language of *Finnegans Wake*, ours is ever increasingly a language whose interior violence is realized and expressed by way of an abstract and electronic modulation, a modulation that is the very silence of speech itself, but nevertheless and exactly thereby a silence that is the full opposite of an original or integral silence.

Yes, ours is an apocalyptic time and world, for it is certainly a time and world of ending, and of ultimate and final ending, but ours is the ending of an apocalyptic joy and hope, or the ending of a plenitude that is nameable as grace, and if center as center has wholly disappeared, ours is a circumference or periphery whose center is nowhere. That nowhere is ours, indeed; but it is not a liberated nowhere, not a nowhere or a circle of eternal recurrence which can be celebrated and affirmed with an ecstatic joy, for it is a nowhere which is not anywhere, and just as a full affirmation of any kind is ever more fully being drawn into an irrecoverable past, Yes-saying and No-saying as such are wholly passing away, and passing into an unspeakable domain which transcends even a naming of Satan.

If we can no longer name Satan, we surely cannot name Christ, for when darkness is unspeakable light is unspeakable as well, and if darkness and light are now unspeakable, that is an unspeakability which speaks in evoking a new nothingness, a new nothingness that is actually present, and actually present as a center which is uniquely our own. For that is a center which we are knowing and realizing to be our own, and if it is an apocalyptic or mystical center, it is so only insofar as it is a negative or empty center, a center which is the center of nothing whatsoever, but precisely thereby a center which is everywhere. Just as we know a Nietzsche or a Joyce to be our precursors, we are ever increasingly knowing them as far distant precursors, and perhaps even as distant as Kierkegaard and Blake. And just as Blake and Kierkegaard are far distant from Milton and Dante, the very totality of our history is disappearing into an irrecoverable past, an irrecoverability that would appear to be irreversibly present, and irreversibly present in a total presence that is a total absence or void. Even as the Christian world dawned as an irreversible negation of all previous worlds and horizons, a new world is now dawning which is an irreversible negation of our history, and if each such dawning is an apocalyptic dawning, that is a dawning which is dawning and ending at once, so that the totality of dawning is inseparable from the totality of ending, an ending that is an inevitable necessity of apocalyptic dawning itself.

Can we speak or evoke the ultimacy and finality of incarnation in our apocalyptic ending? That would certainly appear to be impossible, and not only because of the empty or inverted silence of our speech, but far more so because the very identity of incarnation is an identity of total grace, and even if the incarnation is the absolute paradox, that is a paradox that could only be present to us in a wholly reverse and inverted form; and if we no longer can follow Blake and Joyce in finally knowing Satan as an ultimately liberated joy, nor follow Milton and Kierkegaard in deeply and interiorly knowing Christ as that kenotic Servant who wholly and finally consumes our darkness and guilt, then an absolute paradox to us must surely lie beyond any actual naming of either Satan or Christ.

If *Ulysses* is the epic inauguration of a uniquely modern ending, it is so most clearly in its realization of an anonymous consciousness and society and an anonymous Christ. Now every name and voice is a universal name and voice, a universality which is interior and exterior at once, and so much so that now there is no real distinction between either cosmos and consciousness or Christ and the world. Thereby the name of Christ is unspeakable as such. This unspeakability begins with Milton, but is only consummated in Joyce, and not only in Joyce but in both the imaginative and the conceptual worlds of the twentieth century. But if Christ is unspeakable for us, then so, too, a truly and uniquely individual voice is unspeakable, and if both interior and individual presence have ever more comprehensively disappeared in our painting and literature, that is a disappearance which is the disappearance of a human world and face, so that our world has ever more fully and more finally become an anonymous world, and therewith a world in which an interior and individual voice is silent.

That world can both be understood and enacted as a totally anonymous society, a society in which the only real presence is an anonymous presence, and the only real actor and power is a totally anonymous power, and a power that no longer can be named as the Will to Power, if only because will as such is no longer manifest and real, or no longer can be real as anything which is truly within. Now our world is a totality as it has never been so before, but a totality from which we are absent, or absent as individual and interior wills, or as wills which can actually know either freedom or bondage. The disappearance of an interior freedom and bondage is the dissolution of self-consciousness, the erosion or annulment of that "I" or center of consciousness which is first manifest in Paul, and thence ever more comprehensively becomes the center of a uniquely Western consciousness and society. If the ending of that center is the ending of that Western world, that is the ending of a uniquely Western Christ, and therewith the ending of a uniquely Western God. Neither God nor Christ can be pronounced or evoked in our uniquely contemporary language, so that contemporaneity with Christ can be for us only a contemporaneity with either an absence or a void—unless that very void is for us the deepest manifestation or epiphany of Christ—a void that no longer can be named as either Christ or Satan, for ours is an unnameable void, just as ours is a humanly or interiorly unnameable world.

Yet we are ever increasingly knowing such a void to be our deepest source and ground, and if ground itself could once be named as the creation, now we can know our actual beginning to be the beginning of an abyss, and the beginning of an abyss or nothingness which is an ultimate even if unnameable power, and nothing so evokes the ultimacy and finality of our nothingness as does its very unnameability. That nihilism which was first known by Nietzsche to be our destiny is a nihilism now so comprehensive that it no longer can be named or known as such. Nevertheless, it is evoked and embodied in our every real and actual act, and is most clearly manifest as such in the very disappearance of a uniquely human face and voice. Perhaps something like this disappearance is present in an original Buddhism, a Buddhism negating all images and all interior language, but realizing therein a pure freedom or liberation, a liberation which is a liberation from any possible otherness, and a liberation which is perhaps apocalyptically manifest in the end of the world. While we know that the apocalyptic symbol of the end of the world is present as the very center of an original Christianity, neither Christian imagery nor Christian thinking has ever succeeded in fully or decisively evoking or naming that eschaton or apocalypse. While Buddhism succeeded in coming to know nirvana or Emptiness as an emptiness that is all in all, Christianity has never succeeded in knowing or envisioning an apocalypse that is all in all, unless that has occurred in an all too modern imagination, and there occurred by way of a ground in an absolutely anonymous society and world. If our world is truly empty of an interior center or ground, and even empty of a center or axis of any kind, that is a centerlessness which is truly an abyss, and certainly an abyss which is truly empty of all which we once knew as world, so at the very least we have been initiated into the end of everything which was once our world.

That is an apocalyptic condition and situation, but it could be far more than that, for it may well be the final ending of everything whatsoever which is nameable or realizable as world, and therefore the end of the world as world, or the end of any possible world which is present and actual as world. Such an ending would also be the ending of any possible Christ who is Christ and only Christ, and not only the ending of any form of Christ which is present in our historical past, but also the ending of a Christ who is nameable as Christ, or a Christ who can be known or be envisioned as a Christ who is present or active in the world, for if world itself is no longer nameable, then neither is a Christ who is the redeemer of the world, or a Christ who is the alpha and omega of the world. All too naturally, the Christian in our world has been driven to a Gnostic or spiritual Christ, a Christ who is the dualistic other of the world itself, and thus a Christ who is totally independent of and totally unaffected by ours or any world, and thereby a Christ who can only appear or be manifest with the dissolution of the world. But a Gnostic dissolution of the world is wholly other than an apocalyptic end of the world, for such a Gnostic dissolution is simply a turning away from the world as world, a dualistic withdrawal from the world, whereas an apocalyptic ending is the actual ending of the world as world, an ending which is the ending of world itself, and therefore the ending of any possible dualism or otherness. Our world in its very anonymity would appear to be the ending of any possible dualism, and the disappearance of dualism is the disappearance of otherness; but that disappearance is precisely the disappearance of ourselves, the disappearance of our interiors as the otherness of the world, and the disappearance of our unique and individual "I" as the otherness of an objective universality, for the disappearance of the world as world is inevitably and necessarily the disappearance of everything whatsoever which is the otherness of that world.

If this is apocalypse, it is an apocalypse of death and only of death, and not simply an apocalypse that only can be named as death, but rather an apocalypse that only can be realized as death. A contemporary Gnosticism is a flight from that apocalypse, or a flight from an overwhelmingly interior actuality of death as death, and death as an ultimate or eternal death, a death whose very unspeakability is the unspeakability of death, an unspeakability which is the unspeakability of our interior depths, which now are speakable only as either the absence or the abyss of any truly interior domain or realm. While that is certainly an interior apocalypse of death, is it a total apocalypse of death, a total apocalypse in which life and death are one, even as life and death are one in an original apocalypticism? This is the decisive question to be asked of our apocalypticism, and if we have come to know that an original apocalyptic proclamation and enactment is not a proclamation of the name of Christ—for now we can know that Jesus neither proclaimed himself as Messiah nor even employed the name of Messiah in his parabolic enactment and eschatological proclamation—then is the absence of the nameability of Christ for us, and, indeed, the absence of all nameability whatsoever, an absence that is a necessary and inevitable absence for a full and total apocalyptic enactment?

Just as the full advent of a universal consciousness has ended a uniquely Western and Christian world, has the full advent of apocalypse ended any Christ who is nameable as Christ, an ending which is the ending of a grace which is grace alone? If we can know an ultimate and total death that is nevertheless and even thereby an ultimate and total life, we must necessarily know that life as unspeakable, or speakable at most as the "Lff" of *Finnegans Wake*, and even if that "Lff" is unpronounceable, it nevertheless is evoked, and is evoked in response to an ultimate and unspeakable abyss. Yet that abyss can be and has been named as "Lff," and not only in *Finnegans Wake*, but in every full enactment of a uniquely contemporary imagination, and that naming is naming and unnaming at once, an unnaming which is a full and actual silence, but nevertheless a silence which is a total presence, and a totally actual presence. Thus our uniquely contemporary silence is not a silence which is unheard or invisible, but far rather a silence which is horizon or world itself, and world itself in its very fullness and finality as abyss.

If we are incapable of pronouncing the name of Christ in response to our abyss, that very incapacity could be a decisive sign of the full presence of apocalypse, and the full presence of apocalypse in our abyss, a presence that necessarily and inevitably must end every other presence, and thus must end every act and identity which we have known and named. For a total presence that is an apocalyptic presence must not simply erase but rather reverse any and every possible presence, so that every presence itself is now not simply absence but rather abyss, and if that abyss is overwhelmingly present in what was once manifest and real as an interior domain, that interior domain has itself undergone a reversal, a reversal in which our interior is now becoming manifest as a macrocosm, but a macrocosm which is pure chaos, or which is surely chaos from the perspective of what was once manifest as our interior. Thus insofar as we can continue to speak we can only speak of our world as chaos. Yet the very naming of chaos remains a genuine naming, a naming which itself is now fully paradoxical, and fully paradoxical in its transformation of the silence of chaos into speech, and if that for us is an absolute paradox, it is a paradox that we live in every actual moment, and a paradox that is fully present in that chaos which we can so decisively know to be our own. For to know that chaos as our own is to know absolute otherness as our own; that is certainly an absolute paradox, and an absolute paradox that is for us an inevitable paradox, for only thereby can we continue to act or to speak.

Accordingly, the hearing of abyss as abyss and only as abyss is itself the consequence of grace, and a liberating grace, a grace that liberates us from everything that can no longer be a source of grace, and no longer a source of grace if grace itself is now all in all, an all in allness that must inevitably and necessarily end every grace which is other than itself, and thus must end every grace and every form of grace which is manifest as grace and as grace alone. That grace must perish before grace itself can be all in all, just as Christ must perish before Christ can be all in all, and just as God has perished so that God will be all in all. If our apocalypse is a realization or fulfillment of an original dawning of the Kingdom of God, it could be so only as an absolute paradox, the paradox of a Kingdom of God that is the absolute

inversion or reversal of itself, a reversal manifest in the reversal of an original joy and hope, and likewise manifest in the
reversal of any possible Heaven. Now apocalypse is manifest
and real only as itself, and if such an epiphany is necessarily an
epiphany of abyss, it must necessarily void and erase every
previous identity or naming of apocalypse or grace. If now
apocalypse is *ipsum esse*, then every other *esse* is empty or void, a
voidness which is the inevitable consequence of the fullness of
apocalypse. That act of being which once could be named as
God is now manifest only as abyss, but as an apocalyptic abyss,
and therefore as an abyss comprehending everything which was
once manifest as the acts of God.

Now those acts can only be one act of God, apocalypse itself,
and if that is the eternal act of God, that act is an incarnation
indistinguishable from creation, just as creation is now indistinguishable from crucifixion, and crucifixion is indistinguishable
from apocalypse itself. Full apocalypse could be no less than
this, and if that is an apocalypse initially embodied in an
enactment of the dawning of the Kingdom of God, that is an
apocalypse which must finally realize itself as creation, incarnation, and apocalypse at once. If that realization is an absolute
paradox, that is a paradox which must inevitably appear as a
total abyss, and a total abyss which is a full reversal of everything
standing outside of or apart from this very abyss. Then nothing
whatsoever is nameable or realizable as itself, and if creation is
then manifest as chaos, and a chaos which is total abyss, that
chaos itself is totality, and a totality comprehending everything
which was once named as the acts of God. Now even if those acts
were named or revealed by the Godhead, so those acts are real
in the self-emptying or self-negation of Godhead itself, a
self-negation or self-emptying which could only culminate in
the absolute reversal of the Godhead, a reversal which is a final
apocalypse, and a final apocalypse of the eternal act of God.
That act is the act of Godhead itself, but only as a full reversal of
the Godhead, a reversal which must necessarily and finally end
every potency or echo of a once and for all and irreversible
beginning. While such a pure apocalypse would appear to be
wholly absent from our consciousness, we have come to know an
ending of any possible or actual beginning, as beginning itself is
wholly absent as a possibility for us, and even if that absence is
an inescapable abyss, it nevertheless is even thereby an ending
of every way which is not a way into chaos, and of every voice
which is not a voice of abyss. Apocalyptically envisioned, that
ending is grace, and is a total grace which necessarily must be
absent in anything which is nameable as grace.

So it is that Christ is not a name that can be actually spoken by us, unless it is spoken by a naming of Satan which names a total abyss, but even that naming must perish in a full realization of abyss, for that abyss is unspeakable, unless it is speakable as a nameless abyss. Then the dissolution of naming could well be an embodiment of abyss, and an embodiment of that abyss which is finally apocalypse, just as it could equally be an embodiment of death which is death and eternal death alone. Yet, apocalyptically envisioned, eternal death is eternal life, and if that *coincidentia oppositorum* is at the center of an original apocalyptic enactment, and even at the center of the act of creation itself, that is a center which must finally pass into an absolute centerlessness, a centerlessness which is inevitable in a universal or final apocalypse, and therefore a centerlessness which is finally all in all. That all in all could interiorly only be known as death, and as eternal death, an eternal death that is a final ending, and the final ending of everything that is either within or without.

Now we have reached or are reaching that eschatological end which is either life or death, and now nothing whatsoever ultimately or actually distinguishes life from death, so that there is no way by which we can choose either life or death, or no way by which we can be assured or certain that life is life and death is death. Even if this is a confrontation which ends the individual and interior will, that is an ending which is the ending of every unique and individual identity, and therefore the ending of a life which is only life and of a death which is only death. No doubt namelessness is now truly our own, and if that namelessness is ever more fully a pure anonymity, that anonymity is openly manifest in the erosion of naming, an erosion which is the reversal or annulment of every given identity, and therefore an erosion which is finally a bottomless abyss. Kierkegaard could know such an abyss as the absolute absence or negation of God, just as Nietzsche could know it as the very center of consciousness, and if that negation or that center has subsequently become the very arena or horizon of the totality of consciousness, that horizon is empty of every actual distinction or difference. Therefore that horizon is a pure emptiness, but not a pure emptiness which is an inactual emptiness, but far rather a pure emptiness which is actually empty, and is actually empty of everything which could be celebrated or known as either freedom or grace.

As we have again and again discovered, Gnosticism is an illusory flight from our actuality, and is illusory precisely because of its will to flee, a will that itself forecloses the possibility of such flight, and a will that is the very opposite of its intended destiny. For there is no exit from our darkness, and no possibility for us of even truly apprehending a fragment of light, for whatever light is now present is receding into an irrecoverable past, and if that irrecoverability is manifest as judgment, that is a judgment which is inseparable from our all too contemporary present, and a judgment which is now nothing less than actuality itself. Who could even dream of forgiveness in confrontation with this judgment, or who could know an innocence which is a respite from such experience, or who could envision a peace that would be a calming of our turbulence? Certainly no truly imaginative voice of the twentieth century has even contemplated such illusions, or not done so in its deepest and purest creations, for both the twentieth-century mind and the twentieth-century imagination have unveiled the deep illusion of every way out of our world. Even if that illusion is enacted continually in our society, it is always so manifest as an illusion, and most clearly so when a call to ultimate liberation is apparently enacted or embodied.

Thus if there is no limit to our consciousness, there is no exit from it as well, and not even an exit in what was once manifest as death, for that previous death could only be a transcendent death if it were a freely willed death, and not only is such a free will no longer at hand, but no death lies upon our horizon which is an independent and interior death, and therefore no death which we can interiorly and individually celebrate. Our wake is no longer *Finnegans Wake*, for no resurrection lies readily at hand, and yet our death does lie in the wake of resurrection, and in the wake of an eternal life which is eternal life and eternal death at once; and if that wake is no longer an awakening of the dead, it may well be an apocalyptic transfiguration nonetheless, and an apocalyptic transfiguration which is a transfiguration of our abyss. That we do name our abyss, and name it in a uniquely contemporary silence, is itself an act of transfiguration, and a transfiguration occurring in our dark emptiness, for if that is an actual emptiness, it is an emptiness that is actually at hand, and that is a fullness of time for us, and not a fullness that is simply emptiness, but far rather a fullness that is actually present.

Therein lies what little is present of hope for us, but it is a real hope just because that is a real presence, and not only a real presence but a total presence, and only thereby is apocalypse possible. Here lies our true hope, and not a hope in a future apocalypse, for if apocalypse is truly future it cannot be present in our dark abyss, and certainly cannot be present as our dark abyss. A present apocalypse could only be an apocalypse of our actual emptiness, and therefore an apocalypse which is being enacted even now. When we recall that it was an original apocalypticism that called forth the dark emptiness of the impotent will, we can be prepared for a darkness that is inseparable from light, and a light that can only appear in the heart of darkness, for only the transfiguration of that darkness is an apocalyptic transfiguration. Then even if we cannot say Yes and only Yes, we can say a No that is inseparable from Yes, and while that No for us can never be a pure No-saying, it is precisely that absence which evokes a Yes, and evokes a Yes in the very center of darkness.

Index

Index

absolute beginning, 29, 31, 37, 39, 42, 107; as irreversible beginning, 41–42, 47–48, 50, 52, 54, 59, 66, 76, 109, 111, 184; as once and for all beginning, 41–42, 47–48, 50, 52, 55, 59–60, 66, 76, 109, 111, 113, 118, 184; *see also* 21, 27, 28, 38, 46, 90

absolute emptiness, 93, 95–96, 99, 102–106; as pure emptiness, 98; reversal of, 105–106

absolute negation, 108, 132

absolute newness, 22, 29, 42–43, 46

absolute opposition, 103, 105, 107–109, 112–113, 115, 118–119, 157, 161; *see also* 104

absolute otherness, 62, 85–86, 90–91, 102–103, 105–106, 107–110, 112, 177, 183

absolute paradox, 174, 179, 183–184

abyss, 49–51, 59–60, 173, 180–187; as primordial, 34

act of being, 30, 117, 184

act of God, 11, 29–31, 36–37, 58–59, 74, 85, 101, 104–106, 108–109, 113, 119, 126, 131–133, 141, 150–151, 160, 184; as irreversible, 62; as primordial, 22

actual nothingness, 125–127, 178, 185–187

actuality, 32, 35, 38, 42, 47, 52, 54, 66, 82, 85, 91, 93, 101, 106–107, 109, 112, 128, 130, 138, 171, 175, 185–186; of being, 30; and Buddhism, 89; of death, 42, 47, 52, 85, 110; death as, 32, 34; of fall, 110;

of the fallen will, 130; of the future, 44; and God, 91, 94, 130; of the Godhead, 113; of history, 110, 112, 128; of I AM, 58; origin of, 48–49, 52; pure act as, 37; of resurrection, 91

actualization, 11, 46, 48, 52, 88, 97, 101–102, 107, 131

Aeneid, The, 87

anamnesis, 157

Anna Livia Plurabelle, *see* Plurabelle, Anna Livia

annulment, 37–38, 40, 41, 54, 61, 72, 78–79, 96

anonymous consciousness, 89, 170, 176, 179–182, 185

Antichrist, The, 21, 145–146, 154

apocalypse, 9–12, 24, 59–60, 63, 66, 85–86, 91, 101, 110–119, 121, 153–154, 166, 174–187; historical, 86–90; reversal of, 113

apocalyptic transformation, 112; *see* 26, 65–66, 71, 91–92, 138, 141, 148, 157, 182–187

apocalyptic vision, 9–10, 152–153, 177, 185

apocalyptic Yes-saying, 152, 155–156, 159–160

apocalypticism, 10, 22, 29, 64–66, 89, 166, 182

apostasy, 51, 58, 81

Aquinas, 24–25, 28–30, 36, 127, 168

archaic world, 35, 48, 50, 54, 57–58, 176

Aristotle, 29

ascension, 61, 113, 116